2010 - 2015 Camaro 5th Gen
How to Build and Modify

Scott Parker

CarTech®

CarTech®, Inc.
838 Lake Street South
Forest Lake, MN 55025
Phone: 651-277-1200 or 800-551-4754
Fax: 651-277-1203
www.cartechbooks.com

© 2016 by Scott Parker

All rights reserved. No part of this publication may be reproduced or used in any form or by any means, electronic or mechanical, including photocopying, recording, or by any information storage and retrieval system, without prior permission from the Publisher. All text, photographs, and artwork are the property of the Author unless otherwise noted or credited.

The information in this work is true and complete to the best of our knowledge. However, all information is presented without any guarantee on the part of the Author or Publisher, who also disclaim any liability incurred in connection with the use of the information and any implied warranties of merchantability or fitness for a particular purpose. Readers are responsible for taking suitable and appropriate safety measures when performing any of the operations or activities described in this work.

All trademarks, trade names, model names and numbers, and other product designations referred to herein are the property of their respective owners and are used solely for identification purposes. This work is a publication of CarTech, Inc., and has not been licensed, approved, sponsored, or endorsed by any other person or entity. The Publisher is not associated with any product, service, or vendor mentioned in this book, and does not endorse the products or services of any vendor mentioned in this book.

Edit by Bob Wilson
Layout by Monica Seiberlich

ISBN 978-1-61325-591-9
Item No. SA312P

Library of Congress Cataloging-in-Publication Data Available

Written, edited, printed and designed in the U.S.A.

Title Page:
The 2014 Camaro Z/28 took the 1LE's concept a step or two further, as a purpose-built track day racer that is street and emissions legal. Instead of robbing the parts bin and making a few tweaks, the engineering team was on a mission to create the best handling Camaro possible. They even used the opportunity to improve the aerodynamics significantly, which was subsequently carried over to the base Camaro.

Back Cover Photos

Top:
The first year COPOs were available in five production-based color options, though this Summit White version with blue graphics is perhaps the most recognizable. Year to year the colors and graphics changed.

Middle Left:
The Quarter Master Optimum-SR Two-Disc Clutch (PN 542004) uses two 10.4-inch marcel-type discs with organic rag-type friction and a sprung hub. The vented floater plate and grooved friction surfaces are designed with cooling in mind. Capable of holding 1,400 hp and 1,000 ft-lbs, this is no lightweight, but pedal effort is still minimal. This particular clutch is going into a 650-hp Racing Head Service (RHS) LS7-powered 2010 Camaro SS.

Middle Right:
Texas Speed has a Basic Heads & Camshaft Bolt & Gasket Kit that includes new stock head bolts. You can upgrade to ARP bolts or studs, but the stock ones are fine for naturally aspirated street cars. The downside, though, is that they use a more complicated torque procedure using torque-to-yield bolts. ARP hardware uses only torque (not degrees) to install and is reusable.

Bottom:
After dropping the radiator, fans, and coolers back into place, the heat exchanger slid in behind the bumper support. Redline Motorsports felt it was crucial that the heat exchanger did not affect the air damn and underbody aero. The heat exchanger now lurks behind the Z/28's thin upper grille and emblem, tipping off would-be challengers.

CONTENTS

Preface 4
Acknowledgments 5

Chapter 1: An Overview 6
  Four Generations of Heritage 6
  Fifth-Generation Development 12
  Models 17
  Powertrain 25
  Chassis and Suspension 32
  Modifying 37

Chapter 2: Chassis: Suspension, Brakes,
    Wheels and Tires 41
  Suspension 41
  Brakes 45
  Wheels and Tires 47
  How-To Projects 51
    Rear Bushings Install 51
    Toe Rods and Trailing Arms Install 55
    Subframe Connectors Install 58
    Line-Lock Install 60
    Front Suspension Upgrade 64

Chapter 3: Drivetrain 65
  Differential Upgrades 65
  Transmissions 70
  Solid Axle Conversions 77
  How-To Projects 79
    Driveshaft Safety Loop Install 79
    Torque Converter Install 82
    Clutch Install 87

Chapter 4: Basic Engine Performance Upgrades 90
  V-6 Upgrades 90
  V-8 Upgrades 91
  How-To Projects 101
    Cold-Air Induction Install 101
    160-Degree Thermostat Install 104
    Crank Pulley Install 104
    Long-Tube Header Install 106

Chapter 5: Engine Builds and Swaps 110
  Cylinder Heads 110
  Camshafts 113
  Valvetrains 114
  Crate Engines 116
  Swaps 117
  Cranks and Rods 119
  Pistons 119
  Fuel Options and Compression Ratios 119
  Oiling Systems 120
  Custom Engine Builders 121
  Building Yourself 121
  How-To Projects 122
    Heads and Cam Install 122
    VVT Cam Swap and AFM Delete 127
    Camshaft Degree and Piston-to-Valve
      Clearance 130
    Rocker Trunnion Upgrade 133
    RHS LS7 Build 135

Chapter 6: Power Adders 141
  Nitrous 141
  Superchargers 146
  Turbochargers 153
  How-To Projects 159
    Nitrous Install 159
    TVS2300 Supercharger Install 165
    Custom 4.5L Whipple Supercharger Install 168

Chapter 7: Fuel System, Ignition and Tuning 171
  Engine Management System Tuning 171
  Ignition Systems 175
  Fuel Systems 176
  How-To Projects 180
    Fuel Pump Install 180
    Methanol Injection 184
    The Tuning School Method 185
    Flex Fuel Conversion in EFI Live 188

Source Guide 191

PREFACE

Those were dark days in the early aughts when General Motors canceled the production of the Camaro. General Motors' enthusiasts were forced to make due with a converted Australian sedan and the back-seat-less Corvette. Although both were formidable options, they simply could not replace the Camaro. It is a legendary nameplate with faithful followers who just wouldn't convert. The power of the brand was just so strong that Chevrolet had to bring it back. Enthusiasm had only been building for the LS platform, as stock fourth-generation Camaros were becoming hard to come by. And today no one thinks twice about putting an LS engine in anything from a 1969 Camaro to a Porsche 911. Although some looked at the Camaro's absence as a negativism, today you can look back on it as a caesura in its lyrical history. The pause added punctuation to what had become a literal powder keg.

January 9, 2006, was a momentous day for GM enthusiasts. At the time, I was still a little green as associate editor of *GM High-Tech Performance* (*GMHTP*) magazine when General Motors unveiled the Camaro at Cobo Hall in Detroit, Michigan. But the excitement within our staff and enthusiasts was palpable. It already had a formidable engine to power it, the 400-horse LS2 V-8, so it just needed the new Zeta chassis to call home. A year later General Motors served up the Pontiac G8 GT sedan as an hors d'oeuvre, which used the same chassis and the lower compression, rectangular-port L76.

By the time the 2010 Camaro coupe hit the streets three years later, I was at the helm of *GMHTP*. The production cars were available prior to the press cars, so I arranged to drag test a stick and an automatic with private owners who had placed early orders. By that time, the magazine had been moved to Tampa, Florida, where I located an automatic version and headed to Bradenton Motorsports Park. In the heat and humidity, it went 13.38 at 105 mph. A week or so later, I headed back to New Jersey to test Redline Motorsports' stick car, which went 13.09 at 110 mph at the legendary Englishtown Raceway Park. The stick car later went 12.89 with more seat time and better conditions. Despite some regression from the fourth-gen, the fifth-gen was far superior to the Challenger R/T Classic that was tested on the same day.

At news of the testing, fourth-gen purists cried fowl. Instead of remembering the early days of the LS1, they tended to remember the times run in mineshaft conditions by professional drivers after nine years of familiarity with the platform. As time has gone on, the fifth-gen has proven to be a formidable platform even for drag racing. But it has taken some adjustments and changes in thought. As someone who has owned several fourth-gens, I originally preferred it as a drag racing platform. But the retro modern looks of the fifth-gen, combined with its safety, are particularly appealing if you prefer to drive your Camaro on the street (as many of us do).

Case in point: I wouldn't think twice about strapping my daughter into the car seat in the rear of a fifth-gen. Fourth-gen? Not so much. And if you are building a dedicated race car, it is not hard to drop some serious weight out of the chassis. That's why it is not surprising that as the fifth-gen has become more affordable in the secondary (used) car market, you are seeing more of them at the track.

It has been my privilege to cover the Camaro's rebirth, as well as the gamut of modifications that tuners and builders have undertaken. I was at the first drive of the 2012 Camaro ZL1 at Virginia International Raceway, the 1LE at Gingerman, and countless National Muscle Car Association (NMCA) races, including the Fastest Fifth-Gen Shootout that I conceived and sponsored as editor of *GMHTP*. I hope that the knowledge accumulated from these events, racers, enthusiasts, and experts throughout the industry can help others who love the fifth-generation Camaro for years to come.

ACKNOWLEDGMENTS

Writing a book is a large undertaking, much greater than one man. I would first like to thank Joseph Potak, who basically handed this opportunity to me on a silver platter. Joseph is a stand-up guy who I have known through the industry for years, and I wish him all the best in his globetrotting adventures.

I must also acknowledge the staff at CarTech for putting up with my delays as I launched and grew my business.

Considering the tremendous amount of photography in this book supplied by manufacturers and shops, I clearly owe these ladies and gentlemen some credit as well. That was the glue that kept this book together.

I also owe thanks to my wife and daughter for their continued love, support, and understanding.

Last, I would like to acknowledge General Motors for making this wonderful machine and enthusiasts (like you) who support this industry. Because of you, I haven't worked a day in more than 12 years.

CHAPTER 1

AN OVERVIEW

All photos in this chapter are courtesy of General Motors.

Following an eight-year absence in the market, the fifth-generation Camaro ushered in a new era at Chevrolet. The 2010 Camaro hit the streets amid General Motors' bankruptcy but was not indicative of the old General Motors that built the fourth-generation Camaro, let alone the Pontiac Aztec or made any number of questionable decisions that led to its financial demise. Instead, the fifth-gen was symbolic of a reinvigorated commitment to quality and customer satisfaction. Its long-awaited return brought the world-class performance and craftsmanship in a safer (re: heavier) and better-looking package the public demanded. In fact, its many first-gen styling cues and body lines were so loved that GM brass demanded that as few changes as possible be made from the 2006 concept.

Although this legendary rear-wheel-drive muscle car platform drew to a close during the 2015 model year, it will not only be remembered for its looks, but for its potential as a bona fide supercar. Chevrolet took the fifth-generation platform to the next level with the 2012 Camaro ZL1. The 2014 Camaro Z/28 pushed the limits of the chassis, edging out some of the best in the business on the legendary Nürburgring track. And drag racing–minded critics of the platform got their fill with the return of the COPO Camaro for 2013. The factory-built no-VIN race car was yet another nod to the Camaro's heritage, and a huge boost to the fifth-gen image.

These factory versions of the Camaro demonstrated that the fifth-gen could do anything equally well (on dragstrip, road course, and street), albeit with the right improvements. If your goal is a reliable daily driver that will put a few car lengths between you and your neighbor's Mustang, a bumper-dragging single-digit screamer, or anything in between, you have plenty of options to achieve it. Just like a driving instructor, my job is to show you the driving line. But you have to take the wheel and keep your Camaro shiny side up.

Four Generations of Heritage

In 1960, the Corvair was the sum total of Chevrolet's small-car portfolio until the Chevy II debuted the following year. However, when the Ford Mustang flooded the streets in

The 1969 Camaro Indy 500 Pace Car and its 2011 Camaro SS counterpart, which were featured at the 100th anniversary of the Indy 500 race. A 1967 Camaro RS/SS was the first Camaro to pace the Indy 500, at the 51st race in 1967.

AN OVERVIEW

This is the first Camaro: VIN 100001. This 1967 model was the first of 49 to be hand-built in Norwood, Ohio, in mid-1966 as a "pilot assembly" vehicle. Equipped with a 3.7L inline-six and 3-speed manual, its main function was to introduce the Camaro to the public in August 1966 before going on sale.

The 1969 is widely thought of as the most iconic Camaro of all time, and this particular model would be right up there. Pennsylvania Chevrolet dealer Don Yenko created 200 finely tuned Camaros based on the COPO special order program with an iron-block 427. This is also 1 of 30 to have a Turbo 400 automatic transmission.

1964, it was immediately apparent that the mid-engine coupe should be scrapped for a sportier, front-engine car that would destroy the little pony. In 16 short months GM engineers built and tested the 1967 Camaro from the ground up, based on the hardtop Chevy II. The long-hood short-deck look is credited to Dave Holls, who also designed the 1963 Buick Riviera, and was subsequently promoted. The Camaro debuted on September 29, 1966.

First Generation: 1967–1969

The first-generation Camaro (1967–1969) was the shortest run of the five; however, it was certainly the most memorable. Mechanically speaking, all three model years were nearly identical. The unibody structure had a front subframe with an independent front suspension that used double A-arms and a solid rear axle with the semi-elliptical leaf springs that were popular in its day. Speaking of popular in its day, manual four-wheel drum brakes were standard, though power assist and front disc brakes were available. It wasn't until 1969 that four-wheel disc brakes became optional.

There were many engine and transmission choices starting with a 230- and 250-ci straight-6, a 327-ci small-block, and two 396-ci big-blocks (the most potent sported 375 hp). There was also an SS-350 model with a new 295-horse 350-cube V-8, Chevy's first 350. The Rally Sport

Hugger Orange is easily the most iconic Camaro color.

The Rally Sport (RS) package was available as an add-on during the first-generation Camaro, available with any model, including the V-6, SS, and Z/28. It was an appearance package that included hideaway headlights, backup lights under the rear bumper, and different trim.

(RS) appearance and Super Sport (SS) performance packages could be ordered separately or together (RS/SS). And later in the year, the race-bred Z/28 was introduced with its high-compression and high-revving 302-cube 290-horse V-8.

For 1969 Chevrolet introduced Central Office Production Orders (COPO) 9560 and 9561. The latter (9561) was essentially a stripped-down, base Camaro coupe with a 427-ci iron big-block. GM's records state that 1,015 of these COPOs were delivered to Yenko Chevrolet. The famous Pennsylvania dealership scoffed at the factory-rated 425 hp, squeezing another 25 hp with tuning that was good for mid-13-second times at 105 mph in the quarter-mile.

The rarest Camaro ever built is the COPO 9560, which had an all-aluminum ZL-1 427-ci big-block. Only 69 of these light and extremely quick Camaros left the factory. The ZL-1 reportedly ran low-13-second times with more than 500 hp on tap, though Chevy advertised 430 hp.

Second Generation: 1970½–1981

The second-generation Camaro came a mere three years after the pony car's debut, arriving (late) in February 1970, and lasted more than a decade. Although perhaps not quite as iconic as the first-gen, the 1970½ Camaro offered a split bumper, which has become dear to collectors' hearts, and was available through the 1973 model year before the new government mandated bumper regulations took effect for 1974. A wrap-around style rear window was added for 1975 and was one of the few changes until 1978 when the Camaro was given a new nose. The 1978–1981 models were known as the disco era, and are typically the least sought after today.

Camaro sales peaked with the 1979 model at 282,571. The following year, the fuel crisis plunged sales to 152,005.

Although the second-gens became the first to top the Mustang in sales (for the 1977 model year), engine options became progressively worse through the era. Originally the 155-horse 250-ci 6-cylinder was the base engine with 307-, 350-, and 396-ci options. The most potent of which (the 396 big-block) made 375 hp. The Z/28 model's 350-ci LT-1 was right behind it with 360 horses. The high-compression engine was capable of eclipsing the quarter-mile in 14.2 seconds at 100.3 mph according to *Car and Driver*.

In 1971 General Motors went from the more generous "gross" power ratings to "net," which we use today, on top of dropping the compression ratio of all its engines. By 1972 the LT-1 made a measly 255 hp (net), while the big-block made 240. The SS and its big-block were

The year 1970 introduced the second-gen Camaro and a 360-hp LT-1 V-8 engine. This Hurst Sunshine Special was a prototype for the power-sliding sunroof, as well as front and rear spoilers for the Sports Car Club of American (SCCA) Trans-Am series. It saw considerable time in the wind tunnel.

Although the early split-bumper Camaros are the most sought-after for collectors, the 1977 model saw the return of the Z/28 that emphasized handling. Between the oil crisis and impeding emissions restrictions, the most potent engine option was a 170-hp 350-ci V-8.

AN OVERVIEW

removed for 1973, and the L82 made just 245 hp. The Z/28 was killed for 1975 and the most potent engine, a 350 with a 4-barrel, made just 155 horses. Things didn't get much better than that when the Z/28 returned in 1977 with a 170-horse version of the same engine. Until 1981, the 350 seemed to gain a few ponies every year. Meanwhile a 305 had become a popular engine choice, especially in California where the 350 was not available by 1980 because of the gas crisis.

Chassis-wise, the second-gen Camaro bears much resemblance to its predecessor. Its roots are still in the Nova design: a unibody construction with a leaf spring suspended solid rear axle and a front subframe that used coil springs and A-arms. Although some changes were made to the A-arms, and the steering gear was moved forward. It is also worth noting that the SS and Z/28 models received upgraded suspension.

Third Generation: 1982–1992

The third-gen (1982–1992) Camaro featured many technological advances. The old-style leaf-spring rear suspension was ditched in favor of coil springs, torque arm, and Panhard bar. The torque arm effectively acted like a ladder bar, while the Panhard bar was akin to a Watts linkage. The front end no longer used a subframe, instead replacing it with a MacPherson strut setup. Fuel injection, 4-speed automatic transmissions, and 5-speed manuals all debuted on the third-gen.

In 1982 the hatchback unibody used the Iron Duke 2.5L 4-cylinder as the base engine, 112-horse V-6 as the Berlinetta's powerplant, and 5.0L (305 ci) V-8 with a 4-barrel as the big dog. As if a whopping 145 hp wasn't enough, the Z/28 model used Cross-Fire Injection to add 20 horses. The Z/28 only came with a 3-speed automatic; the carbed 305 was also available with a 4-speed manual. The 5-speed manual wasn't introduced until the following year on the Z/28, along with a more potent L69. The 4-speed 700R4 auto transmission came in 1984, but the best was yet to come. The IROC-Z debuted in 1985, named for the International Race of Champions in which Camaros competed, and came with a 215-horse Tuned Port Injection (TPI) engine and 4-speed auto (available on regular Z/28s, too). Port injection was used on Camaros through the next two generations.

The 350 returned for 1987, making 225 hp with the TPI system, the most since 1974. The 5.7L (350 ci)

The year 1982 marked the introduction of the third-generation, which was the first to use electronic fuel injection in the Z/28. The 5.0L Cross-Fire Injection engine in the Z/28 made 165 hp, while the lower compression 4-barrel version made 145 hp. A 2.8L V-6 and 2.5L 4-cylinder were also available.

The 5.7L returned in 1987, which made 225 hp with Tuned Port Injection (the most power since 1974). The convertible also made a comeback in 1987, and the Z/28 was discontinued for the IROC-Z, which was named after the International Race of Champions. Although other cars were introduced later, the series pitted drivers from different racing series in identically prepared Camaro race cars. The IROC-Z was introduced in 1985 and an instant hit, selling 21,177 in its first year.

CHAPTER 1

The third-gen was closed out with the 1992 model, which was the 25th anniversary. This Z/28 made 245 hp with its 5.7L TPI engine and was also equipped with a 1LE handling package (1 of only 705 in 1992). The optional Heritage Package included the rally stripes, black headlamp pockets, and body-color grille, though all 1992 models had the anniversary badges. The Van Nuys, California, production plant closed after this model year.

was only available with a 4-speed auto; the TPI 5.0L was now offered with the (T5) 5-speed manual. The year 1987 featured yet another comeback on the Camaro, the convertible. The second-gens were completely devoid of this option, as were earlier third-gens.

Throttle Body Injection (TBI) was added to the base Z/28's 5.0L in 1988, which now made 170 hp. Meanwhile, all V-8 Camaros now donned the IROC name, and the 1LE road racing package was offered on IROC models with larger brakes, stiffer suspension, and an aluminum driveshaft. The RS model was brought back in 1989, though as a trim package for the base coupe (V-6 or TBI 5.0L engine options). The 5.7L TPI engines were making 245 hp by 1991 when the Z/28 was reintroduced with its tall wing, side skirts, faux hood scoops, and five-spoke wheels. The B4C police package was also introduced for 1991, which had 1LE handling upgrades and Z/28 powertrain but with the look of an RS.

Fourth Generation: 1993–2002

In many ways the fourth-generation (1993–2002) Camaro was simply the next evolution from the third-gen. The 1993 Camaro improved upon its predecessor's front suspension and steering and had a considerably stiffer chassis. However, the real magic was under the hood, starting with the base engine, which was now a 160-horse, 3.4L V-6. The Z/28 model came with a 275-horse version of the Corvette's 5.7L Gen II small-block LT1 with port injection, one-piece aluminum intake, aluminum heads, reverse-flow cooling, cam-driven water pump, and a unique ignition system (known as Optispark). In its first year the Z/28 model had a similar engine management system as the third-gen TPI, along with the same 700R4 auto. A T56 6-speed manual transmission was also available on the Z/28; a 5-speed manual was available on the V-6. Four-wheel antilock brakes were standard on the Z/28, along with 16-inch wheels, and it was the first Camaro able to pace the Indy 500 without significant modification in quite a while.

Besides the use of rack-and-pinion steering, short-arm/long-arm front suspension, and similar styling, a few other noticeable differences in the chassis include the use of plastic and composite (SMC). The quarter panels and hood were the only pieces of exposed metal on the fourth-gen.

The year 1993 marked the fourth-generation, and the 5.7L LT1, packing 275 hp, had the most power since 1971. The Gen II small-block V-8 was available with a T56 6-speed manual trans and a 4-speed auto. Production moved to the Sainte-Thérèse facility outside of Montreal, Quebec, Canada, which had been retooled and modernized after the G-Body ceased production.

AN OVERVIEW

Later in the LT1's run, output was increased to 285 hp in the Z/28 and 305 hp in the 1996 SS model built by SLP Engineering (shown). SLP converted Z/28 models to an SS by adding a cat-back exhaust, a Hurst short-throw shifter, a Torsen limited-slip differential, and a Level II suspension package with 1LE components and Bilstein shocks.

In 1998, the fourth-gen got a facelift and introduced the Gen III small-block, the 5.7L LS1. The LS1 made 305 hp in the Z/28 model and 320 hp in the SS, now produced in-house by Chevrolet. The all-aluminum engine was lighter and obviously more powerful. Although still a pushrod V-8, it was revolutionary rather than evolutionary like the Gen II. It can be credited with sparking aftermarket interest in modification.

The roof was black on all coupes, and often came with T-tops. This option was extremely popular in the later years.

Although absent from the first year, the convertible returned in 1994 and was much stiffer than the third-gen. Also of note, unlike its predecessors that had been produced in Ohio and California, the fourth-gen was manufactured at the Quebec, Canada, plant.

Other significant changes over the years included the use of a new engine management system and electronically controlled 4L60E auto starting in 1994, which was otherwise the same as the previous 4-speed auto it replaced (700R4). In 1995 the 3800 V-6 (3.8L) replaced the 3.4L, adding 40 hp. The RS returned as an appearance package to the V-6 model in 1996, and the Z/28 gained another 10 hp with an OBD II engine management system.

Even more pivotal, though, SLP Engineering brought back the SS name with conversion packages for the Z/28. A new hood with a prominent scoop and a taller and curvier wing, as well as 17-inch five-spoke wheels with stickier 245/40ZR17 BFGoodrich Comp T/A tires set it apart in appearance. Intake and exhaust upgrades pushed the LT1 to 305 hp, the first Camaro to exceed 300 since 1971. Suspension upgrades further solidified SLP's SS as deserving of the title. The following year SLP up-fitted just 106 SSs with 330 hp LT4 engines (the 5.7L found in the Corvette Grand Sport).

In 1998 the Camaro was given a minor facelift, to the infamous "catfish" design, which signified a much larger change under the hood. Enter the LS1. The Gen III small-block Chevy was different in

The final year of the fourth-gen was 2002, and the 35th anniversary. More than half sold that year had a V-8, which may have been part of its downfall. Chevrolet ceased production on the Camaro due to waning sales.

CHAPTER 1

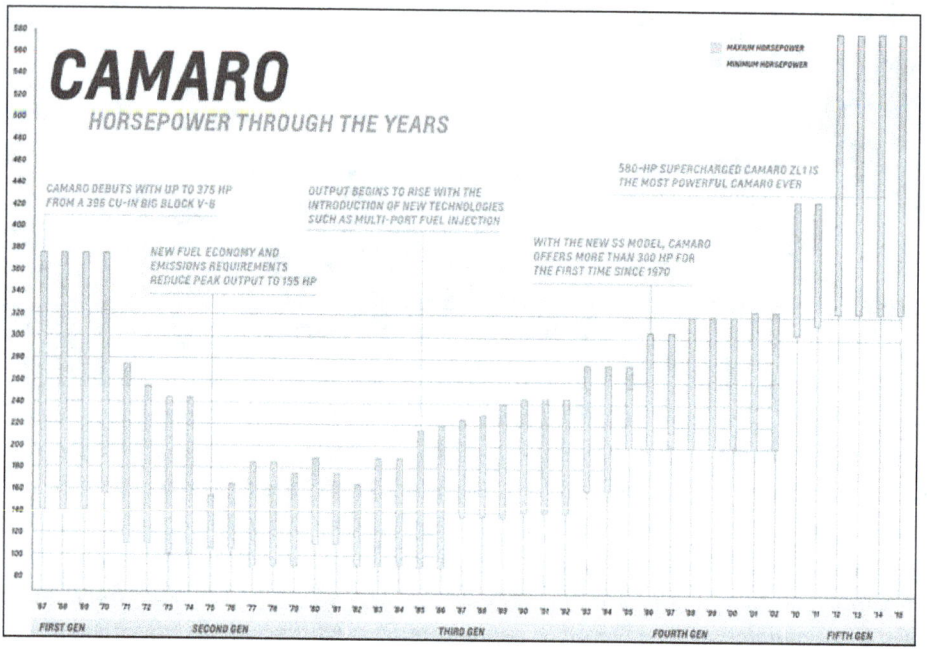

Although sales had declined, horsepower was on the rise. General Motors had struck gold with the Gen III platform, which was just starting to pick up steam. Today it is one of the single most popular choices for engine swaps, no matter what make or model (even imports love LS power!).

and transmissions, little was carried over from the previous generation. The clean-sheet approach is especially apparent in the use of independent rear suspension and the quality of the interior finishes. The retro styling cues and model designations pay homage to the first-generation. Clearly Chevrolet wanted to cut ties with the fourth-gen and conjure up feelings of nostalgia from an older crowd while attracting a new audience tired of homologous forms of transportation.

Powertrain

Because this book discusses performance, it starts with powertrain development. The 2010 Camaro came with three engine choices: 6.2L LS3 V-8, 6.2L L99 V-8, and 3.6L LLT V-6. The LS3 is a Gen IV small-block Chevy, which boasted 426 hp and 400 ft-lbs of torque from the factory.

The similarities are great between the LS3 and its predecessor, the LS1 found in the 1998–2002 Camaro: cam-in-block pushrod V-8 with a deep-skirted aluminum block, 16 overhead valves with a 15-degree angle, composite intake manifold, port fuel injection, and coil-near-plug ignition. A number of improvements in the cylinder head, intake, and exhaust design, as well as the bump in displacement gave it the edge in performance. The LS3 came only on SS models when paired with

pretty much every way from the Gen I and Gen II. There was pretty much no cross-compatibility as there had been between the previous two generations. The LS1 has an aluminum block with ductile iron sleeves, not the traditional iron block. And it used a 3.89-inch bore and 3.62-inch stroke to achieve 5.7L (345 ci) of displacement, not 4.00 by 3.50 inches.

The mains were not the traditional two- or four-bolt, but a deep skirted design with six bolts securing the nodular iron crankshaft. The head bolt pattern is considerably different, as is the intake bolt pattern. General Motors also switched to a plastic intake on the LS1, which bolted to a single-bore 76-mm throttle body and cathedral-style intake runners. The transmission options were identical, though gearing varies in the T56 from year to year, as does the clutch.

Nearly identical in every way to the LS1 introduced on the Corvette for 1997, the Camaro's version had an advertised 305 hp. The more restrictive exhaust may be attributed to some of the difference from the advertised 345 hp in the Corvette. Meanwhile, General Motors took production of the SS out of SLP's hands, offering 320 hp with its Ram Air induction hood. Larger sway bars, ZR1-style 17-inch wheels, and meaty rubber completed the package.

Aside from a change in engine management in 1999, very little changed over the years besides wheel styles and color options. Perhaps the most notable option of this era was the 35th anniversary package offered in 2002, which was red with checkered hood stripes and anniversary logos. Available in both coupe and convertible, it was the fourth-gen's swan song due to decreased sales.

Fifth-Generation Development

Although the fourth-gen Camaro was formidable in its day, the fifth-gen had the benefit of many years of advancement in engineering, manufacturing, and quality control. Aside from the architecture of the engines

AN OVERVIEW

Throughout the run of the fifth-gen, Chevrolet introduced special colors, such as Synergy Green, which was available in 2011 only. It replaced Aqua Blue Metallic, available in 2010 and was superseded by Carbon Flash Metallic for the 45th anniversary in 2012.

This concept inspired the optional ground-effects package, which included unique exhaust tips built into the rear bumper.

These concept wheels helped inspire several optional wheels available through dealers.

a Tremec TR6060 6-speed manual transmission. The TR6060 was the latest evolution of the T56 manual that came in the fourth-gen Camaro (among others), which had two overdrive gears to help tame fuel mileage on the highway.

The L99 was nearly identical to the LS3 in every way except that it had a different camshaft that was attached to a phaser for Variable Valve Timing (VVT), as well as Active Fuel Management (AFM; also known as DoD, displacement on demand) that deactivated half the cylinders on the highway to conserve fuel. The L99's technology cost 26 hp and 10 ft-lbs of torque at peak (while shifting the torque curve), but it was needed to combat the loss of efficiency on 6-speed automatic models. (The automatic of choice was the 6L80E, introduced on the 2006 Corvette.) On the dragstrip, this usually put the bone-stock automatic Camaros in the mid-13s; the manual was a tick faster, right around 13-flat.

The LLT V-6 was even more advanced than the L99, using dual overhead camshafts, four valves per cylinder, piston-cooling jets, and direct injection (in addition to VVT). The LLT was advertised at 302 hp and 267 ft-lbs of torque (using 87-octane) in its first year. It was soon bumped up to 312 hp. For comparison sake, that's 86.67 hp/liter to the LS3's 68.7 hp/liter.

The lighter and more advanced LFX V-6 introduced in 2012 picked up an additional 11 hp (323 total), thanks to its new cylinder head design. All V-6s were available with a 6-speed automatic (6L50) or manual transmission (AY6). The automatic was a lower capacity twin compared to the 6L80 developed by General Motors. The German company Aisin produced the manual, which is more known for its automatics built for the 2007 and later Dodge Ram and various hybrid electric drives.

Chassis and Suspension

The chassis built to house this magnificent selection of powertrains was developed by GM's Australian brand Holden. The Zeta platform debuted in the 2006 Holden VE Commodore, having been introduced in 1999 to replace the Commodore's previous underpinnings. The Zeta architecture, though, was designed to be flexible by accommodating a variety of wheelbase lengths and ride heights.

Case in point: The same architecture was used in the Pontiac G8 sedan, longer wheelbase Chevy Caprice PPV, and the Chevy SS sedan. The 4.5-link independent rear suspension and MacPherson strut with dual ball joint A-arms in the front were common on all models.

Unlike the other Zeta platforms, though, the shorter, 112.3-inch

CAMARO 5TH GEN 2010–2015: HOW TO BUILD AND MODIFY   13

CHAPTER 1

In 2010, V-8 models (1SS and 2SS) represented 58.5 percent of production as enthusiasts clamored for the Camaro's return. The following year the V-6 dominated, at 64.7 percent of production. In both years the automatic trans was the clear favorite, at 67 percent in 2010 and 76.76 percent the following year.

The fifth-gen, like all Camaros, is a unibody construction. The subassemblies contain the engine, front suspension, rear suspension, and drivetrain, which are bolted to the body.

wheelbase Camaro was the only Zeta chassis to be produced in North America. Like most modern cars (and prior Camaro generations), it uses a unitized body frame, with one- and two-sided galvanized steel. According to Lerick Chissus, assistant program engineering manager, every piece of the steel body structure is stamped at the Oshawa, Ontario, Canada, plant. About 370 pieces of steel make up the body structure (400 on the convertible), which are formed using presses and dies, including the massive piece that makes up the quarter panel and C-pillar. Lerick says this is the largest piece in production (at General Motors) with the most draw depth.

GM's best and brightest are required to manipulate the pressure, speed, and weight of the press in order to stretch the metal over the mold without creating tears. "Some of it is an art," says Lerick. "You have to move in synch to understand how it comes together." Eventually all of the formed pieces are placed into a fixture and robotically welded, using spot-welds (and mid-welds along the seam of a joint).

Production of 2010–2015 Camaros was done in GM's Oshawa, Ontario, Canada, plant. The entire complex has more than 10 million square feet of floor. (The Quebec facility had closed in 2002 after the fourth-gen halted.)

AN OVERVIEW

Although the United States had waning interest in Chevrolet's rear-wheel-drive V-8 cars, they were booming in Australia for GM's Holden brand. The Commodore debuted in 1978 and, unlike its previously Opel-based models, the 2006 was completely designed in Australia, including its new Zeta platform. The new independent rear suspension, better weight distribution, 6.0L Gen IV engine option, and even a 6-speed automatic greatly enhanced its performance. This model was basically re-skinned as the Pontiac G8 a few years later, and then used as the basis for the 2010 Camaro chassis with a shorter wheelbase and two doors.

Model designations were made closer to the first-gen Camaro, with the SS being the V-8 model and the RS returning as an add-on appearance package.

The SS model was distinguishable by the "mail slot" in the middle of the front bumper and the SS badge in the grille.

After the body structure is complete, its fate (whether a Summit White 1LS or a Blue Velvet Metallic ZL1) is dependent on which order it fulfills. Despite the array of trim levels, models, and packages, only two body structures are available: coupe and convertible. The structure itself was revised through testing at the Milford Proving Grounds, GM's own version of the Nürburgring, prior to the initial release in 2009. It had a serious leg up on its predecessors in the advancement of computer modeling, according to Lerick Chissus.

Before the fifth-gen Camaro ever touched asphalt, various forms of Computer-Aided Engineering (CAE) established exactly where and how much stiffness was needed in the chassis. In engineering terms, Lerick mentioned "load path," which improves both the suspension dynamics and crash protection. "We are taking load and putting it into the body structure, using it more efficiently through computer modeling."

Although the body structure has not changed since inception, the fifth-gen has undergone a few changes to the suspension and chassis components. The most noticeable change came for the 2014 model year, with a significant facelift and new taillights. Chevrolet used the introduction of the 2014 Camaro Z28 as the perfect opportunity to upgrade the aerodynamics as it had on the 2012 Camaro ZL1, but unlike with the ZL1, those upgrades (minus the rear wing and "Flowtie") were rolled out over the entire lineup. The styling refresh proved to be a good method for reinvigorating sales, as the new models are so easily identifiable by the narrower grille, vented hood, and rectangular taillights.

CHAPTER 1

The LS and LT trim levels offered a variety of wheels, including the standard 20 x 8 wheels on the SS and the 17-inch stealies.

The RS model is recognizable by the halo projector lights.

Other changes include a switch from vacuum to electric-assisted power steering on all models in 2013, which was first introduced on the 2012 Camaro ZL1. Development of the ZL1 also brought about another change, enacted in 2012, to improve the suspension on the SS coupe. Although the 2012 convertible still used the older FE3 style suspension, it benefited from the chassis braces that were developed on the ZL1 convertible for coupe-like torsional rigidity.

In May 2014, Chevrolet announced that the 2015 Camaro would be the last of the fifth-generation. Moreover, it was also announced that production would be moved to Michigan (Lansing Grand River plant).

During the five-year run of the fifth-gen, the Camaro consistently outsold the Mustang and Challenger.

The rear spoiler is also included in V-6 models with the RS package, as are the unique taillamps, body-color ditch molding on the roof, fog lights, and badging.

However, the automotive market has become incredibly competitive, and Chevrolet could ill-afford a stale product in its lineup with a completely new Mustang debuting for 2015 and the Hellcat Challenger making noise with 707 hp.

Sixth Generation

The rumor mill had pegged the sixth-generation 2016 Camaro to be based upon the lighter Alpha platform used in the Cadillac ATS. And with the Gen IV V-8s going out of production, it was likely that the 2016 Camaro would sport the new direct-injection Gen V V-8 architecture used in the 2014 and 2015 Corvette (as well as trucks and SUVs). The 7-speed manual and 8-speed automatic were also likely companions.

Models

From 2010 to 2015, the Camaro coupe was offered in an LS, LT, and SS model. The LS and LT came with a 3.6L V-6, choice of 6-speed manual or automatic transmission, and two trim levels (1LS, 2LS, 1LT, 2LT). The 2010 Camaro 1LS started at $22,995. The SS model was also available with a 426-horse, 6.2L V-8 in two trim levels (1SS, 2SS), either a 6-speed manual or automatic, and an RS Package (that included Bright Silver painted wheels, HID headlights with LED halo rings, and LED taillamps) to bring back the RS/SS.

The Camaro also offered many options, from various stripe packages to shifters, wheels, and a sunroof. The color palette changed from year to year. Three notables: Aqua Blue Metallic was offered only in 2010, Synergy Green Metallic was 2011-only, and Carbon Flash Metallic was offered only in 2012 with the 45th anniversary package. The 2011–2015 Camaro convertible followed the same scheme of trim levels, except it was offered only in LT and SS models.

In 2012, two storied Camaro nameplates were brought back: ZL1 and COPO. The ZL1 represented the pinnacle of performance, combined with the sophistication you'd expect from a $55,000 sports car. Like the SS, the ZL1 was offered (from 2012 to 2015) with a 6-speed manual or automatic, and in either coupe or convertible. A 580 hp, supercharged 6.2L V-8 came under the hood.

A brand-new Magnetic Ride system, revised suspension, forged wheels with larger Goodyear Eagle F1 Supercar G:2 tires, a unique front-end with enhanced aerodynamics, and suede-accented interior were just a few of the other upgrades.

Options weren't quite as extensive as on the SS: exposed carbon fiber hood insert (otherwise painted), bright silver 5-spoke or black 10-spoke wheels, sunroof, and decklid stripes.

The COPO stayed true to its heritage by being a no-VIN, race-only, and limited-run (only 69 produced) vehicle. Engine options changed

It is worth noting that the main gauge cluster was updated in 2012 with more modern typography, after this version drew sharp criticism.

The optional auxiliary gauge cluster was mounted in front of the shifter.

CHAPTER 1

The rearview mirror changed twice during the production run. In 2011, it was changed to project the rearview camera images, but when MyLink was introduced for 2012, the rearview images were transmitted to the LCD radio screen.

The Inferno Orange interior accent color was an option made available from the first year, which appropriately matched the exterior color.

The convertible model was released for 2011, available with a V-6 or V-8. Its most impressive achievement was in improving visibility of the handicapped coupe, and in maintaining torsional stiffness thanks to added underbody bracing.

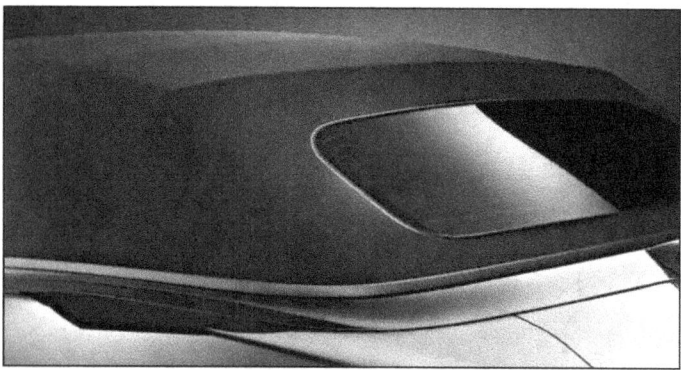

The power top used one twisting lock handle and a rocker switch by the rearview mirror to open and close. It retracted with a "Z" pattern in around 20 seconds. The taut canvas top was made by the same manufacturer as the C6 Corvette's and has an acoustical headliner to reduce noise. The use of composite knuckles and other designs eliminated the appearance of support ribs.

The "45th" logo incorporated the Camaro stripes logo within. Unique red and blue contrast stitching was visible on the outside of the seat.

AN OVERVIEW

The 45th Anniversary Package came only in Carbon Flash Metallic paint for 2012, with its signature stripes, wheels, sill plates, and seat embroidery.

The Camaro ZL1 model was released in 2012. Although it used the same chassis, 30 percent of its parts were replaced or re-engineered from the SS.

The ZL1 convertible followed in 2013. The improvements needed to stiffen the chassis were carried over to the SS model as well.

The unique flat-bottom steering wheel was built for performance driving.

from year to year, but initially included a 427-ci LS7, 327-ci LSX with a 4.0L Whipple supercharger, and a 327-ci LSX with a 2.9L Whipple supercharger. A naturally aspirated 350- and 396-ci LSX, as well as a supercharged 350-ci LSX, were offered from 2013 to 2014 to be more compatible with NHRA's Stock Eliminator and Super Stock classes.

From 2013 to 2015 the 1LE Handling Package was offered on the SS coupe, which used many of the parts developed for the ZL1. In fact, the 1LE was a replica of sorts of an internal test mule (an SS with ZL1 wheels, tires, and sway bars) that the Camaro team knew would be perfect for the road racing enthusiast. For production, the 1LE was only offered with a manual transmission, red brake calipers, and suspension upgrades.

The 2014 Camaro Z28 took that idea one step further. It was the ultimate road racing machine with specially designed R-compound tires, huge carbon brakes, a 427-ci LS7, Recaro racing seats, all sorts of weights savings, race-bred suspension, an adjustable rear wing, and many other aerodynamic enhancements. At $75,000, the 505 hp Z28 was the crown jewel of the collection.

Even the interior was given a makeover, from the flat-bottom steering wheel to the plush suede used throughout.

From the heat-extractor hood with its carbon-fiber insert to its badging, staggered wheels, front bumper, and rocker panels, it is easy to tell the ZL1 from the SS.

The 1LE option package for the SS was created amid development of the ZL1. It was modeled after the famous "mule," an internal development vehicle the Chevrolet engineers used to improve the Camaro's handling. It borrows the ZL1's front wheels and tires (matched front and rear, unlike the ZL1), adds red-painted SS brake calipers, matte-black vinyl-wrapped hood, and has a number of suspension and drivetrain components. Available with a manual trans only, this car was built for enthusiasts with SCCA class racing in mind.

Although handcuffed on the design of the SS, designers had a field day in the wind tunnel with the ZL1. The spoilers, bumper, and grille were all tweaked. And the designers even added a belly pan to enhance the underbody aerodynamics.

AN OVERVIEW

The 2014 Camaro Z/28 took the 1LE's concept a step or two further, as a purpose-built track day racer that is street and emissions legal. Instead of robbing the parts bin and making a few tweaks, the engineering team was on a mission to create the best-handling Camaro possible. They even used the opportunity to improve the aerodynamics significantly, which was subsequently carried over to the base Camaro.

The adjustable spoiler was unique to the Z/28 and offered more than 110 pounds of downforce at 125 mph and above. The front splitter and wheel flare moldings also worked with the wider wheels and body shape to move air around and enhance downforce. There's even a belly pan with NACA ducts and brake cooling ducts.

The standard Recaro seats were later offered as an option on SS models. Although mainly used to better hold the driver in place at extreme g-forces, they were also integral to the Z/28's extensive weight loss.

Like the ZL1, a carbon-fiber heat extractor was incorporated into the hood to eliminate lift and enhance cooling.

The smaller upper front grille and bumper design, which was developed with Computational Fluid Dynamics, was carried over to the other models and enhanced cooling. When incorporated with the hood vent and the Z/28's other improvements, it produces 440 pounds of downforce. By contrast, the SS was negative (producing lift).

CHAPTER 1

The "Flowtie" is unique to the Z/28 and has a hollow center to allow better airflow. It is emblematic of how dedicated the team was at improving the Z/28's performance in every way imaginable.

Although a radio is intact, it actually had only one speaker to save weight. Air conditioning was optional. Anything that wasn't essential was stripped.

The heat extractor, though not carbon fiber, was carried over from the SS, as was the thinner upper grille and reshaped bumper.

The taillights were the biggest difference incorporated throughout the 2014 lineup. From the square double light to these large, rectangular versions, this gave a refresh to the fifth-gen's styling, along with the new front end.

This refresh was a last hoorah for the Camaro, now that the sixth-gen was on the horizon.

AN OVERVIEW

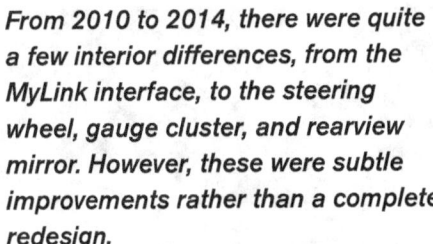

From 2010 to 2014, there were quite a few interior differences, from the MyLink interface, to the steering wheel, gauge cluster, and rearview mirror. However, these were subtle improvements rather than a complete redesign.

The 1LE still used a matte-black hood, albeit with a hood scoop.

The addition of the Z/28 also meant you could have Recaro seats in other models.

The 2014 Camaro 1LE package was not immune to the overhaul and looked like a mini Z/28.

CAMARO 5TH GEN 2010-2015: HOW TO BUILD AND MODIFY   23

CHAPTER 1

The COPO Camaro program was reintroduced in 2011. It is built strictly for racing and does not carry a VIN (so it is unable to be registered for street use). Since its inception, there have been several changes, but the overall specs remain the same. It has a Strange Engineering 9-inch solid axle, several engine configurations, manual and automatic trans options, Aeromotive fuel system, long-tube headers, special fiberglass hood, and lightweight 15-inch drag wheels with either a 30 x 9-inch radial or bias-ply slick (depending on trans choice).

For the first year, COPOs were available in five production-based color options, though this Summit White version with blue graphics is perhaps the most recognizable. Year to year the colors and graphics changed.

Several engine configurations were available over the years depending on NHRA rules, including a few Whipple supercharged combinations. One even used a specially designed 4.0L supercharger with a 327-ci LSX; the 2.9L is shown here. In 2013, the COPO switched from the Delco ECM to a Holley HP processor, and went with three naturally aspirated combos. For 2014 and 2015, a Whipple supercharged combo was brought back but packing 350 cubes this time.

The COPO Camaro is very much a turnkey race car, built in Michigan. It comes with everything it needs for NHRA legality, including a certified chrome-moly roll cage, window net, and restraints.

AN OVERVIEW

Powertrain

The compact and lightweight nature of the pushrod V-8 architecture kept the LS series of engines in production for more than 15 years, originating with the 1997 Corvette and 1998 Camaro/Firebird. In fact, the Gen V LT1 in the 2014 Corvette Stingray isn't exactly a radical departure. Many of the same basic design attributes can be found in the Gen III and Gen IV engines, such as the LS3, L99, LSA, and LS7 found in the fifth-generation Camaro.

The Gen IV small-block Chevy LS3 first appeared on the 2008 Corvette. The Camaro version is nearly identical with four notable exceptions: the oil pan, exhaust manifolds, air intake, and accessory drive system. These differences account for the variance in horsepower from the 2008–2013 Corvette to the 2010–2015 Camaro, although the exhaust system is mostly to blame. Chevrolet saved the freer flowing exhaust

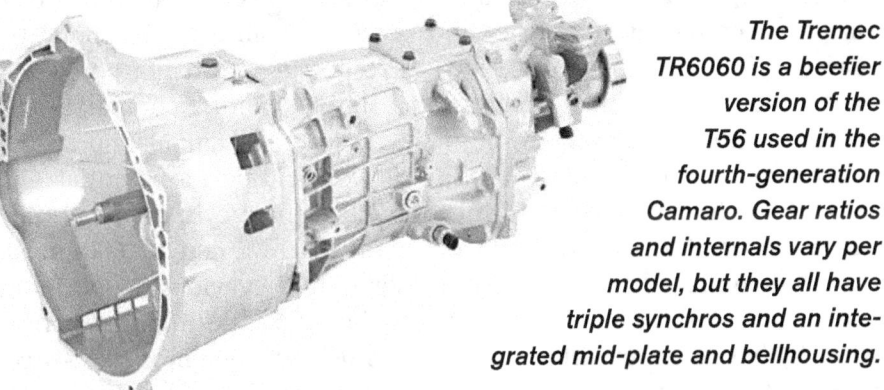

Even the automatic in the Camaro SS had six speeds. General Motors named it the 6L80; the "6" stood for the number of gears and the "80" was a strength rating. The extra gears kept the engine in its powerband longer, while cruising on the highway with a conservative rear-end ratio. General Motors is already up to eight gears now, which may seem excessive. However, it is an effective way of increasing fuel efficiency without losing performance.

The Tremec TR6060 is a beefier version of the T56 used in the fourth-generation Camaro. Gear ratios and internals vary per model, but they all have triple synchros and an integrated mid-plate and bellhousing.

Internally there was no difference between the 6.2L LS3 V-8 in the 2010 Camaro SS and the 2008–2013 Corvette. The L99, however, was specific to the Camaro SS and came only with an automatic transmission. Although it looks no different from the LS3 from the outside, its Variable Valve Timing (VVT) camshaft and Active Fuel Management (AFM, formerly known as DoD, Displacement on Demand) made the internals quite a bit different. In case you are wondering, the accessory drive system, oil pan, exhaust manifolds, and engine cover are unique to the Camaro.

CHAPTER 1

The 3.6L LLT V-6 powered the LS and LT trim levels, and was every bit deserving of the "high-feature V-6" title. This was the Camaro's introduction to direct injection.

systems for the ZL1 and Z28. Both versions even rely on the same camshaft (204/211 duration at .050, .551, and .525-inch lift, 117 LSA) and composite intake manifold with a 90-mm electronic throttle body. The LS3 uses a 4.065-inch bore and 3.62-inch stroke for 376 ci of displacement. For those unfamiliar, the LS3 is a traditional cam-in-block arrangement with hydraulic roller lifters, pushrods, and 1.7-ratio steel rocker arms commanding two valves per cylinder (for a total of 16).

The cylinder heads on the 6.2L V-8 were the most notable improvement over the outgoing Corvette (6.0L LS2) engine. Although the cathedral port used on the LS2, as well as all Gen III applications, excelled in the area of port velocity, it simply couldn't compete with the LS3's larger, rectangular port for overall flow and power potential. Out of the box these cylinder heads flowed more than 300 cfm (at .600-inch lift), something previously unachievable without CNC porting. In essence the LS3 heads were a more cost-effective version of the LS7 heads, which has its origins in the C5R program, and a higher performance version of the L92 and L76.

Massive 2.165-inch intake valves took advantage of LS3's larger 4.065-inch bore and used a hollow stem, a necessity given the size and RPM. The exhaust runner also changed from an oval to a more traditional D-shape, and used a 1.59-inch stainless steel valve. In stock form, these formidable heads supported more than 600 hp naturally aspirated and more than 1,000 with forced induction.

The LS3 found in the 2010–2015 Camaro SS shares many similarities with other Gen III/IV LS series engines. An aluminum alloy block uses ductile iron cylinder liners and six-bolt iron main caps. The block's deep skirts that house the main caps make for an extremely sturdy bottom end far superior to the Gen I/II two-and four-bolt designs. It only needs reinforcement in the most extreme of applications (more than 2,000 hp). This deep skirt required moving the oil pump to the front of the crank. The factory crankshaft is made of nodular iron with undercut and rolled fillets, which is another sturdy piece capable of more than 1,000 hp.

The powdered-metal connecting rods are another story. Although far stronger than those in Gen I/II engines, they give up the ghost with a little bit of detonation in a

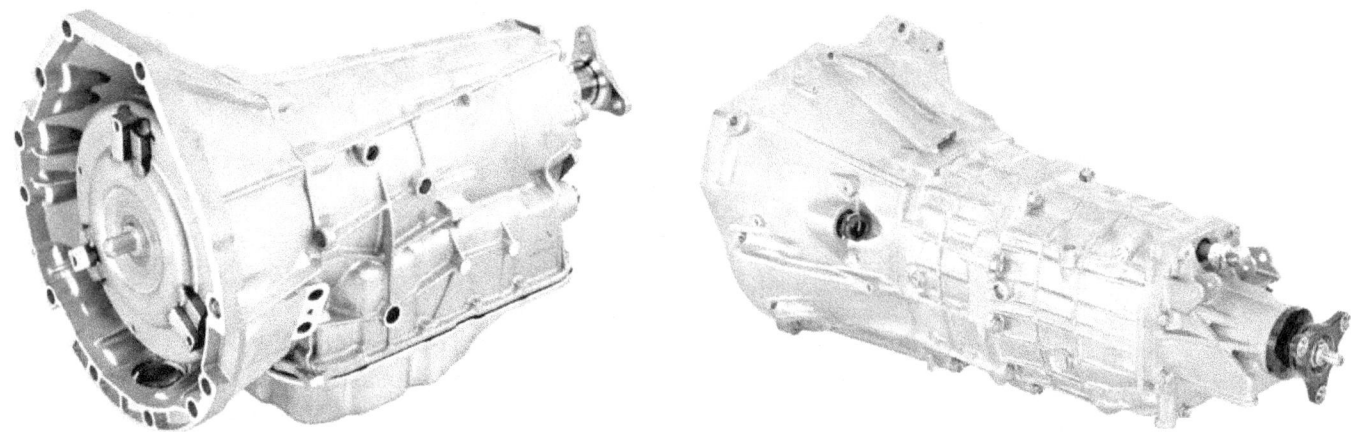

Like the SS, the LS and LT came with two 6-speed options: the 6L50 automatic and the Aisin Warner AY6 manual.

forced-induction application. The same could be said of the hypereutectic aluminum pistons. Naturally aspirated builds typically only have to worry about a connecting rod bolt failure. The factory Multi-Layer Steel (MLS) head gaskets are sturdy enough for most applications, as is the arrangement of the four head bolts per cylinder. High-quality, reusable gaskets are used throughout the engine.

The electronics are one of the most notable differences between Gen III and Gen IV engines. Like all LS engines, the LS3 is topped with an individual coil ignition system, mounted on the valvecovers. The coils are revised from previous versions. The Mass Airflow (MAF) sensor is another improvement, switching to a slot-style with much better range. The coils, MAF sensor, MAP sensor (located at the back of the intake manifold), Intake Air Temperature (IAT) sensor (in the air box), cam sensor (in the timing cover), 42 lbs/hr fuel injectors, and four oxygen sensors (fore and aft of the catalytic converters) are just a few of the inputs to the E38 computer (also used with the L99 and LS7).

The 6.2L L99, which uses the LS3 as a foundation, was created specifically for the 2010 Camaro SS and is unique to the brand. The L99 adapted the VVT and AFM systems used on other LS applications as early as 2006. GM's VVT is the first pushrod application to go into production and uses a phaser that is integrated with the cam sprocket and mounts to the front of the camshaft behind the timing cover. A large single "bolt" retains the camshaft and acts as a valve for controlling oil and telling the phaser how far to advance or retard the timing (up to 52 degrees).

The valve works off pulse-width modulation; when no pressure is present, it is locked and the cam is fully advanced. The camshaft itself has holes in the barrel to help channel this oil to the phaser. This

Many thought this engine cover was too plain; Chevrolet dealerships later offered color-matched versions for an upcharge. Both the V-6 and V-8 used a similar air-intake arrangement with a sealed box and flat filter. Also notice the ECM and fuse box to the left, but no battery. All Camaros have the battery mounted in the trunk.

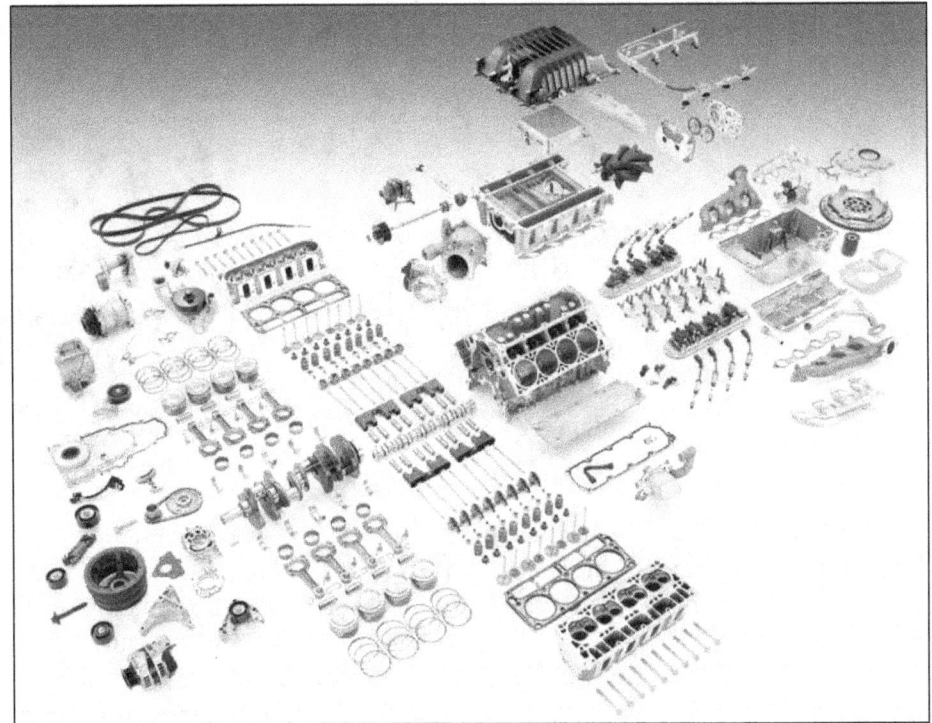

This is an exploded view of the Camaro ZL1's LSA, which was released to celebrate its many improvements over the LS3, including the Eaton TVS 1900 supercharger. The long-block was identical to the Cadillac CTS-V's with roto-cast cylinder heads, reinforced block, forged connecting rods, and crank. The supercharger lid and intercooler were a considerable improvement over the V, hence its higher horsepower rating (556 versus 580 hp).

CHAPTER 1

The ZL1's LSA uses a similar accessory drive system as the LS3 and L99, making it a fairly easy swap if not for the ECM.

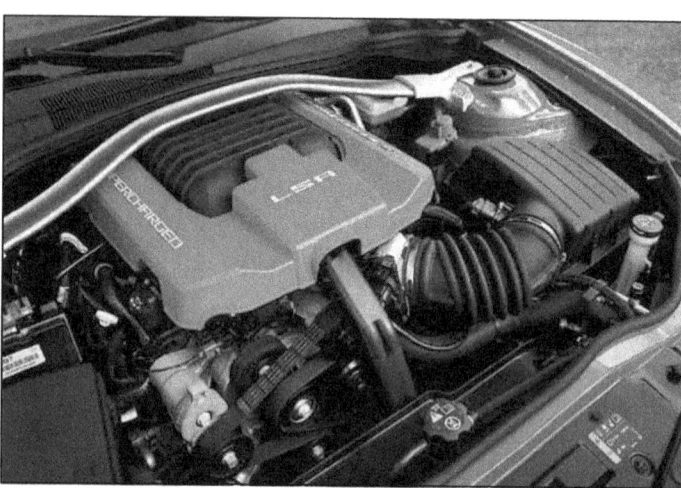

This air-box appears no different than the one on the SS as well, which is perhaps why the aftermarket has had such luck improving upon it.

The 3.6L LFX replaced the LLT V-6 for 2013, which boasted a number of improvements throughout. Most notably, the exhaust manifolds were cast into the cylinder heads, the intake port was reshaped, larger intake valves were used, and longer duration camshafts were added.

All in all, the LFX was lighter and more powerful than the LLT.

technology is not only effective in boosting power "under the curve," but in working with AFM to improve fuel economy.

AFM has its roots in the 1981 Cadillac L62's "V8-6-4." A unique set of lifters deactivates four cylinders (preventing the valves from opening) under light-load conditions that are also controlled by oil, which comes from solenoids mounted in the valley cover.

Side by side, the LS3 and L99 vary in only a handful of areas. As mentioned, the L99 uses a separate set of lifters (for AFM) and a valley cover. The timing cover with its unique sensors, the timing set with the cam phaser, the cam "bolt," and the camshaft itself are also unique to the L99. One downside to the AFM and VVT system is that it limits the amount of cam lift. The L99 cam specs .499/.499-inch lift on the non-active AFM cylinders and .510/.510-inch lift on the active AFM cylinders. Duration is a mild 198/201 at .050.

Because piston-to-valve clearance is a concern with VVT, Chevrolet also increased the combustion chambers on the L99 heads to 70 cc (from 68 cc on the LS3). This effectively brings the compression ratio from 10.7 to 10.4:1. The more conservative cam specs and compression limit the L99 to 6,200-rpm redline,

AN OVERVIEW

while moving peak torque to 4,300 rpm (from 4,600 rpm). As the result, solid intake valves are used instead of hollow-stems to cut cost.

Whereas the L99 added technology to the basic LS3 design for greater fuel economy, the 2012–2015 Camaro ZL1's 6.2L LSA V-8 adds strength to the LS3 architecture to stand up to the Eaton TVS 1.9L supercharger. Starting with the block, the bulkheads were strengthened by 20 percent while also enlarging the windows to enhance bay-to-bay breathing and decrease pumping loss. The block is made of 319-T5 aluminum with cast-iron cylinder liners (cast into place) that are actually machined with a deck plate.

Although the pistons are still (high-silicon alloy) hypereutectic aluminum, they are dished for proper air/fuel mixture and a 9:1 compression. The top ring land is anodized to deflect heat, and the piston skirt is coated to prevent cylinder wall scuffing. The floating wrist pin also contributes to a quiet and durable piston, as does oil-spray cooling. The LS9 is the only other LS engine to use these jets to pressurize engine oil and reduce piston temperature.

Like the LS9, the LSA also uses a forged 3.62-inch-stroke crankshaft with a proprietary flange. Instead of the traditional six-bolt flange, the LSA uses eight bolts to connect to the flywheel and flexplate (the LS9 uses nine bolts). The connecting rods are a forged powder metal that is both light and strong. The oil pump capacity was increased to 33.8 gallons per minute.

In addition to the bottom end, the LSA boasts many other improvements over the LS3. The cylinder heads, for example, are nearly identical aside from the actual casting process itself. Just like the LS9, premium A356-T6 alloy is rotocast; the mold is rotated as the molten alloy cools to eliminate porosity. The camshaft is relatively mild (.480/.480-inch lift, 198/216 duration at .050, 122 lobe separation angle) for the purposes of being more quiet and smooth than its naturally aspirated counterparts. The Eaton Gen VI supercharger and its twin four-lobe rotors belting out 9 psi of boost afford this luxury. The new rotor design was a 20-percent improvement in airflow over the previous generation.

Although the Camaro ZL1's LSA is nearly identical to the 2009 Cadillac CTS-V in which the engine was originally designed, several improvements were made to the air-to-liquid intercooler as well as the lid. Hence its different appearance. It also uses cast stainless steel exhaust manifolds, which help account for the bump in power. However, like the CTS-V's, the ZL1's LSA uses a center-feed fuel system with a dual fuel pump that is pulse-width modulated (changes pressure according to throttle input) and an additional pickup. Other common features include: an 87-mm throttle body, direct-mount LS7 ignition coils, dedicated eight-rib supercharger drive system, and E67 computer.

The legendary 7.0L LS7, originally developed for the 2006 Corvette Z06, was adapted for use in the 2014–2015 Camaro Z/28 with a new accessory drive system, engine covers, Tri-Y headers, and open-element cold-air intake. No expense was spared to make the ultimate small-block with titanium rods and intake valves, high-port heads based on the C5R design, billet main caps, dry sump oiling, and the best OEM Gen III/IV intake manifold ever made.

CHAPTER 1

Like the LS3, the 7.0L LS7 was first implemented on the Corvette before finding a home in the 2014–2015 Camaro Z28. The LS7 is the first engine to use dry-sump oiling on the Camaro.

As it was for the 2005–2013 Corvette, the LS7 is an engine built for the track, which made it the perfect choice for the purpose-built Z28. At 427 ci, the LS7 pushes the limit of cylinder wall thickness, since it is still bound to the 4.4-inch bore spacing, as are all LS engines. Being a small-block, though, it is still a fairly high-revving engine, maxing out at 7,100 rpm. A 4140 forged steel crankshaft, secured by forged steel main caps, provides 4.0 inches of stroke to forged titanium connecting rods and hypereutectic pistons. Titanium 2.20 intake and sodium-filled 1.61-inch exhaust valves in the C5R-derived cylinder heads complement these lightweight materials.

The LS7's smaller CNC-ported runners are the highest flowing factory cylinder head in the LS lineup (and possibly ever made by General Motors). Raised intake runners and a 12-degree valve angle required matching intake manifold and 1.8-ratio rocker arms. As you'd expect, the camshaft is the biggest yet at .591/.591-inch lift and 211/230 duration at .050, cut on a 121 lobe separation angle.

In the 2014–2015 Camaro Z28, the LS7 appears more like something built from the Chevrolet Performance catalogue rather than an actual production car. Instead of the typical OEM air box, the Z28 uses an open element K&N air filter with a straight intake tube that clamps to the 90-mm throttle body. Even the ZL1's stainless steel exhaust manifolds pale in comparison to the high-flowing Tri-Y headers used on the Z28, to say nothing of the dual-mode 2.75-inch exhaust with which it connects.

Further adding to the custom feel of the Z28's powertrain, all LS7s are hand-built in the Performance Build Center in Wixom, Michigan. And to protect these high-dollar 427s from oil and fuel starvation, they were given a specially designed oil tank and fuel pump to account for the incredible g-forces in which the Z is capable.

The 2010–2011 Camaro LS and LT featured the highest horsepower naturally aspirated V-6 General Motors has ever built. The 3.6L direct-injection LLT is part of the High Feature V-6 engine family, which is a far cry from the 3800 V-6s of yesteryear. Although the 3800 is a 90-degree pushrod engine with two valves per cylinder, such as any small-block V-8, the High Feature engines use a 60-degree "V" with 24 valves and dual overhead cams.

The Cadillac CTS was among the first U.S. applications for the High

Engine Options

	LLT	LFX	LS3	L99	LSA	LS7
Type	V-6, dual overhead camshafts	V-6, dual overhead camshafts	V-8, overhead valve, 2 valves per cylinder, cam-in-block, hydraulic roller	V-8, overhead valve, 2 valves per cylinder, cam-in-block, hydraulic roller, VVT, AFM	V-8, overhead valve, 2 valves per cylinder, cam-in-block, hydraulic roller, 1.9L Eaton supercharger, air-to-water intercooler	V-8, overhead valve, 2 valves per cylinder, cam-in-block, hydraulic roller
Displacement	3.6L (217 ci)	3.6L (217 ci)	6.2L (376 ci)	6.2L (376 ci)	6.2L (376 ci)	7.0L (427 ci)
BorexStroke (inches)	3.70x3.37	3.70x3.374	.065x3.62	4.065x3.62	4.065x3.6	4.125x4.00
Bore Center (inches)	4.05	4.05	4.4	4.4	4.4	4.4
Compression	11.3:1	11.5:1	10.7:1	10.4:1	9.1:1	11.0:1
Horsepower @RPM	312@6,400	323@6,800	426@5,900	400@5,900	580@6,000	505@6,100
Torque (ft-lbs @RPM)	278@5,200	278@4,800	420@4,600	410@4,300	556@4,200	481@4,800
EFI Type	Sequential Direct Injection	Sequential Direct Injection	Sequential Port Injection	Sequential Port Injection	Sequential Port Injection	Sequential Port Injection
Fuel (octane)	87	87	91	91	91	91
Weight (pounds)	361	345	403	TBD	467	454
Assembly Site	St. Catherines, Ontario, Canada	St. Catherines, Ontario, Canada	St. Catherines, Ontario, Canada	St. Catherines, Ontario, Canada	Silao, Mexico	Wixom, Michigan

AN OVERVIEW

Feature V-6, and ultimately received the LLT two years prior to the Camaro's initial release. The LLT is an incredibly efficient engine, capable of running on 87-octane with an 11.3:1 compression ratio thanks to direct injection (DI). By placing the fuel injectors into the combustion chambers, a more complete burn with a leaner mixture occurs at the same power level. The impetus for the system is a high-pressure mechanical fuel pump.

Other key features of the LLT V-6 include VVT, silent (inverted tooth) cam drive, and oil-spray cooled and coated pistons. As with the LSA, pressure-activated jets spray the underside of the cast aluminum pistons with oil to reduce the temperature for increased longevity. A polymer coating on the piston skirts, floating wrist pins, sinter forged connecting rods, and a forged steel crankshaft make up the rotating assembly. A319 aluminum alloy is used to cast the cylinder heads and block, which has six-bolt mains, cast-in iron cylinder liners, and bay-to-bay breather vents such as on an LS block.

The 2012–2015 Camaro LS and LT received a slight upgrade with the LFX V-6. The new design swapped the aluminum intake manifold for composite, used longer duration camshafts, and revised the cylinder head design. Improved intake runners were matched with larger valves, and on the exhaust side things got even more radical: casting the exhaust manifolds directly into the heads. This dropped 20 pounds and gained more than 10 hp. Other revisions made at that time included a new fuel pump and injectors, isolated fuel rail, stronger and lighter connecting rods, and improvements to the camshaft cap and throttle body design. The engine is even stronger externally, with improved structural front cover and block.

CAFE standards being what they are, it is no surprise that every fifth-gen Camaro came with a 6-speed transmission. With the V-6 LS and LT, it gave Chevrolet the opportunity to use some fairly aggressive gearing to keep the peaky engine in its powerband. The Aisin AY6 manual seems to use gears you'd usually see in a truck transmission, using an extremely steep 4.48:1 first gear. The 6L50E automatic mirrors the SS's 6L80E fairly closely, which uses the close ratios down low for optimum acceleration and two overdrive gears, along with a 3.27:1 rear gear for better highway mileage. In fact, most Camaro models used 3.27 rear-end gears, with the exception being the manual-trans SS and 2LS, as well as the ZL1 and Z/28.

The 6L80E and 6L90E automatic transmissions represent a real departure in design for General Motors. Both are extremely strong, which is denoted by the second number (80 or 90). You can guess what the first number signifies. Both transmissions replace the 4L80E truck transmission (and the Turbo 400 before it), adding two gears. A compound planetary that functions as three planetary sets in one is the modus operandi (larger gears in the 6L90E's output carrier give it increased holding power). Internally it is more than just a few extra gears that separate the two transmissions.

The 6L80E and 6L90E are increasingly reliant on electronics for operation, rather than hard parts that can wear out or be overwhelmed by engine torque. As a result, it uses no bands, just clutches, which must engage at the exact time another disengages. This requires precision transmission calibration. The 6L80E was first used in the 2006 Corvette before finding a home in various Cadillacs, trucks, and the Camaro. The 6L90E was introduced in the 2009 Cadillac CTS-V, which shares the ZL1's LSA powerplant. In addition to the output carrier, its holding power is increased by way of a strengthened output shaft, strengthened input gear set, additional clutch plate, and two additional pinion gears.

The Camaro features many variations on the Tremec TR6060 manual transmission. Contrary to popular belief, all TR6060s were not created equal. The original version was built for the 2008 Corvette and built to handle 600 ft-lbs of torque. Its predecessor, the T56, was only good for 450 ft-lbs of torque in the most potent GM applications. A few key upgrades include wider cluster gears with larger front/rear bearings, wider fifth- and sixth-gears, thicker second gear, larger input bearing, larger 3-4 synchros with more teeth, larger 31-spline main shaft, and a thicker case.

Transmission Options

	Aisen AY6 Manual	Tremec TR6060 (M10)	Tremec TR6060 (MG9)	GM 6L50E Auto	GM 6L80E Auto	GM 6L90E Auto
First:	4.48	3.01	2.66	4.06	4.03	4.03
Second:	2.58	2.07	1.78	2.37	2.36	2.36
Third:	1.63	1.43	1.30	1.55	1.53	1.53
Fourth:	1.19	1.00	1.00	1.16	1.15	1.15
Fifth:	1.00	.840	.740	.850	.850	.85
Sixth:	.750	.570	.500	.670	.670	.67
Reverse:	3.67	3.28	2.90	3.20	3.06	3.06

In addition to receiving different gear ratios from the SS version (M10), the ZL1 version (MG9) comes with an air-to-liquid cooler and is 30-percent stronger. The output shaft, rear housing, additional roller bearing, and triple synchros highlight those improvements. The 1LE Handling Package equipped SS models with the smoother shifting MM6, as did the Z/28, which has the same ratios as the MG9 and many of the same improvements.

Connecting the Camaro's transmission to the rest of the drivetrain is a two-piece driveshaft with rubber couplers that are extremely effective at isolating vibration and noise. The rear-end housing on the LS, LT, SS, and Z/28 is aluminum with an 8.5-inch ring gear. The automatic-equipped SS, manual V-6, and most automatic V-6s came with 3.27-ratio gears (2LT had 2.92). Manual-equipped SSs had 3.45; the ultra high-performance 1LE and Z/28 had 3.91 gears.

All models came with limited-slip differentials. But the Z/28 uses a unique, zero-preload diff with a concentric helical gear set in lieu of traditional clutch plates and springs. This design allows for continuous torque biasing, generating "friction proportional to the input torque." This is particularly useful at a corner exit, which helped make the Z/28 one of the fastest production cars on the road course. Complementing this track-worthy diff is a specially designed cooler with an integral heat exchanger (inside the housing), which effectively removes more than 100 degrees from the diff fluid. All CV axles have a 30-mm diameter on the driver's side and 40 mm on the passenger's side to reduce wheel hop, though the 1LE and Z/28 version has a much beefier CV joint.

As the most powerful in the Camaro lineup, the ZL1 necessarily has the strongest rear end. The ring gear measures a whopping 9.84 inches, and the housing is made of cast iron. The manual trans version comes with 3.73 gears; the automatic has 3.27s. A heavy-duty differential and stacked plate cooler are also capable of providing 100 degrees of relief. The axles, though, are by far the most impressive of the bunch. Measuring 60.5 mm on the passenger's side and 33.25 mm on the driver's side, the axles look like baseball bats. For the CV joints, the engineers attempted to pirate some from a turbo diesel 4 x 4. But even those weren't strong enough, so they started from scratch. One engineer told me that this rear end is as strong as they know how to make. Given the challenges involved with an independent rear suspension, that is saying something.

Chassis and Suspension

The basic design and components of the fifth-generation Camaro's fully independent suspension carry over to all models. The front suspension uses a "multilink strut" and dual-ball joints, foregoing a traditional upper control arm, such as a MacPherson strut. A radius rod (aka front trailing arm) and lower control arm locate the strut-mounted spindle (and bolt to the K-member). The lower control arm works longitudinally and laterally during suspension travel; the radius rod acts upon fore and aft movement during acceleration or braking. The sway bar (or stabilizer bar) uses a long end link to connect halfway up the strut, enacting roll resistance during cornering. It bolts to the K-member via brackets and bushings. The struts and springs are a coil-over style, mounting directly to the body structure and spindle and keep the tires planted during changing road conditions.

Although the front suspension bears close resemblance to other Zeta-based applications, the 4.5-link rear suspension was developed exclusively for the Camaro. In lieu of a double A-arm setup, such as on the Corvette, the Camaro uses a bulky L-shaped (stamped steel) upper control arm with a traditional lower control arm, trailing arm, and toe rod to

When equipped with the optional wheels, it could be difficult to tell a V-6 model from an SS. Although it is worth noting that the suspension and brakes were different altogether, not just the engine and drivetrain. Softer bushings and springs, thinner sway bars, etc., were also used.

AN OVERVIEW

The single-piston, floating calipers were a dead giveaway to V-6 models. The upside is that they also make great drag brakes, allowing for smaller and lighter drag wheels.

All SS models came with fixed, four-piston Brembo brakes. Although substantially sized, the weight of the SS made them simply adequate.

The 1LE offered many handling improvements over the SS, which was based on an in-house test-mule for the ZL1's new suspension.

Sway Bar Options

Suspension	Front Sway Bar (mm)	Rear Sway Bar (mm)
FE2 (LS, LT)	22.2	21.7
FE3 (SS convertible)	23.0	23.0
FE4 (SS coupe)	23.0 (solid)	24.0 (solid)
FE6 (1LE)	27.0 (solid)	28.0 (solid)
FE5 (ZL1)	25.0 (solid)	28.0 (solid)
Z/28	25.0 (solid)	26.0 (solid)

locate the hub/wheel. The control arms guide vertical movement, the trailing arm acts upon everything else. The toe rod simply sets the toe angle of the rear wheels. The rear sway bar bolts to the cradle and connects to the lower control arms via end links to control body roll. The rear and front cradles are double-isolated from the body structure by rubber bushings, in addition to the rubber bushings found throughout the suspension. This does wonders to reduce NVH (Noise Vibration Harshness).

As for model variations, four suspension packages were offered on the fifth-gen Camaro (Camaro ZL1 and Z/28 also received unique components). All LS and LT V-6 models received the FE2 suspension. The SS convertible and 2010–2011 coupe came with FE3 suspension, 2012–2014 SS coupe used FE4 parts, and the 1LE came with FE6 parts. Each of the four used different sway bars, spring rates, and shocks to achieve different outcomes.

The V-6 models are known to have a smoother ride and the SS is noticeably stiffer. This is directly related to the FE2's 25 N/mm spring rate and 96 mm of suspension travel in the front, and 53 N/mm rear springs enabling 115 mm of travel.

The FE3's lowered ride height puts it at 84 mm of travel using 27 N/mm springs in the front, and 100-mm travel with 55 N/mm springs in the rear. Initially hollow sway bars were used to reduce weight; later models used solid bars for additional stiffness. The sway bars, shock valving, and spring rates are matched to the size and grip of the tires, as well as the weight of the car and other factors.

As formidable as even the Camaro SS coupe's FE4 suspension is on a road course, the Camaro team certainly wasn't done. The FE6 in the 1LE package builds upon this

CHAPTER 1

Goodyear Eagle F1 G:2 Supercar tires were designed especially for the ZL1 and 1LE, which greatly improved braking, as well as overall grip and handling. The specially designed wheels helped shave rotating mass. Despite the two wheel styles, it's actually the same design; one has extra machining to cut out the center piece of the spokes.

foundation by first tweaking the sway bars to dial in the handling as close to neutral as possible.

It is worth noting that the FE4, FE6, ZL1, and Z/28 use a revised rear sway bar design that moves the drop links outboard of the control arms. Camaro program engineering

The ride height, spring rates, bushing durometer, sway bar stiffness, and geometry were all optimized for the ZL1.

Contrary to appearances, the 1LE's red brake calipers were otherwise identical to the SS.

The ZL1 also had six-piston Brembo brakes with a two-piece rotor. Even with its increased weight, it still stopped on a dime. Both wheels used the same casting with different machining, which helped cut costs and weight.

Although the ZL1 was incredibly fast on the track, the 1LE was the pure track car.

AN OVERVIEW

manager Tony Roma said it "makes a bar with the same diameter four to five times more effective" than the previous design. A matched set of sticky, 285-mm Goodyear Eagle F1 Supercar G:2 tires complement the bars, rather than using the staggered Pirelli P-Zero's on regular SS coupes. Although the suspension bushings and spring rates carry over, heavier-duty wheel bearings, toe links, and rear shock mounts are borrowed from the ZL1. The rear shocks are switched to monotube (from twin on the SS), symbolic of the 1LE's singular purpose.

By comparison, the Camaro ZL1 and Z/28 are completely different animals from even the road racing–inspired 1LE-equipped SS. The ZL1 is a high-tech marvel that provides the "best of both worlds" approach to handling by using Magnetic Ride Control. This sophisticated electronic system changes the shock valving on the fly using Magneto-Rheological fluid that changes viscosity by way of an electromagnet.

The ZL1's MR system is not simply a warmed-over version of what was found in the C6 Corvette. The old single-wire design was replaced with a dual-wire version 3.0 that uses two smaller magnets and new ride height sensors. This MR is part of a new Performance Traction Management (PTM) that integrates it with launch control, traction control, stability control, and the electric power steering. The new PTM is so fast

That was until the 2014 Z/28 was created.

The forged 19-inch Z/28 wheels were the lightest of the bunch and combined with massive carbon ceramic brakes for unparalleled performance.

As the sun sets on the fifth-gen platform, it will be remembered for its combination of cutting-edge technology, impressive performance, and nostalgic looks that helped reinvigorate the muscle car wars.

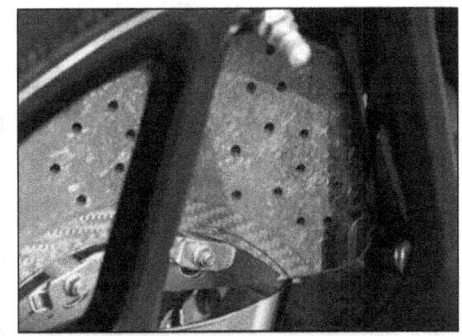
The Brembo carbon ceramic brakes are one of a handful of parts not available to the general public, helping to ensure there are no Z/28 clones.

you can actually floor it at a corner exit and let the computer do all the work, managing the vehicle dynamics. PTM can modulate engine torque 1,000 times per second to reach the very edge of traction.

In terms of hard parts, stiffer cradle and suspension bushings were used to match the increased grip. A set of 25-mm front and 28-mm solid sway bars match the staggered 285- and 305-mm Supercar rubber. And the stiffer progressive-rate rear springs spec at 70 to 45 N/mm. The front is identical to the FE3/FE4's 27 N/mm.

The Camaro Z/28 takes the ZL1's passion to the next level. Minus the use of Magnetic Ride, the Z/28 uses the same advanced Performance Traction Management system as the ZL1, but calibrated for the Z/28's components and intentions. Multimatic Dynamic Suspensions Spool Valve dampeners, such as those used in Formula One racing, have a more singular purpose than Magnetic Ride: track domination. Hundreds of hours of hot lapping and combing through data allowed the engineers to precisely tune the inverted monotube struts and aluminum-body monotube shocks. These dampeners are designed to be consistent lap after lap in providing optimum wheel control and are stiffer and more responsive than the 1LE, for example.

The springs are also considerably stiffer, at 50 N/mm front and 91 N/mm rear because ride quality isn't a real concern. This allowed a smaller set of 25-mm front and 26-mm rear sway bars. The key, though, is a set of R-compound Pirelli PZero Trofeo R tires that measure a whopping 305 mm at all four corners.

With 1.08-g capable during lateral acceleration, higher durometer bushings are needed to keep from distorting and possibly even tearing. The lower control arm ride link "travel limiter" (aka front sway bar end link) bushing is 50-percent stiffer, which also improves steering feel. The rear upper control arm bushings

Model	Tires	Wheels	Curb weight (pounds)	Brakes
LS coupe (manual)	P245/55R18	18x7.5	3,719	Single-piston; 12.64x1.18-inch front, 12.4x.9-inch rear vented rotors
LS coupe (auto)	P245/55R18	18x7.5	3,702	Single-piston; 12.64x1.18-inch front, 12.4x.9-inch rear vented rotors
LT coupe (manual)	P245/55R18 or P245/50R19	18x7.5 or 19x8	3,738	Single-piston; 12.64x1.18-inch front, 12.4x.9-inch rear vented rotors
LT coupe (auto)	P245/55R18 or P245/50R19	18x7.5 or 19x8	3,722	Single-piston; 12.64x1.18-inch front, 12.4x.9-inch rear vented rotors
LT convertible (manual)	P245/55R18 or P245/50R19	18x7.5 or 19x8	4,015	Single-piston; 12.64x1.18-inch front, 12.4x.9-inch rear vented rotors
LT convertible (auto)	P245/55R18 or P245/50R19	18x7.5 or 19x8	4,002	Single-piston; 12.64x1.18-inch front, 12.4x.9-inch rear vented rotors
SS coupe (manual)	P245/45ZR20 front, P275/40ZR20 rear (1LE: P285/35ZR20)	20x8 front, 20x10 rear (1LE: 20x10 front, 20x11 rear)	3,908	Brembo 4-piston; 14x1.26-inch, 14.4x1.1-inch vented rotors
SS coupe (auto)	P245/45ZR20 front, P275/40ZR20 rear	20x8 front, 20x10 rear	3,946	Brembo 4-piston; 14x1.26-inch, 14.4x1.1-inch vented rotors
SS convertible (manual)	P245/45ZR20 front, P275/40ZR20 rear	20x8 front, 20x10 rear	4,172	Brembo 4-piston; 14x1.26-inch, 14.4x1.1-inch vented rotors
SS convertible (auto)	P245/45ZR20 front, P275/40ZR20 rear	20x8 front, 20x10 rear	4,209	Brembo 4-piston; 14x1.26-inch, 14.4x1.1-inch vented rotors
ZL1 coupe (manual)	P285/35ZR20 front, P305/35ZR20 rear	Forged 20x10 front, 20x11 rear	4,120	Brembo 6-piston; 14.6x1.26-inch front, 14.4x1.1-inch rear rotors
ZL1 coupe (auto)	P285/35ZR20 front, P305/35ZR20 rear	Forged 20x10 front, 20x11 rear	4,149	Brembo 6-piston; 14.6x1.26-inch front, 14.4x1.1-inch rear rotors
ZL1 convertible (manual)	P285/35ZR20 front, P305/35ZR20 rear	Forged 20x10 front, 20x11 rear	4,374	Brembo 6-piston; 14.6x1.26-inch front, 14.4x1.1-inch rear rotors
ZL1 convertible (auto)	P285/35ZR20 front, P305/35ZR20 rear	Forged 20x10 front, 20x11 rear	4,403	Brembo 6-piston; 14.6x1.26-inch front, 14.4x1.1-inch rear rotors
Z/28	P305/30ZR19	Forged 19x11 front, 19x1.5 rear	3,837	Brembo 6-piston; 15.5x1.4-inch front, 15.3x1.3 rear carbon rotors

AN OVERVIEW

are 400-percent stiffer; a 25-percent increase to the inner and outer lower trailing link bushings help prevent toe change under high loads. Like the 1LE, the Z/28 also comes with a strut tower brace for additional chassis stiffening. It has less weight to carry around the track thanks to a strict diet plan. Thinner rear window glass (from 3.5 to 3.2 mm), lightweight rear seat with no trunk folding/pass-through, no air conditioning, removed wiring/sound system, and a 19-inch wheel include some of the measures taken by the engineering team to strip around 100 pounds.

From the Z/28 all the way down the lineup, the Camaro offers impressive braking. The Z/28's carbon ceramic Brembos are, of course, the best of them. Measuring 15.5 inches in the front and 15.3 inches in the rear with six-piston front and four-piston rear calipers, brake fade is not a concern on the Z/28. In addition to face-planting occupants at 1.8 g and stopping from 60 to 0 mph in less than 100 feet (according to *Motor Trend*), the carbon brakes also shed more than 21 pounds in unsprung weight.

Two-piece rotors, though steel, were used on the ZL1 for the same reason. The ZL1 is no slouch, using a similar set of six- and four-piston calipers, but with smaller (14.6-inch front, 14.4-inch rear) rotors.

The SS also uses a fixed aluminum caliper from Brembo, with four pistons in the front and a single piston in the rear to clamp 14- and 14.4-inch one-piece rotors. The LS/LT fills its 18- and 19-inch wheels with 12.64-inch front and 12.4-inch rear brakes with floating, single-piston alloy calipers. Although dwarfed by the rest of the lineup, by normal standards these are a pretty substantial set of brakes.

Modifying

Whether you are an avid road racer, drag racer, or street enthusiast, the fifth-gen Camaro has the capabilities to perform admirably. From its intimidating lap times at the Nürburgring, success in the Grand-Am and SPEED World Challenge series, countless wins in the NHRA, and the sheer volume of cars sold in the United States, the 2010–2015 Camaro is hell-bent on domination. And the origin of this success is sheer determination. From inception, the Camaro was built with adversarial intentions and not much has changed.

Out of the box, the fifth-gen Camaro SS made more power and was a vastly superior handling car to the little Blue Oval pony. The Mustang's live rear axle proved to be its Achilles' heel in terms of handling and ride quality. Unfortunately, though, the Camaro's straight-line acceleration suffered due to its weight. The lighter pony car was at least .1 second faster in the quarter-mile (and frequently .2 faster for 0–60) when the 2011 model debuted. The even-heavier Dodge Challenger suffered the same fate and was usually one- to two-tenths slower than the Camaro in the quarter-mile. Its weight and softer suspension also proved to be a detriment to handling, despite its independent rear suspension.

When comparing the ZL1, outgoing 662 hp GT500, and the 700 hp Challenger Hellcat, things become more interesting. Despite being the heaviest of the group, the Hellcat had the second fastest (11.7 at 125 mph during a *Motor Trend* test) run on the GT500's heels. In the same test, the ZL1 ran a respectable 12.2 at 116 mph. Typically the GT500 runs in the range of 11.6 at 125 mph. But the straight axle Shelby and the understeer-happy Hellcat can't hold a candle to the ZL1 through the twisties. Testing consistently shows that the Camaro can outrun both cars thanks to its tremendous grip and composed handling.

Perhaps the most impressive thing about the fifth-gen platform is its high ceiling with modifications, particularly on V-8 models. Although V-6 models can easily rival their larger displacement counterparts in stock form, with the help of supercharger and turbocharger kits, the lack of aftermarket support for direct-injection fuel components constrains the power potential. The Gen IV V-8, on the other hand, is perhaps the most supported engine the aftermarket has ever seen. From whisper-quiet 1,500-hp fuel pump setups to big-block type displacement, LS engines are peerless in the aftermarket community. A simple cam swap can yield 50 to 100 hp, and even more with a good set of headers and cylinder heads. It is downright easy to make great power increases.

As impressive as the Coyote 5.0L and the late-model Hemi are, there are no 1,000-hp naturally aspirated Coyotes, 1,500-hp Hemi street cars, or 800-hp Pro Touring cars running around with either engine. Yet this is not at all uncommon in the LSx community. LSx engines offer incredible power potential and the reliability and variety of modifications is extensive. You can build the ultimate fifth-gen Camaro to do whatever you want, from drag racing, to drifting, road racing, autocross, circle track, standing mile, top speed racing, hill climbs, rallies, and just about anything else you can dream of. This book provides the tools to make those dreams a reality.

CHAPTER 1

Sixth-Gen: A Look Ahead

The 2016 Camaro was unveiled on Belle Isle in May 2015 amid throngs of onlookers and reporters. It was announced that the lighter Alpha platform would be used in production at the Lansing Grand River Assembly Plant, though employing 70-percent unique components.

The basic structure is a unitized body frame with one- and two-sided galvanized steel. The length was reduced from 190.6 to 188.3 inches, height by 1.1 inch (to 53.1), and the wheelbase from 112.3 to 110.7 inches. The new architecture was credited for losing more than 200 pounds (133 in just the body) and gaining 28 percent of structural rigidity. Aluminum suspension pieces and a laser-brazed roof were just a few added measures to shed mass.

Like the later fifth-gens, the sixth-gen has a narrow upper grille and hood vents on the SS for a very slippery design. The front fascia has an "air curtain" to guide air around the wheel rather than through the wheelhouses. The sixth-gen spent 350 hours in the wind tunnel to achieve its shape, which reduces drag on the LT (for better fuel efficiency) and improves downforce on the SS (for better performance).

Despite some speculation that CAFÉ standards were just too strict, Chevrolet proudly announced that the Gen V LT1 small-block would power the SS. Sporting 455 hp and 455 ft-lbs of torque, the direct-injection 6.2L V-8 has every bit of muscle that the SS needs to stay true to its heritage while embracing the latest technology.

Like its pony car competitor at Ford, Chevrolet announced that the LT1 would be joined by a turbo 4-cylinder, as well as the latest 3.6L V-6. At 275 hp and 295 ft-lbs of torque, the 2.0L turbo LTG Ecotec is on par with the V-8s of only a few generations ago. The new LGX V-6 makes an impressive 335 hp and 284 ft-lbs of torque. A Tremec TR3160 6-speed manual and 8L45 8-speed auto are the transmissions of choice for the smaller two engines, while the SS wields a TR6060 6-speed manual again and an 8L90 8-speed auto. Originally released on the 2015 Corvette, the 8L90 has Active Rev Match to blip the throttle during downshifts just like an F1 car. The torquey 11.5:1 LT1 and lighter weight allows for a 2.66 first gear on the TR6060, unlike the previous SS, along with 3.73 rear gears. The 8L90 affords a conservative 2.77 rear gear with its steep 4.56 first and 2.97 second.

The suspension is new and improved, though not a complete departure. An independent five-link rear suspension with twin-tube shocks and a stabilizer bar enhance the previous iterations by reducing "squat" during acceleration and reducing mass by 26 pounds. Magnetic Ride with monotube shocks are available on the SS for the first time, capable of reading and adjusting at 1,000 times per second as with the previous ZL1. The front suspension is a new double-pivot MacPherson-type strut arrangement with dual lower ball joints, stabilizer bar, and twin-tube

After months of teasing, the 2016 Camaro was introduced at the 2015 Detroit Belle Isle Grand Prix. Thus the sixth-generation was born.

AN OVERVIEW

struts; Mag Ride with inverted monotube struts is available on the SS.

Along with the new quick-ratio electronic steering assist, the SS was designed to be lighter and more nimble feeling. The engineering team also used the terms *linear* and *com-municative* to describe the steering feel on the sixth-gen. The 20-inch wheels are still the standard with Goodyear Eagle F1 Asymmetric 3 run-flat tires, and 18-inchers with all-season Goodyears on the LT. Brembo brakes are available on all models, topping out at 13.6 inches on the SS. ∎

From extensive testing, Chevrolet knows that switching the lower grille angle from 20 to 13 degrees creates a 1-percent improvement in cooling. A belly pan is used underneath the car that stretches from the grille to the center of the car to reduce lift by 30 percent, as well as drag. Although the hip line is reminiscent of the fifth-gen, the lines are unique and seem to hint at the new era of aerodynamic testing and thought.

Brembo brakes are available on all models, up to 13.6 inches on the SS.

The greenhouse isn't a huge improvement in site line, but Chevrolet did manage to update the interior appropriately. This treatment is less nostalgic and more cutting edge.

CAMARO 5TH GEN 2010–2015: HOW TO BUILD AND MODIFY   39

Sixth-Gen: A Look Ahead CONTINUED

Three engine options are offered for the 2016 Camaro: 455-hp V-8, 335-hp V-6, and 275-hp turbo 4-cylinder. All three are fuel-efficient direct-injection engines with Variable Valve Timing. The LT1 V-8 also has Active Fuel Management like the previous L99.

Despite commonalities of the Alpha platform, 70 percent of the Camaro is unique, including the dimensions, suspension geometry, and powertrain.

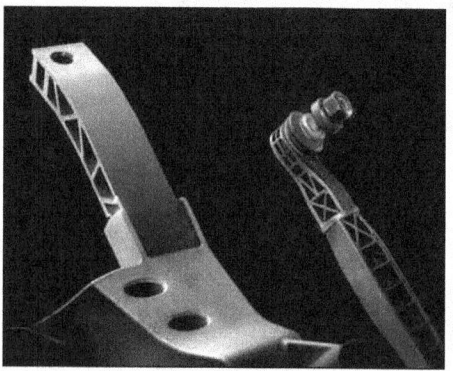

Aluminum front and rear suspension pieces with composite links reduce weight by 21 percent.

CHAPTER 2

Chassis: Suspension, Brakes, Wheels and Tires

As I mentioned in the Introduction, the fifth-generation Camaro came factory-equipped for world-class handling. Those demanding even greater capabilities can often look to the next model in the line, though aftermarket variants certainly have their advantages as well. In this chapter I cover how to swap from other models, as well as aftermarket options to enhance the Camaro's handling. In addition, I also cover how to adapt the fifth-gen's suspension and other components for use on street/strip and dedicated drag racing setups.

Although conventional thought led many to believe an independent rear suspension (IRS) could not survive under severe drag racing duty, there are now 6-second Outlaw Drag Radial cars with IRS and it won't be long before a Camaro goes as fast in the quarter-mile. The COPO program has helped make a solid axle swap for dedicated race cars a reality without months of expensive fabrication work. Options are truly plentiful for fifth-gen Camaro owners looking to go fast.

Suspension

Many of the standard modifications such as springs, sway bars, and bushings are extremely effective on the fifth-gen platform. However, serious enthusiasts should also consider shocks, trailing arms, and control to gain full control of the Camaro's chassis.

Springs

Lowering springs are typically the first stop for any street performance enthusiast wanting to improve handling. Although the manufacturer is concerned with ground clearance and ride quality, enthusiasts don't care about these things. So whether you are talking about a V-6, SS, or even a ZL1, lowering springs is a cost-effective means of improving the look and handling of your Camaro. Thankfully the market is flooded with springs to suit your needs.

Chassis turning a solid axle COPO and a Camaro with factory independent rear suspension are quite different, but make no mistake, hard launches and wheelies are still possible at the dragstrip.

Industry staples such as Eibach, H&R, and Hotchkis, as well as companies specializing in GM muscle cars such as Detroit Speed & Engineering, BMR Suspension, SLP Performance, MTI Racing, LSR Performance, and LG Motorsports all make lowering springs for the fifth-gen. Installation cost is usually quite reasonable because you can reuse the factory shocks, but a fresh alignment is required.

As you may know, the springs establish the ride height on any car. However, they also work in concert with the sway bars to control body roll, as well as the shocks to control wheel travel. A quality lowering spring lowers the center of gravity, which is easy to imagine by comparing the handling of an SUV to your Camaro. An SUV feels top-heavy and nervous, and fails to inspire confidence to take a turn at a high rate of speed.

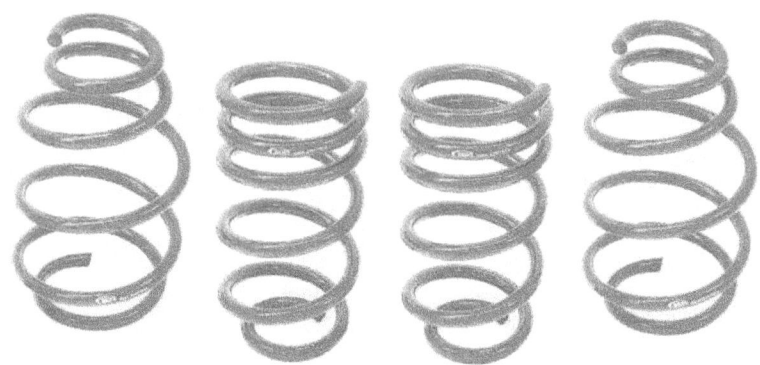

BMR offers several springs for the Camaro, including these springs with 220 lbs/in at the front (PN SP023) and 460 lbs/in at the rear (PN SP024) that provide 1.4 inches of drop. Chrome silicon high-tensile spring wire is cold wound on a CNC coiling machine, compressed solid twice, stress-relieved at 750 degrees, shot-peened, and computer tested for height and spring rate. (Photo Courtesy BMR Suspension)

Again, picturing the SUV, think of how much the body leans going around turns or how much it leans forward under hard braking. This exaggerated body roll demonstrates the need for stiffer springs. However, the springs cannot be too stiff. Spring rates must be optimized for the car, as the springs are responsible for keeping the tires in contact with the road. The springs need some measure of compliance to the contours of the road or the shock can't do its job. Plus, if you plan on street driving your Camaro and don't want to rattle all your fillings loose, it helps to have something a little more forgiving.

Air suspension became popular for this very reason because you can have a lowered stance without the punishing ride quality. The downside is that they add weight (compressor tank and wiring), not to mention complexity. Air Lift Performance and Ridetech offer quality fifth-gen kits. Although these certainly improve the performance of an LS, LT, or SS, they are generally considered more for their aesthetics, which is why they are not a focus in this book.

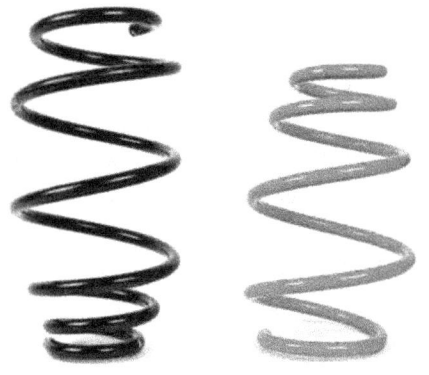

It is easy to see the difference between a stock spring and a lowering spring. Although it should be noted that the spring is not simply shorter, it is also stiffer, which helps reduce brake dive and (to some extent) body roll. Stiffer is not always better, though, as the springs can greatly affect ride comfort. Even on a race car where comfort isn't a huge concern, spring rates need to be compliant enough for proper weight transfer. (Photo Courtesy Phastek Performance)

Coil-Overs

Although aftermarket shock choices are limited, quite a few coil-overs are on the market that combine lowering springs with optimized valving and adjustability. Although it comes at a price, coil-overs allow the user to adjust the ride height by raising or lowering the spring's mounting point. Most coil-overs also have some adjustability to the shock's rebound and compression. Being able to adjust the shocks allows the user to compensate for changing conditions, other modifications to the car, driver taste, or use.

For example, if your Camaro pulls double duty on the autocross course and dragstrip, it comes in handy. At the dragstrip you want to set the shocks much softer to help squat and transfer weight to the rear tires. On the autocross course, however, you want it considerably stiffer for optimum handling. Street driving may be somewhere in between. For the ultimate drag racer or road racer, aftermarket coil-overs are the ticket. For drag racing, check out Strange Engineering, Lakewood, QA1, or Lingenfelter Performance Engineering

CHASSIS: SUSPENSION, BRAKES, WHEELS AND TIRES

(LPE). Road racing enthusiasts can select among MTI Racing, BC Racing, Megan Racing, AFCO, LG Motorsports, KW, Bilstein, Detroit Speed, and Chevrolet Performance's 1LE and high-zoot Z/28 offerings.

BC Racing is one of a few companies that make coil-overs aimed at the street crowd, rather than those strictly race oriented. Phastek Performance sells these BR coil-overs with very livable spring rates, though custom rates are available if you don't like your kidneys. Thirty levels of adjustment alter the rebound and compression to your satisfaction. A 56-mm body houses 46-mm pistons with spring steel valves, T6061 aluminum locks, and patented concave lower locking ring. (Photo Courtesy BC Racing)

The Camaro 1LE Track Pack from Chevrolet Performance (PN 23123397) allows the SS, or even the LS and LT (PN 23123398), to achieve 1.01 g-forces similar to those of its namesake. This SCCA-approved package features a 27-mm solid front and 28-mm solid rear stabilizer bars along with ZL1 rear shock mounts and toe links. The 1LE sway bars are more neutral than the understeer-happy SS counterparts, and the stiffer durometer bushings provide much better body control and more predictable handling. Early fifth-gens need the later FE4-style rear control arms to be compatible with the sway bar.

A complete Z/28 kit (PN 23464729) is available for a pretty penny, including the DSSV dampeners, springs, sway bars, and much more. This kit is top-of-the-line and can hang with anything the aftermarket offers. (Photo Courtesy Chevrolet Performance)

Sway Bars

The sway bars, sometimes referred to as stabilizer bars or anti-roll bars, control body roll and give the car its balance. A stiff front bar induces understeer, which is the front end's tendency to slide in a turn. A stiff rear bar causes oversteer, which is the rear end's tendency to slide or "drift" in a turn. The thickness and material (solid or hollow) greatly affects the stiffness of the bar; its shape also affects the handling characteristics. It is extremely important to match the bars correctly front to rear, but also to the rest of the suspension components, such as the springs and the tires. Whenever possible, the newer style rear sway bar employed on the FE3 SS, 1LE, ZL1, and Z/28 is preferable for optimum handling.

In a drag racing application, the front sway bar is basically dead weight and the rear sway bar plays a much different role. As the car launches from a standstill and the rear tires grip, the chassis twists with the

The FE4 lower rear control arms from Chevrolet Performance (PN 20942237) have a different mounting point for the rear sway bar, which greatly improves body control and feel. Even a stock 2012–2015 SS sway bar is an improvement over the early design. This 2010 SS, though, has a Pfadt ZL1 bar.

rotation of the driveshaft. A true anti-roll bar counteracts that by keeping the chassis level and maintaining traction in both rear tires. Some adjustable versions even allow you to preload one side if the chassis requires it.

BMR Suspension is one of the few companies making a true anti-roll bar for fifth-gen Camaros, which has three separate adjustments for the stiffness. BMR, LSR, MTI, LG, Detroit Speed, Eibach, Whiteline, Hotchkis, and Chevrolet Performance offer OEM-style sway bar upgrades better suited to street driving, road racing, and autocross.

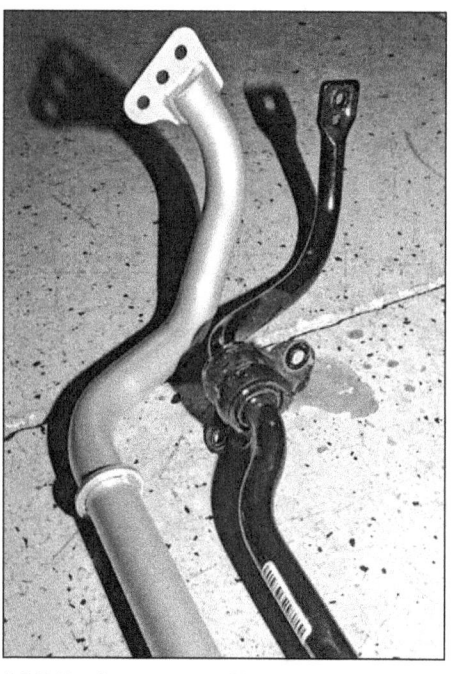

LSR Performance offers these adjustable front sway bars with settings for 159-, 212-, and 285-percent stiffer than the stock SS. The bars are manufactured from 4130 chrome-moly tubing. The ends are made of billet, which has been stamped and TIG welded for maximum strength. Three-way adjustable rear bars are available for 2010–2011 and 2012–2015 Camaros as well. Energy Suspension urethane bushings are included, along with brackets and a lifetime warranty.

Bushings

Although softer durometer rubber bushings may have kept the general public from complaining about ride quality, they tend to negate road feel and enhance deflection. Vague feedback, wheel hop, and instability can be addressed by swapping to polyurethane, Delrin, or solid aftermarket bushings. A good place to start is in the subframe and differential with options from Energy Suspension, Whiteline, and BMR. Recently Pfadt Racing's suspension parts have started resurfacing, which includes the only solid aluminum bushings on the market.

Because most companies do not offer any aftermarket version of the front radius rod or control arm, this is also an area where a bushing upgrade would be beneficial. There is no shortage of upgrades to

the Camaro's rear suspension, often scorned for its wheel hop. The upper and lower control arms, which guide vertical movement, are partially responsible. Swapping out the upper control arm bushings and the lower control arm altogether go a long way toward improving the situation.

Control and Trailing Arms

If you plan to switch to the later style sway bar or run 15-inch drag wheels, swapping the lower control arms is a must. The trailing arms are perhaps the weakest link in the rear suspension, known to deflect under acceleration or hard cornering. Because the trailing arms locate the wheel, the alignment is altered as these flimsy pieces give way, which leads to inconsistent handling as well as wheel hop. The toe rods are another weak link that negatively

aFe Power has re-released Pfadt suspension products, including these rear trailing arms. These fully TIG-welded, 14-gauge trailing arms are made of 304 stainless steel and optimized for weight. Thanks in part to the graphite-impregnated polyurethane bushings, these trailing arms reduce deflection by 32 percent, according to aFe/Pfadt. These trailing arms reduce the dreaded wheel hop, as well as improve corner-exit acceleration by allowing smooth application of power to the ground. Both the trailing arms and matching toe rods work on any year or model Camaro. (Photo Courtesy aFe Power)

A combination of Pfadt and custom-made pieces allow Redline Motorsports' ZL1 to fit 15-inch drag wheels. BMR Suspension and Carlyle Racing have since offered similar lower control arms.

affect the dynamic alignment (specifically the toe angle) under heavy cornering. Both a stiffer, boxed replacement with stock style eccentric bolts and adjustable rod end versions are available in the aftermarket. Suppliers include BMR, Whiteline, Hotchkis, Spohn, UMI, Lakewood, QA1, and LSR, to name a few.

Subframe Connectors

Although subframe connectors are actually not a part of the suspension, they do allow the suspension to do its job. By tying various critical points of the frame together, chassis flex is minimized. In doing so, that energy is transmitted to the shock absorbers and other moving parts designed to control it. Just as with bushing or control arm deflection, chassis flex can lead to uncontrolled movement, manifested as erratic handling.

For precise handling and straight launches, you want to keep that under control with subframe connectors and braces from BMR Suspension, Lakewood, SLP, Hotchkis, and LSR Performance. Strut tower braces are available through Chevrolet Performance, Hotchkis, SLP, QA1, LSR, BMR, and Spohn, to name a few. However, they are not nearly as effective as underbody bracing (and not of value to straight-line performance).

In various forms of racing, the Camaro's 4.5-link suspension has proven to be quite capable with modification. In the Sports Car Club of American (SCCA) World Challenge GTS class and the Grand-Am GS class, Camaros could frequently be seen at the front of the pack when they weren't so heavily sanctioned with weight penalties. In both classes, cars are heavily regulated to stay very close to their factory counterpart. In the drag racing world, there have been some incredibly fast street-based Camaros that retain the factory independent rear suspension, including Terri Mensing's 2010 SS, built by IPS Motorsports.

Aside from the American Racing Headers/Farks Supercars 7-second supercharged SS, the fastest fifth-gens use a solid axle. Like the COPO Camaro, a four-link solid-axle rear is a pretty standard swap for any serious chassis shop. The benefits are unlimited gear selection, simplicity, durability, and unlimited power potential. It's the preferred method of Outlaw 10.5 and Pro Mod classes (more on this in Chapter 3).

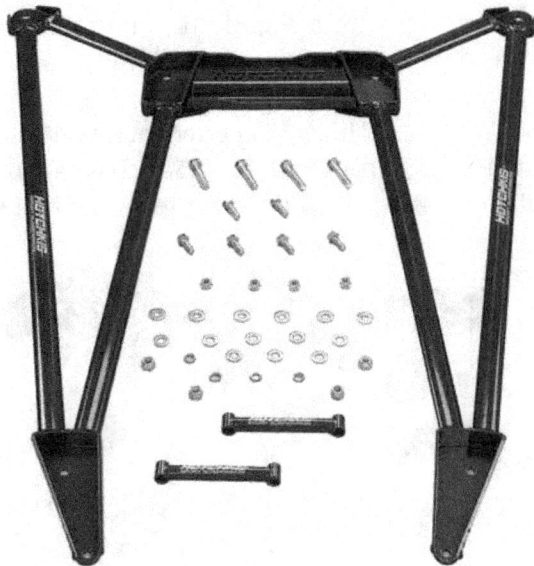

Hotchkis, BMR, and several others offer subframe connectors, just as with the last few Camaro generations. Although it adds weight, tying the subframe helps reduce chassis flex. By placing that energy into the suspension, which is designed to handle it, you can improve the stability and predictability. This is effective on a road course, dragstrip, or even the street. Designs vary by manufacturer. The Hotchkis Chassis Max Brace (shown) is unique in that it is made of elliptical aluminum tubing and laser-cut CNC-machined aluminum brackets. (Photo Courtesy Hotchkis Performance)

Brakes

The Camaro has substantial factory offerings in the brake department, many of which are available through Chevrolet Performance. For example, the Camaro SS Brake Kit (PN 23120542) brings a V-6 model up to SS specs with 14-inch rotors and Brembo four-piston calipers. The Camaro ZL1's brakes (PN 22959672 front, 22989384 rear) take it a step further with 14.6-inch front, 14.4-inch rear rotors, and six-piston Brembo calipers. The rear kit even includes a new master cylinder and backing plates.

None of these Chevrolet Performance kits void your warranty. For drag racers, using V-6 rear brakes on SS models is a fairly common modification to fit 16-inch drag wheels. Others have retrofitted C5 Corvette (1997–2004 models) rear brakes to fit the more common 15-inch drag wheels.

For the ultimate in braking performance, you have to turn to the aftermarket. You may not be able to purchase the Z/28's carbon ceramic brakes, but Wilwood Engineering has the next best thing. Wilwood's C/SiC is made of a proprietary blend of ceramic matrix composite material. It has been engineered to resist distortion, warping, and cracking at extreme temperatures while shaving substantial weight. Wilwood's traditional big front brake kit (PN 140-11269-DR) uses drilled or drilled-and-slotted iron rotors in 14.25 x 1.25 inches along with the AERO6 six-piston calipers. The AERO4 rear brake kit (PN 140-11270-DR) uses the same diameter with a slightly thinner rotor and four-piston calipers, while utilizing the OEM parking brake.

If bigger is better then you want to check out the 15-inch kits from Baer, Brembo, StopTech, and SLP/Brembo. Prices range from $3,300 to $4,500.

Perhaps the ultimate big brake kit is offered by AP Racing through Stillen (PN AP7720). At a whopping 16.15 inches, you have more braking power than any OEM vehicle. Despite its size, it still works perfectly with the OEM master cylinder and ABS. And it is on par with other high-end kits on the market at around $3,650.

AP Racing also offers a kit for hardcore road racers that trades the full-floating rotor for a patented strap drive (PN AP7700). These 14.5-inch J-hook, drilled, or drilled-and-slotted rotors are designed to make the most of the space afforded by 18-inch track wheels and still utilizing a six-piston caliper.

Although all of the aforementioned work perfectly on the street and track, there are some important considerations to take into account for racing. Brake pad selection is crucial to safety on a road course. There is nothing more terrifying than entering a turn midway through a session with no brakes. High-temperature pads are essential to lasting through any track event. Hawk Performance is a sure bet for track pads, though some also prefer StopTech, Carbotech, and EBC. Although the Hawk HPS and HP Plus are great street/autocross pads, you want something more aggressive, such as the DTC-70, for longer road courses that are hard on brakes.

Bleeding the brakes and adding high-temperature fluid also goes a long way toward surviving a track day. Motul, Amsoil, Wilwood, Castrol, and Brembo make fluid with a 300-degree dry boiling point. The fluid you choose affects the firmness of the brake pedal; the pads determine the bite. Changing just these

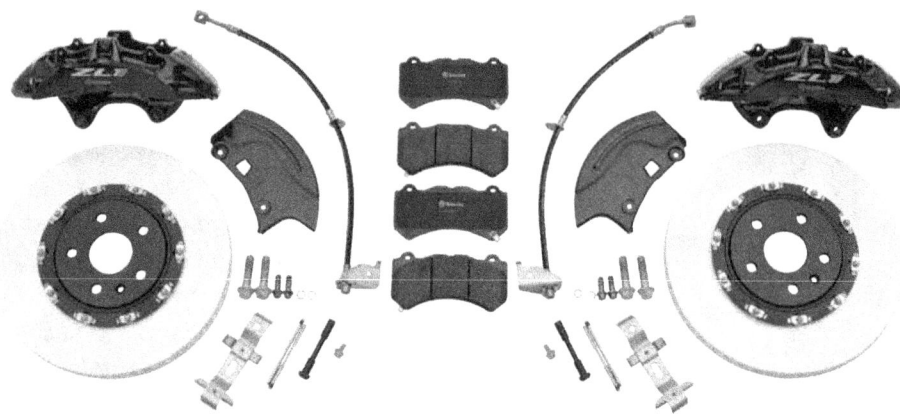

Although SS or 1LE brakes are a fine upgrade for V-6 models, why not jump right to ZL1 brakes? The Brembo six-piston, 14.6-inch front (PN 22959672) and four-piston, 14.4-inch rear (PN 22989384) brakes add tremendous stopping power and resistance to brake fade. Admittedly, the rear brakes are identical to those on the SS model minus the color and logo, so it is mainly marketed as an upgrade for the V-6. Twenty-inch wheels are required, but the kit comes with everything you need to install it, including brake lines, pads, and hardware. And it will not void your warranty. (Photo Courtesy Chevrolet Performance)

Wilwood offers nearly the same performance with a slightly smaller 14.25-inch six-piston front (PN 140-11269-DR) and four-piston rear (PN 140-11270-DR) kit at a much lower price point. (Photo Courtesy Wilwood Engineering)

If size matters, you want the AP Racing 16.15-inch six-piston front brake kit from Stillen (PN AP7720). Many professional road racing teams use AP Racing brakes; a smaller set is available for the hardcore crowd required to run 18-inch wheels. (Photo Courtesy Stillen)

Despite the number of aftermarket brake options, do not underestimate stock Brembos on an SS. With a good set of brake pads, you can make it through a full weekend of road racing without a hint of brake fade. Depending on the pad formula, it can actually add a lot more bite, too, which is also helpful for autocross or street driving. Ask fellow racers for pad advice, as it varies by track. Because some tracks, including Sebring and Road Atlanta, require pretty aggressive pads, you want a separate set if you plan on street driving your Camaro. Another helpful tip is to bleed the brake fluid, replacing the OEM fluid with high-temp variations. It's not snake oil; that stuff could literally save your life.

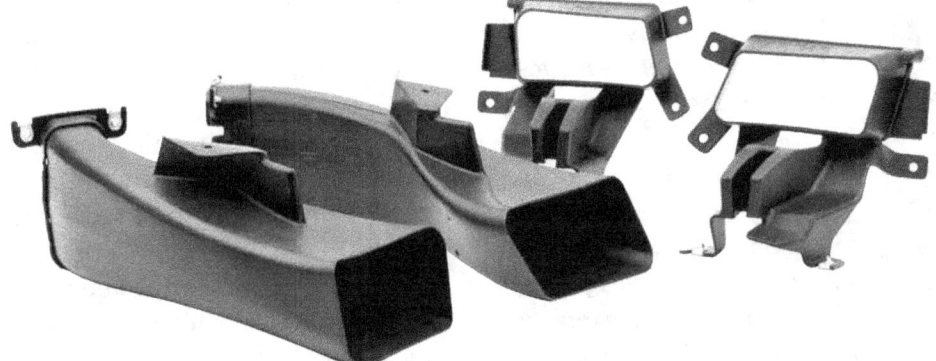

The Camaro Z/28 brake cooling ducts can also help prevent brake fade. Because the front bumper on the Z/28 and SS are shared, these cooling ducts simply attach and grab high-pressure air. The ducts dump air on the back of the rotors to help dissipate heat in the vanes. (Photo Courtesy Chevrolet Performance)

two components on your Camaro can dramatically change the braking feel and performance.

Rotors and brake lines are minor players in the braking system in terms of upgrades. It should be noted that a set of braided stainless steel brake lines can also improve pedal feel. Rotors are more of a wear item. Some gains can be had in rotor design, particularly if you switch to a two-piece that saves weight. Aftermarket rotors often have more material so that they can be cut periodically and reused, rather than just discarded once they warp. Some tend to be better at resisting warp, but eventually they all warp. If you plan on road racing, drilled rotors should be avoided. The holes can become the source of cracks and premature replacement.

In drag racing, braking power and fad resistance is less of a concern, as weight and fit is a larger priority. Because even the V-6 Camaro can't accommodate a 15-inch drag wheel, several aftermarket manufacturers have jumped on the opportunity. BMR Suspension offers a full rear package using Wilwood calipers and rotors, modified rotor hats, fabricated caliper brackets, and modified OEM spindles. TCE Performance Products offers a similar kit with Wilwood components; Carlyle Racing uses SSBC calipers. All of these are street friendly and retain the OEM parking brake. Baer offers an 11-inch SS4 front package, which is ideal for a drag car that sees some street time.

The COPO Camaro's Strange Engineering manual brake package is what you want for a dedicated track car for the ultimate in weight savings. With some fabrication, other options are available.

Wheels and Tires

The proportions of the fifth-gen and the large brakes make any wheels smaller than 18 inches in diameter a tricky situation at best. Chevrolet dealers typically offered several wheels in addition to the many factory offerings. The Camaro was so hot, though, that nearly every aftermarket manufacturer jumped at the opportunity to offer wheels.

Tire Rack offers dozens of wheels from the more economical $200 to $300 American Racing wheels, up to BBS, O.Z., and Enkei Racing in the $400 to $600 range. In addition, there are plenty of $150 to $200 knock-off wheels in the early SS style with larger sizes and a greater range of colors.

Lug nut style varies by wheel, which is the only consideration for a direct-fit wheel besides (of course) style. Pirelli P Zero tires, which come standard on the SS, as well as the

CHAPTER 2

Street Legal Performance (SLP), famous for making the fourth-gen SS, offers these 20 x 8 front and 20 x 9 rear to fit stock SS tires for those who simply want to add a different look. At around $1,400, these are certainly one of the more affordable, yet quality bolt-on options. For plus-size models, Tire Rack is a better source. The Hurst Stunner looks similar but is available in 20 x 9 front and 20 x 11 rear for a few bucks less. (Photo Courtesy SLP Performance)

The JDP Motorsports Camaro regularly competed in the Ultimate Street Car Association series using a set of Forgeline GA1Rs. These custom wheels are a forged one-piece monoblock design that combines strength, stiffness, and light weight. Like all Forgeline wheels, these are made of forged 6061-T6 aluminum. Although they look amazing, it is important to emphasize the safety aspect of using quality wheels for racing. The extreme stress can bring out imperfections in a lesser wheel, which can prove to be disastrous on the track. The GA1R is engineered for 2,100 pounds of load per wheel. (Photo Courtesy Forgeline Motorsports)

When ordering a custom wheel, it is a good idea to use a measuring tool such as Percy's Wheelrite. You can buy one from Summit Racing for around $75. It simulates the wheel and tire to help you select bolt pattern, wheel diameter, wheel width, backspacing, and tire profile.

Continental ExtremeContact DW, BFGoodrich Sport Comp-2, and Firehawk Wide Oval Indy 500 are available in the standard 245/45/20 and 275/40/20 sizes. These are all performance summer tires. BFG, Firestone, Continental, and General make all-season rubber for those who drive in the northern climates.

For optimum handling in the heavy fifth-gen, you want the largest front wheel you can fit to accommodate the largest tire. As the ZL1 proved, a 20 x 10–inch is about the largest wheel the fenders can afford. Any wider than that and you need some flares as on the Z/28, which has 19 x 11–inch wheels. Thankfully the rear wheelwells can stow 11-inch-wide wheels without any modifications. Wider rear wheels require flares. With the right sway bar setup, a staggered 20 x 9.5 front and 20 x 10.5 rear works exceptionally well using 275-mm front and 315-mm tires, although there is no denying that the 1LE's matched 20 x 10 setup with 285-mm tires is extremely well balanced.

Chevrolet chose the 20 x 11 rear wheels and 305-mm tires on the ZL1 to offset the supercharged 6.2L V-8's tremendous grunt. Owners of higher horsepower cars would be wise to do

When selecting wheels and tires, ABS and TPMS compatibility are two concerns for street-going Camaros. These Weld wheels have tire pressure sensor provisions and these Nitto NT05 275/40/20 front and 315/35/20 rear tires have nearly the same diameter as stock yet are a whole lot stickier. The Weld Racing RT-S line carries a lower price than Forgeline but have a forged billet center and cold forged rim shell that exceeds SAE J2530 standards. Sizes from 15 to 20 inches are available.

The Goodyear Eagle Supercar G:2 tires are OEMs on the ZL1 and also an excellent tire. You can see how the asymmetric pattern resists hydroplaning yet provides maximum grip toward the outside edge, where you need it most under hard cornering. (Photo Courtesy Goodyear)

the same. The right sway bar setup is needed to maintain handling balance.

The factory Goodyear Eagle F1 SuperCar G:2, BFGoodrich G-Force Rival, Nitto NT05, and Hankook Ventus R-S3 tires seem to be the stickiest available street tires. Some R-compound tires are also suitable for limited street use, such as the Toyo Proxes R888, Continental ContiForceContact, Dunlop Sport Maxx Race, P Zero Corsa System, and Michelin Pilot Sport Cup 2. For maximum grip, though, you want to downsize to 18- or 19-inch wheels to run full slicks, such as the BFGoodrich g-Force R1, Hoosier R7, and Kumho Ecsta V710.

For a plus-size wheel that may see some time on a road course or autocross, you want to steer away from aftermarket cast wheels. Typically these one-piece wheels are made using a gravity casting process, which has less density than other methods. Weight is increased to compensate.

Low-pressure casting is a better approach, but requires the additional work of the flow-forming method (also known as spun-rim or rim-rolling technology) to provide enough strength for the track. By spinning the initial casting while heating the outer portion and using steel rollers to press against it, the final width and shape is created with the strength of a less expensive forged wheel.

O.Z., Weld Racing, Inspiri, and Forgestar use this process almost exclusively. However, high-end companies such as BBS and HRE have been getting in on the action, too. In fact, BBS actually pioneered the process, which it uses on OEM wheels for BMW, Audi, Ferrari, and Porsche.

The Toyo R888 is an R-compound tire, with very low tread wear, that is available in 20-inch sizes and suitable for the street. Although it's not ideal for a daily driver, it is suitable for a weekend car or one that you drive to and from the track (provided there's no rain). Most other R-compound tires have even less tread than this and are strictly for road course or autocross. (Photo Courtesy Toyo Tires)

CHAPTER 2

For drag racing, Nitto offers the 555R and the stickier NT05R drag radials in 20-inch and smaller sizes for stock wheels, so you can actually drive to and from the track on them. A dedicated set of wheels and tires for the track with a meatier sidewall is recommended. With stock brakes the SS and ZL1 can also fit up to an 18 x 11–inch rear wheel and 305/45/18 drag radial. There is an abundance of affordable 18-inch Camaro and Corvette knock-off wheels, which makes this is a workable option for weekend drag racers looking to swap back and forth for daily driving. In terms of weight or strength, this option is not ideal, and you run the risk of breaking a wheel at speed. These are factory C6 Corvette Z06 front wheels (painted), which are a safer option, and spec 18 x 9.5 inches, just big enough to fit these 305-mm NT05s. (Photo Courtesy AntiVenom Racing)

A 15-inch wheel is the most ideal setup for drag racing because it allows for sticky tire options with meaty sidewalls and less weight. A Mickey Thompson or Hoosier drag radial allows for the best 60-foot times with an automatic. A bias-ply slick is more ideal for stick shifts because the soft sidewall can absorb the initial drivetrain shock. This ZL1 has C5 Corvette rear brakes to fit the Weld RT-S wheels and 325/50/15 ET Street Radials.

It is tight, but some 17-inch wheels fit on the SS as well. Texas Speed ran these Weld RT-S 17 x 10–inch wheels with a Hoosier 28 x 10 slick and matching 17-inch skinnies up front. The ZL1 requires 18-inch skinnies. (Photo Courtesy Joseph Potak)

Generally, General Motors uses one-piece forged wheels on its high-end cars such as the Camaro ZL1 and Z/28. Many aftermarket companies, including HRE, CCW, Forgeline, ADV.1, BC Forged, BBS, 360 Forged, Invo, and Modulare, make custom one-piece as well as pricier three-piece forged wheels. Some companies can help with choosing the right offset; however, you may need to purchase a wheel fitment tool such as Percy's Wheelrite.

In drag racing, safety, strength, and weight are also concerns. Although unsprung weight isn't nearly as detrimental, reducing rotating weight (rear wheels) and rolling resistance can be helpful in lowering elapsed times. To ensure safety and strength, you can look no further than the SFI Foundation for its seal of approval. The SFI tests for dynamic cornering fatigue, radial fatigue, and deflection. If the wheel meets these standards, it is given the SFI-approved sticker.

Weld Racing, Bogart, Forgeline, and CCW offer great options in 16-, 17-, and 18-inch diameters to fit over stock brakes. A rear brake conversion that allows for 15-inch wheels opens the full gamut of choices, including Holeshot and Billet Specialties, the latter of which makes a 17-inch front wheel if you want to keep the stock front brakes. Beadlocks are recommended on the rear wheels for 1,000-hp dedicated drag cars to keep the tire from spinning on the wheel.

Choosing the right tires can make nearly anyone feel like a hero at the dragstrip. Launching a fifth-gen Camaro on even the stickiest set of tires with 20-inch wheels can be a tricky proposition. The lack of sidewall makes the window for nailing the launch even smaller. With a stick shift, you want to run a 15- or 16-inch drag wheel with full race slicks and the appropriate driveline upgrades. Automatic transmissions can be much more forgiving and work well with a drag radial. Plus the heavier weight of the fifth-gen lends itself better to a stiffer sidewall.

For track only, Hoosier DOT Drag Radials, Mickey Thompson ET Street Radial, Radial Pro, and Pro Bracket Radial are excellent options. Street/strip applications have a wide variety to choose from, including the Mickey Thompson ET Street Radial, M&H Racemaster Drag Radial, Nitto NT05R and 555R, Toyo Proxes TQ, and, of course, the original BFGoodrich g-Force T/A. These are all available in various sizes, from 15- to 20-inch wheels. Although not appropriate for a daily driver due to poor wet traction and wear, these tires are plenty capable for weekend jaunts and driving to and from the track.

How-To Projects

Rear Bushings Install

All photos for this project are courtesy of Joseph Potak.

To make the Camaro's ride quality palatable for non-enthusiasts, Chevrolet uses soft durometer bushings throughout the chassis and suspension. For optimum performance, this is problematic for several reasons. Under hard acceleration, the rear end is prone to wheel hop (aka axle hop). Instead of the rear simply squatting as the weight transfers, it bounces so quickly and violently that it typically breaks axles and CV joints. During hard cornering these bushings also tend to deflect erratically, which becomes substantially worse with grippier tires. This is why the ZL1, 1LE, and Z/28 have harder durometer bushings than other models. As the bushings deflect, the dynamic alignment can be altered substantially and handling is less predictable.

The solution is to use solid aluminum bushings and rod ends, which may not be right for every owner, enthusiast or not.

Polyurethane is a nice compromise and is offered by several suppliers. For this build I went with BMR Suspension's Rear Cradle Bushing Kit, Street Version (PN BK001, BK016). For less than $200 you can help eliminate wheel hop in hours. The cradle inserts are much easier to install than the full bushings in BMR's Pro Version, which take hours of removal time for the factory bushings. Unlike the cradle, the differential bushings are considerably easier to remove. The only difference between the Street and Pro Version is the durometer.

This Street Version, according to BMR, is good for up to 450 rwhp (your typical bolt-on or cam-only fifth-gen) with its 68 durometer. A 95 durometer and Delrin version is available for high-horsepower Camaros. As for the suspension bushings, I chose to upgrade the trailing arms and toe rods all together because they cost around $200 for both. The amount of time and labor spent removing the old

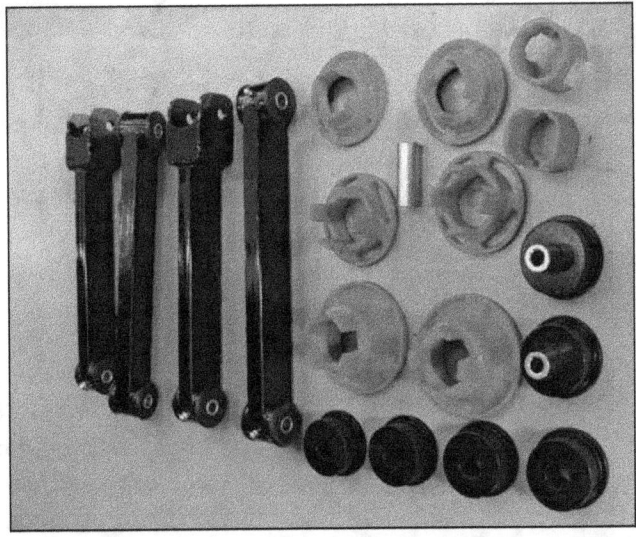

1 *For this build I chose BMR Suspension's Rear Cradle Bushing Kit, Street Version (PN BK001, BK016). For less than $200 you can help eliminate wheel hop in hours. The cradle inserts are much easier to install than the full bushings in BMR's Pro Version, which takes hours of removal time for the factory bushings. You can replace the rear trailing arm and toe rod bushings as well, but the time and labor involved doesn't justify the small cost savings.*

bushings doesn't justify the price difference to have a part with inferior performance.

Toe rods and trailing arms are the number-one and number-two suspects in the Camaro's soft and sometimes unpredictable handling (more on this in "Toe Rods and Trailing Arms Install").

2 With the Camaro supported by a lift, remove the rear wheels first.

3 Next remove the exhaust to allow the rear cradle to drop down. Unclamp the rear pipes from the mid-pipe, and unhook the mufflers from the hangers.

4 Unbolt the lower shock mount from the lower control arm, then remove the brake calipers and tie them out of the way.

5 Unbolt the driveshaft from the differential at the rubber coupler with an 18-mm wrench and socket.

6 You can use a flat dolly, but these roll-around auto dollies are the best. A set of 5-hole dollies cost about $100 on Amazon. When using a lift, three-pole jacks are also sufficient, although you need to put the subframe on the ground to work on it. The auto dollies skip the potential back injury, but you need to crawl around on the ground for the next step.

CHASSIS: SUSPENSION, BRAKES, WHEELS AND TIRES

7   Now that the cradle is supported, it is time to remove the four bolts that hold it to the chassis with a 21-mm socket. Next, Simply lift the body up and away from the subframe. To get enough height to pull the subframe from under the car would be difficult without a lift, but BMR says you can pull most of this install off with a hydraulic jack and two stands. Thankfully the instructions are pretty explicit.

8   After removing the bolts that connect the differential to the subframe with an 18-mm wrench and socket, you can see that the differential has flimsy rubber bushings with a steel center.

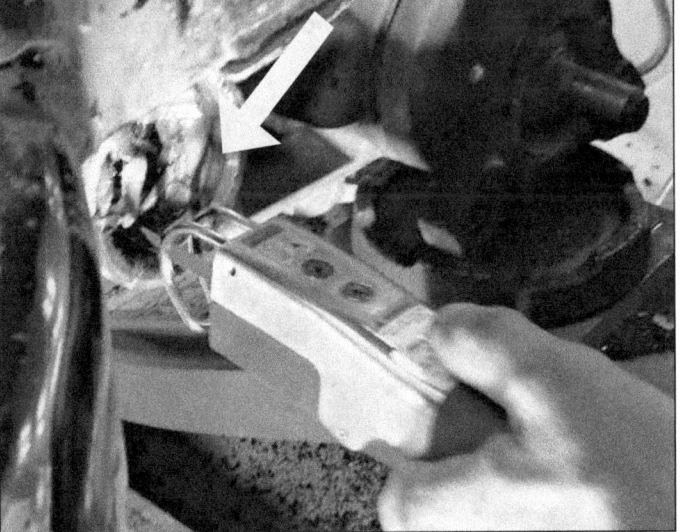

9   A small reciprocating saw or a 2-inch hole saw attachment can make short work of the OEM bushings. There is also an aluminum bushing shell that needs to be removed with a screwdriver after all the rubber is removed. BMR's urethane bushing halves slide in from each side and are greased to complete the install.

10 If you are attempting this without a lift, you need the subframe lowered by 3 inches to fit the inserts. There are both front and rear bushings (four total), and this insert goes on the top of the rear bushing with a generous amount of lube. The lube is essential to minimize squeaking.

11 This is the top of the front bushing.

12 The bottom of the front and rear (shown) bushing look similar, and are much more substantial pieces of urethane.

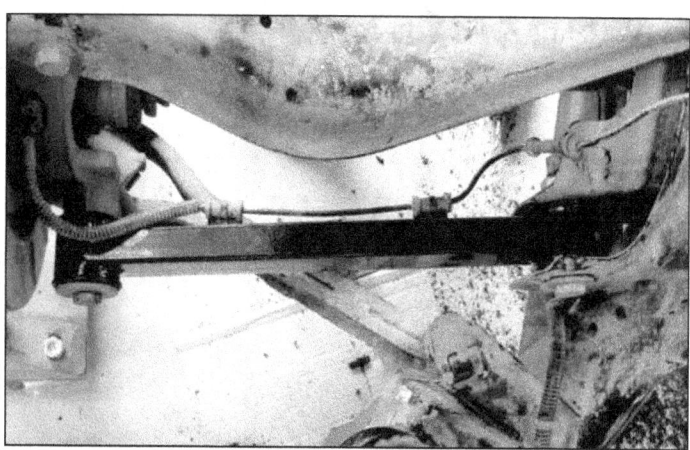

13 These non-adjustable toe rods are cheap and easy to install once the subframe is out, making it a no-brainer. The same goes for the trailing arms (not shown).

14 After lowering the body down, using the rear dowels to align it, tighten the bolts to 110 ft-lbs of torque. Because the inner bolt controls alignment, it is important to mark the washer and subframe for reference prior to unbolting.

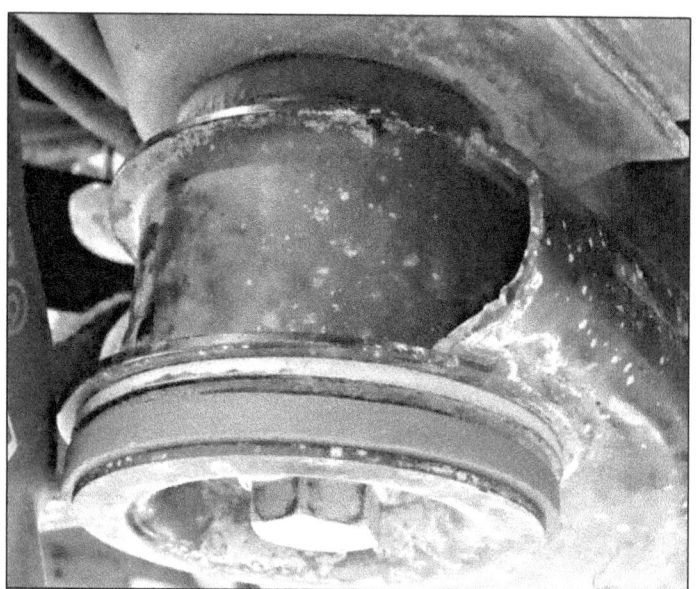

15 With the bottom bolt and cup in, you can see why the lower portion of the insert is so much larger.

Toe Rods and Trailing Arms Install

All photos for this project are courtesy of Joseph Potak.

As I mentioned in "Rear Bushings Install," the toe rods and the trailing arms are the biggest culprit in the fifth-gen's sometimes unpredictable and soft handling. The toe rod sets the toe angle, an important piece of the wheel alignment. Ideally you'd like its position to be as fixed as possible under load. With a factory stamped steel toe rod and its rubber bushings, it causes instability, whether during launches, cornering, or braking.

BMR uses boxed 1 x 2–inch Drawn Over Mandrel (DOM) steel with spiral fluted polyurethane bushings in its economical, non-adjustable toe rods (PN TR002), suitable for most street cars. In terms of handling, this, along with sway bars and springs, are your best bang for the buck. For straight-line acceleration, though, you want to combine toe rods with a good set of trailing arms. Again, the non-adjustable versions (PN TCA026) are plenty for most applications, and they are one of the easiest and quickest to install. BMR says that 1 hour is average.

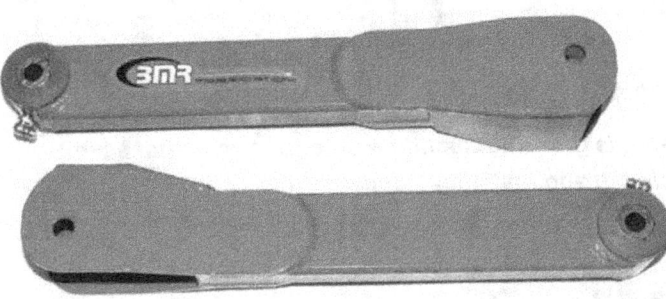

For straight-line acceleration you want a good set of trailing arms. The non-adjustable version trailing arms (PN TCA026) are plenty for most applications, and they are one of the easiest and quickest to install. BMR says 1 hour is average.

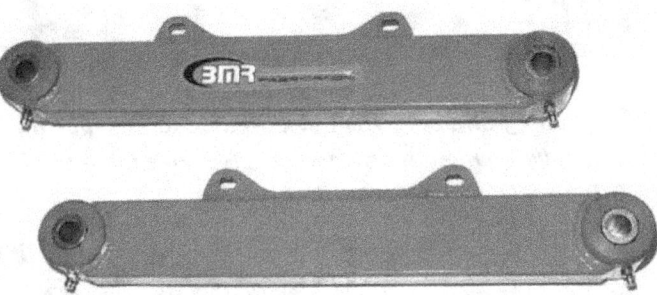

Like the trailing arms, BMR uses boxed 1 x 2–inch Drawn Over Mandrel (DOM) steel with spiral fluted polyurethane bushing in its economical, non-adjustable toe rods (PN TR002), suitable for most street cars. In terms of handling, this, along with sway bars and springs, are your best bang for the buck.

Like the toe rods, BMR uses 1 x 2–inch DOM boxed steel and 95 durometer polyurethane bushings that are also internally fluted to more evenly distribute the lube to keep them from squeaking. Although you might not see a direct drop in 60-foot times from swapping these two parts, your launches will be more consistent, which is almost as good.

1 You can either raise the car on a lift or put it on a set of jack stands so that the weight is off the tires. It is easier to remove them, but they can also stay on. Use an 18-mm socket and wrench to loosen the bolt and nut on the outer bolt of the trailing arm that attaches to the spindle.

CHAPTER 2

2 Using the same socket, completely remove the front trailing arm bolt. The nut is welded to the subframe, so you have no need for the wrench. Remove the outer bolt last. The trailing arm then slides out.

3 Once the BMR trailing arm is back in position, install the bolts with 80 ft-lbs of torque. The last step is greasing the fitting on each arm. If that seems simple and fast, that's because it is.

4 Next, loosen the rear subframe bolts and remove the front ones with a 15/16-inch socket. The extra room gives access to the inner toe rod bolt. It is important to support the cradle prior to this step.

5 The ABS wire needs to be popped loose of the toe rod by squeezing the retaining clip.

CHASSIS: SUSPENSION, BRAKES, WHEELS AND TIRES

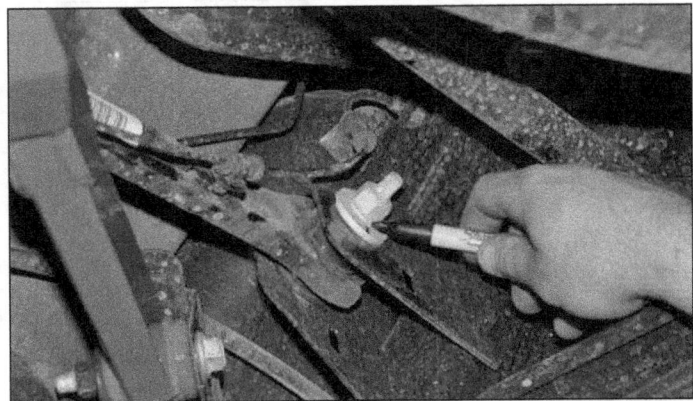

6 Because the toe rods are an essential part of the rear wheel alignment, you need to mark the washer and subframe as a reference point. Upon reinstallation you want to put this back to spec for the time being. If you plan on road racing, a more aggressive alignment is another great bang-for-the-buck. It can dramatically enhance the responsiveness of the steering, if nothing else.

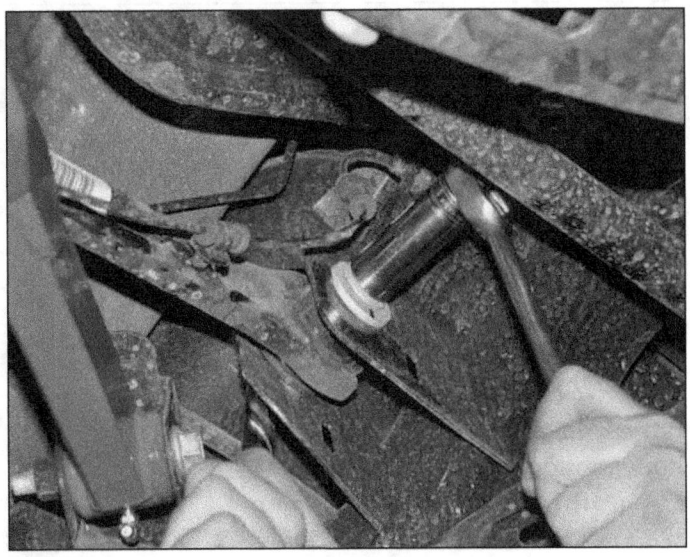

7 Remove the inner bolt with a 22-mm wrench and socket. Next, remove the outer bolt with an 18-mm socket.

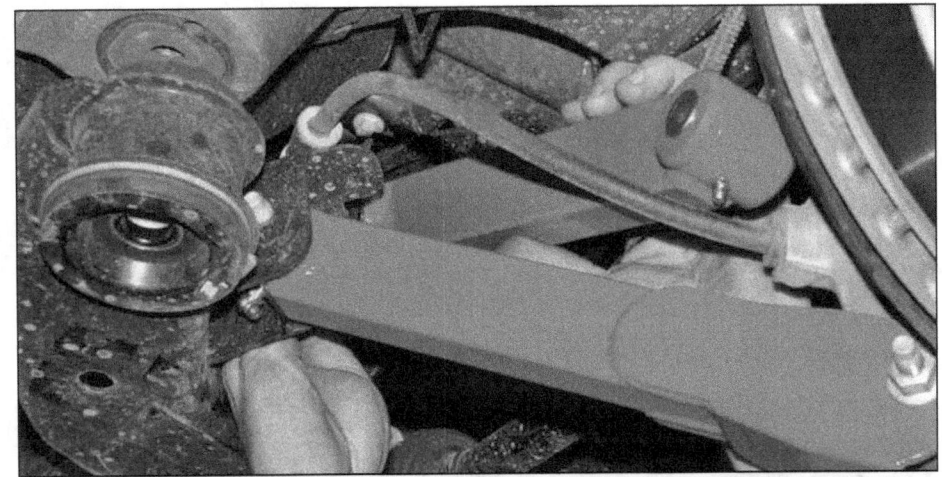

8 Install the BMR toe rod with the grease fittings pointed down and the ABS tab on top using the stock bolts.

9 The front cradle bolts go back in and all four are torqued to 130 ft-lbs. Then use a 10-mm wrench to align the cam washer on the toe rod to the marks before tightening to 85 ft-lbs, and then the outer bolt to 95 ft-lbs. Clip in the ABS and grease the bushings to complete the install.

Subframe Connectors Install

All photos for this project are courtesy of Joseph Potak.

Although the fifth-gen Camaro often draws criticism for its weight, the chassis is considerably stronger than in previous generations. It was the first to receive a five-star crash rating. It is also more efficient at directing kinetic energy to the suspension rather than generating undesirable body motion.

In the fourth-gen, for example, chassis flex had many negative effects, from handling and launch consistency, to turning the interior into a complete rattle-trap, especially if you had a T-top. In a third-gen with any mileage you'd be hard-pressed to open the doors when it was on a lift from chassis flex. But even though the fifth-gens have aged much better thus far and appear considerably stiffer, it doesn't mean they couldn't use a little extra help.

Road racers and drag racers alike should consider BMR's bolt-on subframe connectors (PN SFC015), which triangulate the front subframe, carrier bearing, and rear subframe where the cradle mounts. The connectors tie these three key areas together with 1 x 1–inch, .120 wall rectangular tubing and 3/16-inch CNC laser-cut steel plates. Because this is a bolt-on affair that uses existing holes, installation is only about an hour.

And while you are at it, for about $60 you might as well complete the job with BMR's Driveshaft Tunnel Brace (PN DTB004), made from 1 x 2–inch, .083 wall rectangular steel with 3/16-inch CNC laser-cut plates. This is a direct replacement for the thin stamped-steel factory piece.

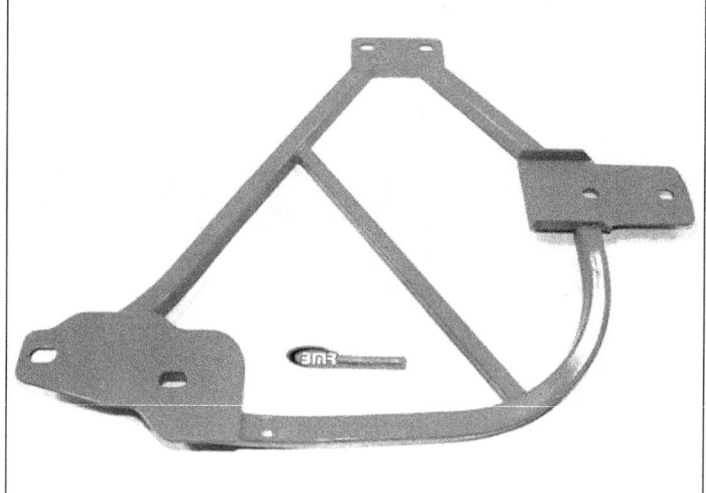

1 Road racers and drag racers alike should consider BMR's bolt-on subframe connectors (PN SFC015), which triangulate the front subframe, carrier bearing, and rear subframe where the cradle mounts.

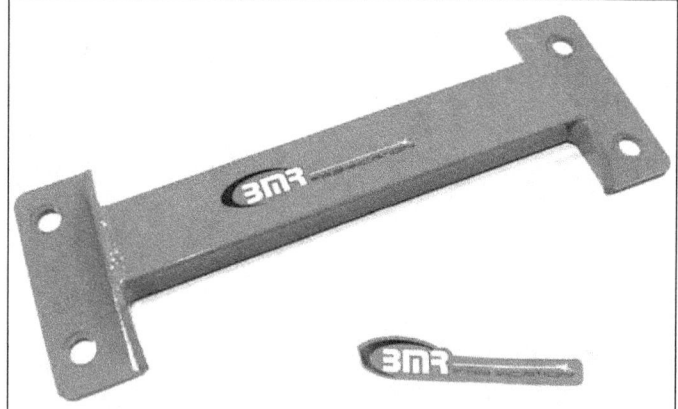

2 For about $60 you might as well complete the job with BMR's Driveshaft Tunnel Brace (PN DTB004), which is a direct replacement for the thin, stamped-steel factory piece.

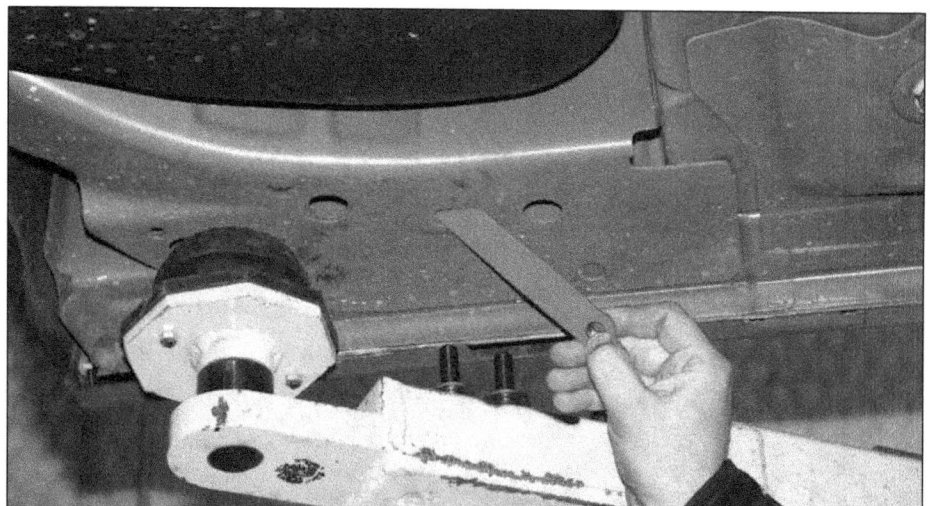

3 With the vehicle on a lift, preferably a four-post with the suspension loaded, begin by slipping the frame inserts into the frame rails. The larger ones fit the front, the smaller ones go toward the rear.

CHASSIS: SUSPENSION, BRAKES, WHEELS AND TIRES

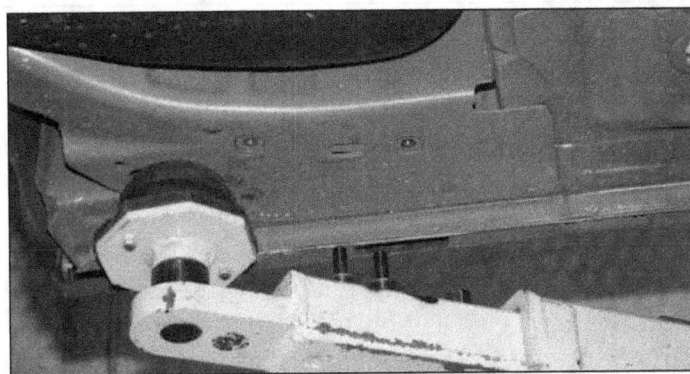

4 With the frame inserts in place, you can see how they use the factory holes but add a threaded surface to which you can bolt the subframe connectors. The frame rail changed slightly here from the 2010–2011 models to the 2012 and later, so be sure to use the appropriate insert. Early models like this use a flat insert.

5 Threading one of the supplied 1/2-inch Allen head bolts and washers temporarily helps keep the inserts in place when you install the connector.

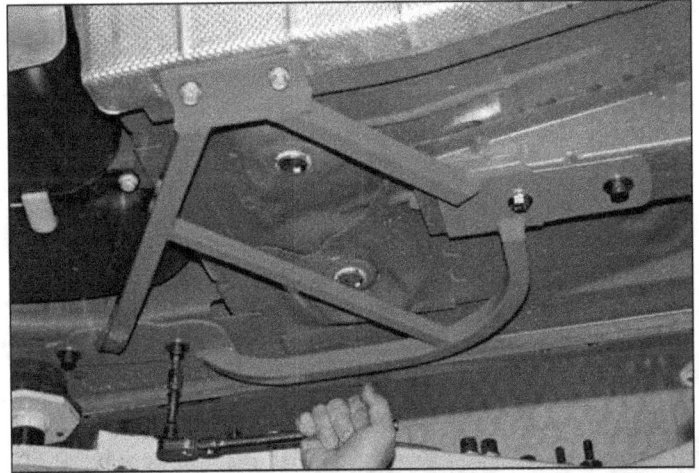

6 With the subframe connector in place, loosely thread all the bolts (rear to front) before giving a final 45 ft-lbs to the Allen bolts.

7 After removing the 10-mm bolts again, the BMR driveshaft tunnel brace bolts to the connectors and joins them. Torque the 10-mm bolts to 48 ft-lbs. From this vantage point it is easy to see that the full benefits of the connectors cannot be realized without the tunnel brace as well.

Line-Lock Install

All photos for this project are courtesy of Joseph Potak.

The recipe for big smoky burnouts is a line-lock kit, a healthy amount of horsepower, and maybe even a little water. Besides drawing the admiration and respect of fellow car guys, burnouts also have a functional purpose at the dragstrip. Drag radials and slicks need heat to be sticky.

There's actually science behind this: certain compounds operate best at a specific temperature range. Watch NHRA or serious heads-up classes and you'll see one of the crew members put a heat gun to the tires after the burnout. Plus, a burnout cleans off the road debris that clings to the gummy rubber. One pass through the pits after a run is enough to coat a set of slicks with tiny pebbles and sand. If you change tires at the track, you know this all too well.

Normally you might simply plop your left foot down on the brake pedal while stomping the gas pedal to do a burnout. Quite a bit of finesse is required to keep the car from moving while also not slowing the rear wheels too much. With a stick shift, you also have to worry about dumping the clutch prior to applying the brakes.

The advantage of the line lock is that it negates the nuances of brake application, making the burnout a simple and routine operation. You hold down the brake, flip the switch, give it gas, and flip the switch when the car gods say enough. The line lock operates by locking the front brakes only, so you are not fighting the rear brakes or wearing out the pads.

To show off the installation, I am using a 2010 Camaro line-lock kit from SJM Manufacturing. To complete the install you need DOT 3 brake fluid, zip ties, 1/4-inch wire covering, and an ATM fuse accessory add-on tap. Hand tools, a drill, and preferably a brake vacuum bleeder are needed for the 2- to 3-hour install.

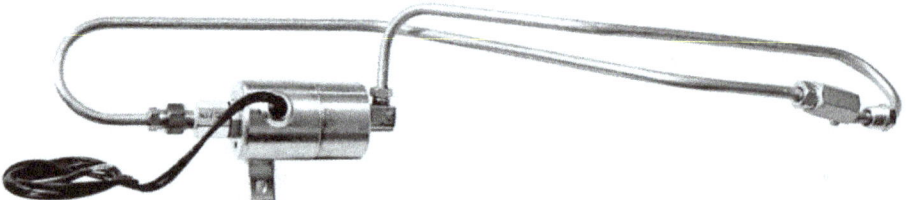

The advantage of a line lock is that it negates the nuances of brake application, making the burnout a simple and routine operation. To show off the installation, I am using a 2010 Camaro line-lock kit from SJM Manufacturing.

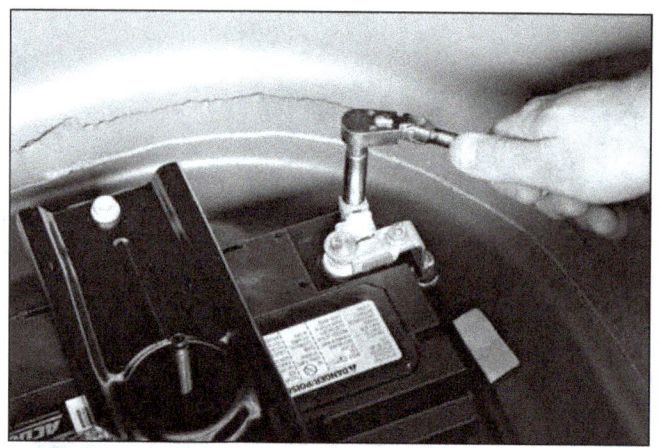

1 *Whenever you touch electric components, you should always disconnect the negative battery cable first, which is located in the trunk. A 10-mm socket does the trick.*

2 *You need a 13-mm wrench to loosen the brake line marked "MC1" on the ABS module. Some brake fluid may leak out, so it is a good idea to use a shop towel to absorb it.*

CHASSIS: SUSPENSION, BRAKES, WHEELS AND TIRES

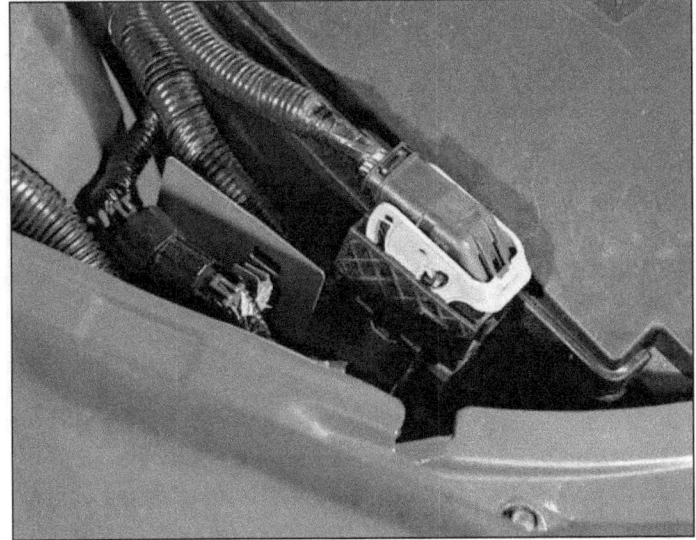

3 Turning your attention to the fuse block, the two bulk wiring connectors on the bracket next to it need to be unclipped and set aside.

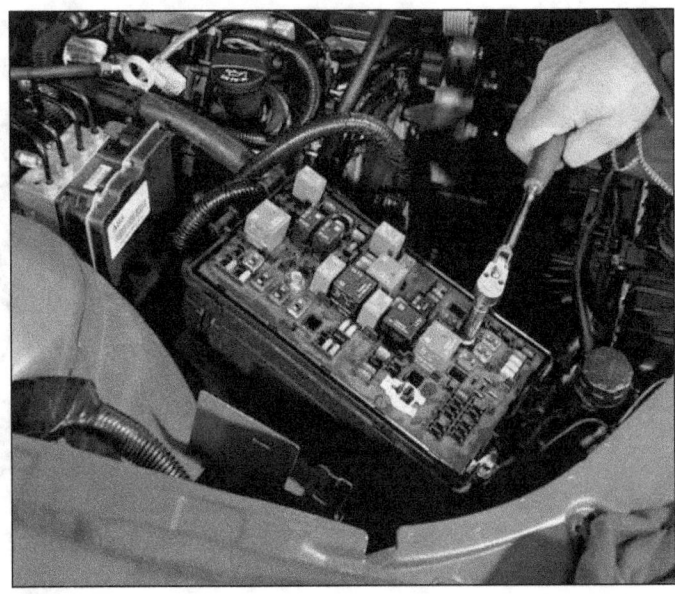

4 Remove the fuse box cover using a 10-mm socket on the two fuse block screws.

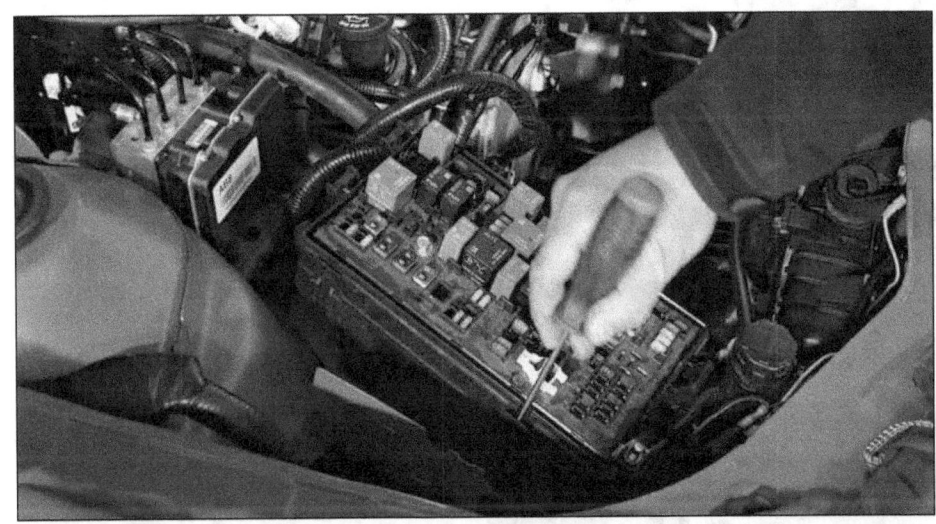

5 Use a flat-blade screwdriver to unclip the tabs that secure the upper part of the fuse box to the lower housing. Then, pulled it up and to the right, away from the housing.

6 Use a 13-mm socket to remove the lower fuse box housing.

CAMARO 5TH GEN 2010-2015: HOW TO BUILD AND MODIFY

CHAPTER 2

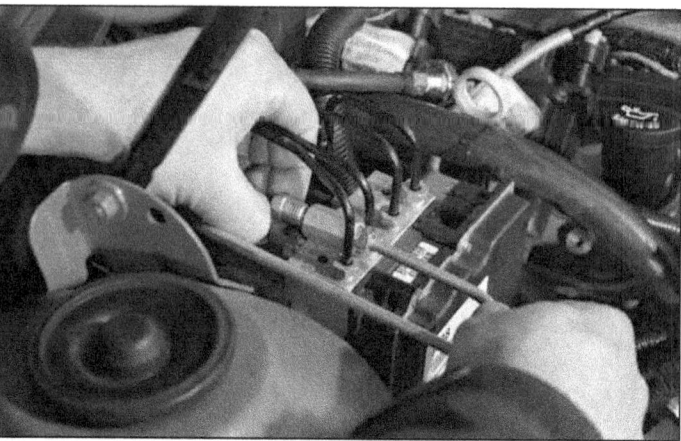

7 Set the line-lock assembly into place with the lines going toward the ABS module.

8 The factory line that was removed from the ABS module threads into the double-sided brass union that leads to the inlet for the line-lock. Thread the other line leading from the line-lock into the ABS module.

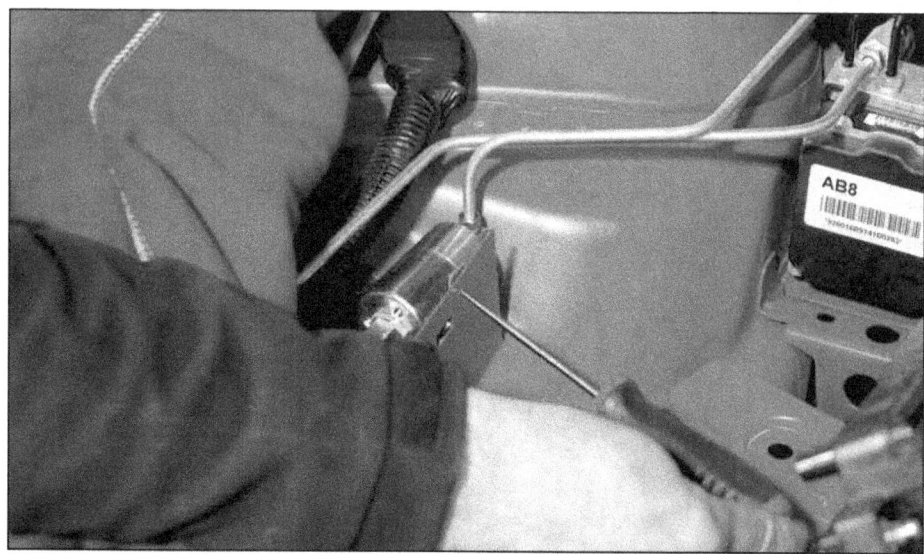

9 Mark the OEM bracket where it aligns with the mounting tab on the line-lock.

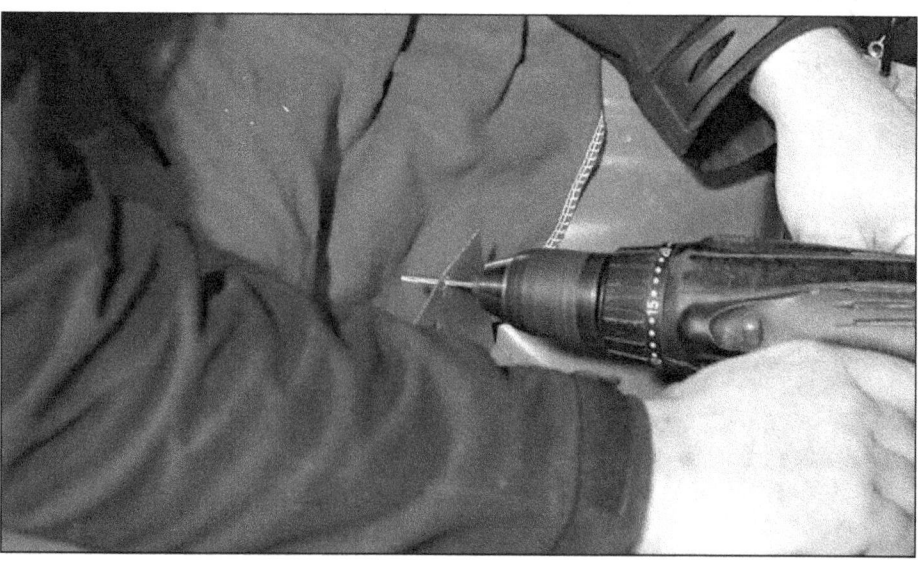

10 Using a 3/16-inch drill bit, make a hole in the marked location. Be sure to protect the line-lock and catch the metal shavings as best you can. De-burring the hole is also recommended.

CHASSIS: SUSPENSION, BRAKES, WHEELS AND TIRES

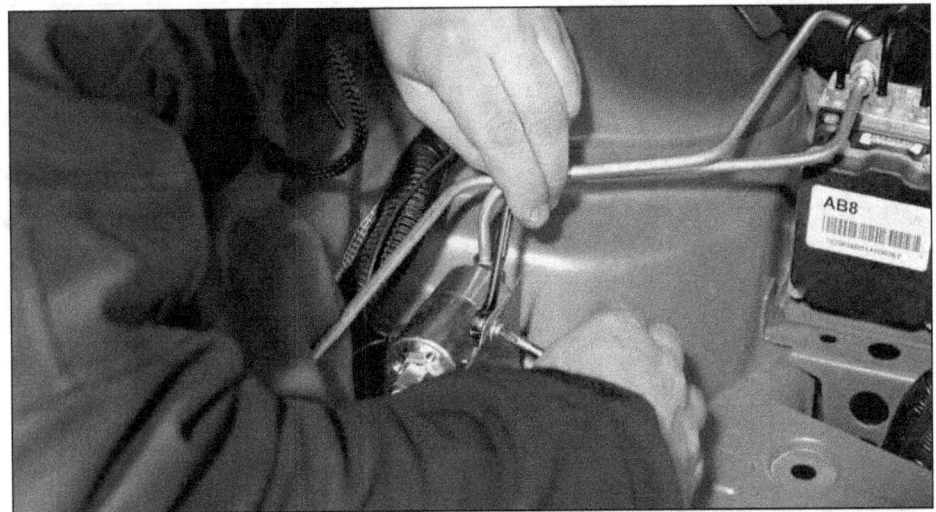

11 The supplied screws mount the line-lock.

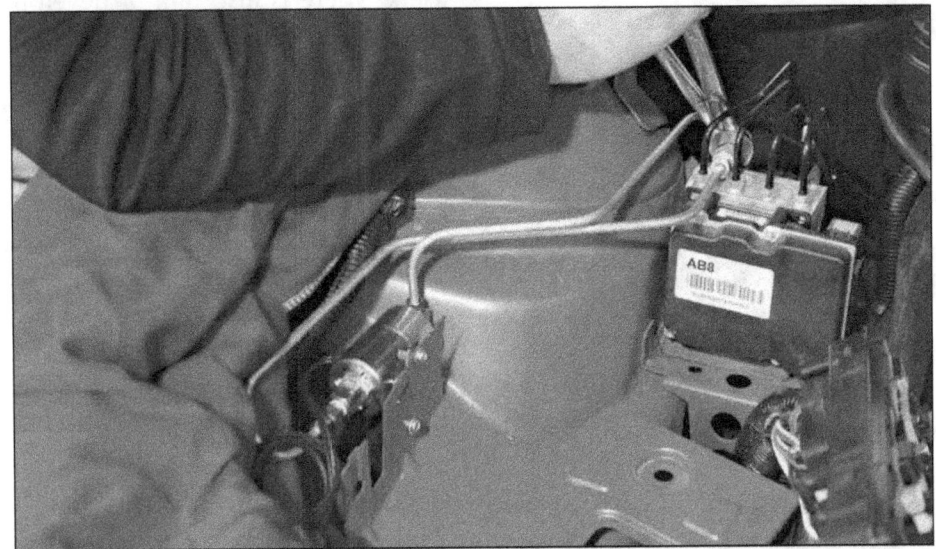

12 The brake line fittings can be tightened to 12 ft-lbs or a one-sixth turn past finger tight.

13 Reinstall the fuse box as it was removed. Connect and zip-tie the bulk connectors. This is a good time to vacuum bleed the front brakes and refill the brake fluid master cylinder.

The last step is wiring up the solenoid and mounting the switch. You need a 12-volt power source, such as a cigarette lighter, or you can connect it directly to the fuse panel (under the left dash bezel) with a fuse tap from an auto parts store. The switch needs to be within arm's reach of the driver, preferably near the shifter.

CHAPTER 2

Front Suspension Upgrade

With all this talk about suspension work that focuses on the Camaro's independent rear suspension components, you may be wondering about the front end. Well, aside from the bushings, sway bar, and coil-overs, that's about it. The factory parts work so well, there isn't much need for upgrades here. But in the weight-conscious world of drag racing, the engine cradle does leave some room for improvement.

Xtreme Innovations & Fabrication designed a bolt-in cradle to drop weight off the nose. The cradle is fully TIG-welded 4130 chrome-moly. Separate versions are available for street cars and drag cars, though the street car version already drops 28.5 pounds (a 45-percent reduction).

A full front suspension kit for drag cars adds a manual steering rack, double adjustable struts, strut hat adapters, tubular lower control arms with billet mounts, and four-piston brakes with aluminum hubs. Xtreme says that a set of skinnies lightens the Camaro by 170 pounds.

The record-setting ATI Performance COPO #008 is one of many users. There is also talk of developing a tubular rear cradle, though a solid axle conversion has been first on the agenda.

Xtreme Innovations & Fabrications designed this bolt-in cradle to drop more than 28 pounds off the nose of the fifth-gen Camaro. With a full drag setup, you can lose a total of 170 pounds with a manual steering rack, tubular lower control arms, and aftermarket brakes.

The aftermarket engine cradle is made from tubular 4130 chrome-moly and fully TIG welded. Other fabricators have found similar gains in both the front and rear, but these are usually reserved for serious drag cars.

CHAPTER 3

DRIVETRAIN

The 2010–2015 Camaro came with some robust drivetrain options, though depending on the model and application, it may not be exactly what is needed. The most notorious shortcoming of the V-6 and SS models is the rear end. The factory differential housing is aluminum, prone to flex, and equipped with a very weak posi unit. The weight of the vehicle combined with the weight of the large rolling stock can burn out the clutches after just a few burnouts at the dragstrip. On the Z/28 model, General Motors opted for a heavy-duty helical gear set (in lieu of clutch packs) and coupled that with a cooler built into the diff cover.

The axles are another huge issue with the V-6 and SS rear ends. Although a sticky tire and a hard dragstrip launch surely break the factory CV axles, these have even been known to break on the street. The 1LE and Z/28 both received stronger versions. Between the ZL1's baseball bats for CV axles and massive cast-iron 9.9-inch differential, it does not experience the same issues. GM engineers tested it over and over again at the dragstrip using drag radial tires. Since then many 8- and 9-second ZL1's have used an entirely stock drivetrain, which is why Chevrolet Performance offers it as an upgrade.

Differential Upgrades

The aftermarket is also full of upgrades for the SS's rear end. GForce Engineering and The Driveshaft Shop are the two most prominent makers of CV axle upgrades, ranging from your basic 1,000-hp-capable 28-spline axles to 1,800-hp custom 33-spline units. The inner and outer stubs are one weak point, which can be replaced with a billet one-piece configuration. Typically the cages are upgraded as well on the CV joint with 4340 or 300M billet and polished.

GForce uses a high-alloy aerospace steel for the axle material itself because it has "better torsional

Although the LS/LT, SS, and Z/28 use an 8.5-inch differential with an aluminum housing, the ZL1 has this massive 9.9-inch cast-iron unit. Engineers designed it to be nearly bulletproof, even going so far as to test it with drag radials on a prepped surface. The transmission options are equally as robust on the Camaro. (Photo Courtesy General Motors)

CHAPTER 3

The ZL1's 3.73-geared manual (PN 22959394) and 3.23 automatic (PN 22959395) Camaro ZL1 HD Driveline Kit is available through Chevrolet Performance. The asymmetric axles are a baseball bat–like 60 mm (hollow) and 33 mm (solid) with heavy-duty CV joints. The various thicknesses and compositions have different torsional stiffness rates that combat wheel hop by dispersing stored energy. Even the couplers on the driveshaft have been upgraded. Thanks to a heavy-duty limited-slip differential and cooler that can drop temps by more than 100 degrees, the ZL1 diff is equally at home on the road course and the dragstrip. (Photo Courtesy Chevrolet Performance)

twisting abilities than 300M." The Driveshaft Shop favors 300M with CNC-rolled splines. This process is superior to cutting because it does not remove material or the "inherent grain structure that it's made with."

The Driveshaft Shop also offers a Ford 9-inch conversion kit that includes a bolt-in housing, axles, and an upgraded driveshaft. This allows for a multitude of posi options (even a spool) and virtually unlimited gear ratios. This is a nice advantage because few aftermarket manufacturers make gears for the Camaro diff, and some who have did not enjoy much success due to durability concerns.

Axles are a recommended upgrade for any modified SS. Like General Motors, Gforce Engineering employs varying axle diameters to combat wheel hop. The standard 1,000-hp axles are made of "high-alloy aerospace steel" that is similar but has better torsional twisting properties than 300M with billet one-piece inner and out stubs. The 28-spline CV joints are made in-house with 4340 cages and high-alloy center races that are heat-treated. The 33-spline Outlaw axles are also available. (Photo Courtesy Gforce Engineering)

The Chevrolet Performance 1LE 3.91 gear kit (PN 19301504) is a great upgrade for the SS rear end. Torque multiplication increases by 13 percent on the manual and 20 percent on automatic models. By getting the 6.2L into its powerband quicker, the SS accelerates quicker off the line. The only downside is a reduction in fuel mileage. Some others in the aftermarket have struggled with manufacturing the ring and pinion; however, Chevrolet obviously knows what it is doing. Lingenfelter's 3.70 and 3.91, made by American Axle, have also proven to be reliable. (Photo Courtesy Chevrolet Performance)

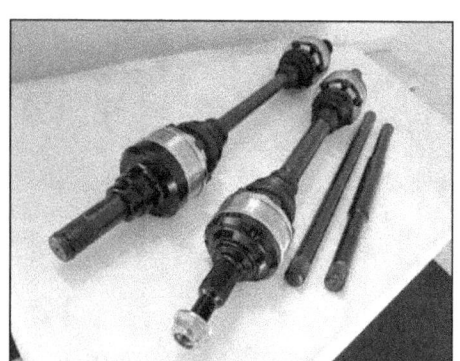

The Driveshaft Shop offers its own 1,000-hp axles that also use staggered thickness, but 108-mm CVs on both ends and 300M center bars. The 1,400-hp Level 5 axles step up to 30 splines with certified 4340AQ cages that are REM polished. A 300M center race, CNC rolled splines, and extensive real-world testing have helped these axles hold up in some of the fastest Camaros in the world. These axles are offered for the 9-inch, 12-bolt, and other conversions. (Photo Courtesy The Driveshaft Shop)

DRIVETRAIN

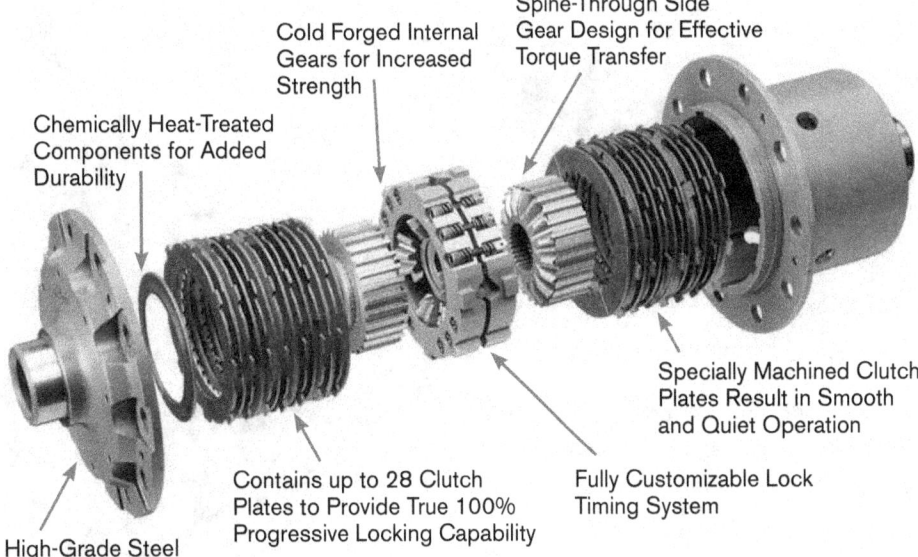

You can also rob the parts bin for the Camaro Z/28's rear differential module cooler kit (PN 23216684), which fits the differential on any SS with a manual trans. The RDM cooling system circulates trans fluid through the heat exchanger mounted into the diff cover. By dropping temps more than 100 degrees, the cooler keeps the fluid and internals intact during track sessions. (Photo Courtesy Chevrolet Performance)

Although you can simply rebuild the stock clutch-type posi, aftermarket options offer complete replacement upgrades. Many road racing and drifting professionals have relied on OS Giken's Super Lock limited-slip diff (PN CH061), packed with up to 28 friction plates using a patented lock-timing system. The standard spec combines low preload and progressive 100-percent lock capability, so it feels stock at low speeds and street driving but transmits power perfectly under load. By distributing power more effectively, it even makes the car more stable in bad weather. (Photo Courtesy OS Giken)

The Eaton Detroit Truetrac is a helical-gear style of diff, just like the Z/28 uses, available for the SS rear end. As with any limited-slip diff, it transfers power to the high-traction wheel under load (when traction is uneven). However, it uses multiple helical-shaped gears to mesh with increasing force to slow or stop the excessively spinning wheel, instead of a friction material. The Detroit Locker was perhaps the first aftermarket diff to bridge the gap between an OEM posi and a full-on spool. Its operation is comparatively unrefined and has fallen out of favor among street-going enthusiasts but is still popular in the off-road world. With electronic differentials already making their way onto performance cars such as the C7 Corvette, the Locker seems archaic by comparison. (Photo Courtesy Eaton)

This Moser spool, though beautifully machined, is an even more crude and simple device than the Locker. It simply locks both axles together and is really only suitable for a dedicated drag car. Because it does not allow the wheels to spin at different speeds, turns must be taken cautiously. On the dragstrip, where turning is undesirable, its simplicity means 100-percent reliability. When stepping up to a 9-inch or 12-bolt, many lightweight spools and differentials are available. (Photo Courtesy Moser Engineering)

The Driveshaft Shop offers a host of different driveshafts for the Camaro, including this 3⅜-inch carbon-fiber version for the manual trans SS. At only 15.5 pounds, it is extremely light yet strong thanks to a new bond technology and a Porsche-style 930 joint made from a proprietary aerospace-grade material similar to 300M but 15-percent stronger. Note the lack of rubber couplers, which The Driveshaft Shop says are not needed thanks to its precise machining of billet couplers that are even better than any U-bolt–style yoke. (Photo Courtesy The Driveshaft Shop)

The Driveshaft Shop offers 10 variations on the 9-inch conversion. The bolt-in kits include a powder-coated housing with the rear bracket and polyurethane bushing, powder-coated front mount with polyurethane bushings, 1,400-hp axles, 31-spline diff stub axles with O-ring bushings, and your choice of driveshaft. (Photo Courtesy The Driveshaft Shop)

A Strange "S" series center section is available separately with various gear ratios, Wavetrac or Trutrac. The immense selection of gear and diff options, which is easy to swap in and out, is a huge advantage with any 9-inch swap. (Photo Courtesy The Driveshaft Shop)

The Gforce Engineering 9-inch IRS kit uses 35-spline stub axles standard (31-spline optional), proprietary-design 1,500-hp axles, and a one-piece Dynotech driveshaft in carbon fiber or aluminum. The heavy-duty front mount uses BMR polyurethane bushings. The TIG-welded housing is a complete bolt-in affair, available with a Strange or Moser center section. (Photo Courtesy Gforce Engineering)

DRIVETRAIN

Strange offers its own IRS differential, based on its popular S60, essentially a Dana 60. This massive 9.75-inch ring gear is nearly bulletproof and available in a variety of ratios. (Photo Courtesy Strange Engineering)

The Strange housing is cast from 206-T4 finned aluminum and is stuffed with billet 2024-T351 aluminum main caps, 35-spline axle stubs, an S-Trac differential, 1350-style driveshaft yoke, and an O-ringed cover. The housing accepts OEM and aftermarket bushings, and the 9-inch axles from Gforce and The Driveshaft Shop bolt right up. (Photo Courtesy Strange Engineering)

Lingenfelter was an early player in the differential game with this aluminum 9.5-inch, manufactured by American Axle with its TracRite GT helical-gear limited-slip diff. This heavy-duty diff comes with street/drag racing bias or a no-preload version for road racing in 3.42, 3.73, 4.10, or 4.56 ratios. (Photo Courtesy Lingenfelter Performance Engineering)

This bolt-in design requires The Driveshaft Shop 1,400-hp axles and either a single- or two-piece driveshaft specific to the diff. (Photo Courtesy Lingenfelter Performance Engineering)

The HammerHead is the lightest of the bunch and doesn't absorb as much horsepower. Based on the GM 12-bolt, the ring gear is only 8.875 inches (stock SS is 8.5 inches), but many users have found this sufficient for more than 900 hp thanks to its superior aluminum casting design. Because it is a 12-bolt, it has the benefit of many gear-ratio options from 3.42 to 4.88, Eaton TrueTrac, WaveTrac, and even a spool with 9310 alloy Pro Gears for race cars (4.11 to 5.00 ratios). Various packages are available with The Driveshaft Shop axles and driveshafts. (Photo Courtesy The Driveshaft Shop)

CHAPTER 3

The Lingenfelter cast aluminum 9.5-inch differential is available in four ratios, mates to The Driveshaft Shop axles and driveshaft, and is another bolt-in solution. LPE's diff is probably the lightest solution next to the ET Enterprises Hammer-Head, which is also aluminum. This 12-bolt-based design also enjoys a plethora of gear-ratio and posi options, and mates to The Driveshaft Shop parts.

Transmissions

Factory transmissions are plenty capable on V-6 models, even with some modifications, given the limits of the direct-injection system. The SS, on the other hand, received the weakest version of the Tremec TR6060 (M10). The MM6 TR6060 manual transmission included in the 1LE package and the Z/28 model, as well as the MG9 in the ZL1, boasts some improvements that make it the best choice for high horsepower and racing, though the M10 can be upgraded to MM6 or MG9 specs.

Of particular importance is the upgraded output shaft and additional roller bearing. Because the main shaft is not supported internally at the rear of the transmission as with the MG9, it is prone to breakage. The MG9 is rated to 560 ft-lbs of torque, the MM6 to 500 ft-lbs, and the M10 to 430 ft-lbs according to Tremec. Although these figures may be conservative, it is worth noting that there are internal differences among the three versions. Additional upgrades can be made to any version with a quality builder, including the use of micropolishing, cryogenic tempering, bronze fork pads, carbon blocker rings, a Corvette ZR1 pickup tube, billet main shaft, and SFI bellhousing.

For race applications, you can even face-plate the gears or convert to a sequential transmission for clutch-less shifting. With the proper upgrades, a TR6060 transmission can withstand more than 1,000 rwhp and plenty of abuse. The same cannot be said for the automatic counterparts.

The 6L80E and 6L90E automatic transmissions are stout internally, akin to the Turbo 400 and 4L80E, except with no bands and two or three extra gears. The control methods, though, are vastly different from the previous electronic transmissions, such as the 4L80E and 4L60E. By eliminating bands, the 6L80E and 6L90E require precise engagement and disengagement of the clutches. Heat and increased power levels can easily make the clutches slip during initial application, which skews the timing. So tuning becomes an essential part of having a healthy and working transmission.

Initially few tuners knew their way around the complicated new controls, but with trial and error, that has changed. Mechanical upgrades such as clutch packs are typically needed for high-horsepower builds. The 3-5-Reverse clutches, 4-5-6 clutches, and the spline area of the 4-5-6 hub are all known weak points. With some new clutch packs, as well as the 6L90E's larger output carrier and gears, these transmissions are routinely capable of 900 hp.

Circle D Specialties is one of a few companies that offer a billet 4-5-6 hub and piston assembly with a billet hub shaft for more than 1,000

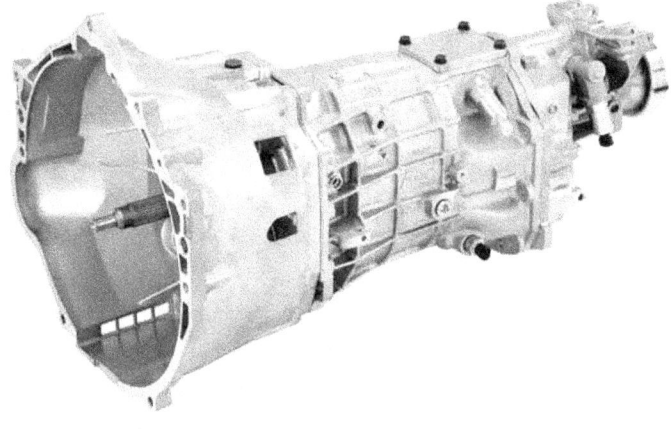

The Camaro came with some solid transmission options, and with just a few upgrades, the TR6060 and 6L80E can hold up to some serious torque. The ZL1, 1LE, and Z/28 came with the strongest variations, but with a few upgrades the SS can be brought up to spec and beyond. (Photo Courtesy General Motors)

DRIVETRAIN

hp. Originally Circle D and Century Transmissions were the only two games in town and owners of all the fastest times. However, recently more builders have been getting in on the action. Unfortunately, though, unlike its predecessors, the 6L80E and 6L90E make poor transmissions for racing. The simplicity of a Turbo 400 is often favored in high-powered drag cars, though many have great success with 4L60E and 4L80E swaps in both dedicated drag cars and those that see street time.

A conversion wiring harness is available from PCM of NC that reduces the cost of using a stand-alone transmission controller with 4L60E/4L80E swaps. Either way, converting to any other transmission requires custom tuning to the ECM and a new trans crossmember.

With increased modifications, an upgraded clutch and torque converter can become necessary. The factory components work well, to a point. Unfortunately the precise moment that you need to upgrade the parts depends greatly on the application, driving style, and use. An aftermarket torque converter helps optimize the performance of any combination by increasing torque multiplication as it goes through the automatic trans. The stall speed can also be finely tuned to the combination.

As aftermarket camshafts and turbochargers raise the operating range of the engine, a higher stall speed allows the car to accelerate from the sweet spot in the powerband, much like changing the rear gear ratio. It is imperative to run some sort of multidisc converter from a reputable builder with the 6L80E and 6L90E transmissions given their unique design. Excessive slippage could result in transmission damage.

An external trans cooler is also highly recommended. Both transmissions tend to run hot. The factory clutch in the SS and Z/28 is a fairly stout single-disc unit, but the weight of the fifth-gen can play a big factor in premature wear. If you plan on racing or adding forced induction, an aftermarket unit is in your future. Twin-disc clutches, such as the one in the ZL1, are ideal for maintaining street-friendly pedal feel, effort, and maximum power-holding capacity. Triple-disc clutches are even available for 1,000-hp builds.

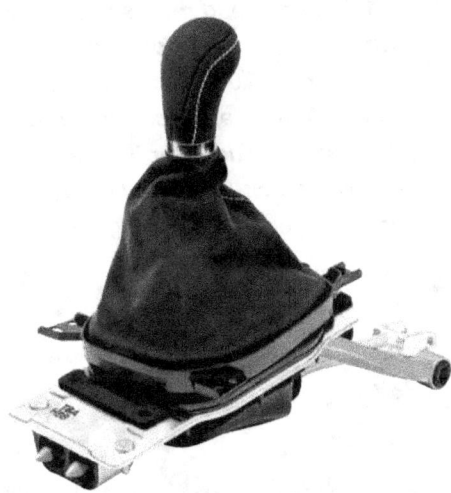

GM's own short-throw shifter used on the ZL1 is available through Chevrolet Performance with either a suede (PN 19299460) or leather (PN 23157703) knob and contrast stitching. All the hardware needed is included to install the 5.1:1 shifter into a TR6060-equipped SS. (Photo Courtesy Chevrolet Performance)

For your typical bolt-on street car, an SFI-certified bellhousing is total overkill. But way too many 700- to 1,000-hp Camaros are still using the stock bellhousing on the TR6060. Because the TR6060's bellhousing is integrated into the front plate, the previous T56 bellhousings were incompatible. Rockland Standard Gear makes a kit (PN TUEP18201, TCCM10150) that adapts a custom Quick Time SFI steel bellhousing using Rockland's front plate with internal pump for cooling. (Photo Courtesy Rockland Standard Gear)

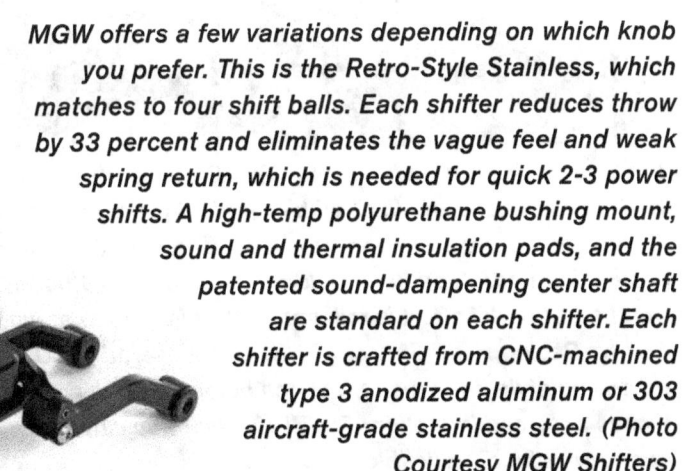

MGW offers a few variations depending on which knob you prefer. This is the Retro-Style Stainless, which matches to four shift balls. Each shifter reduces throw by 33 percent and eliminates the vague feel and weak spring return, which is needed for quick 2-3 power shifts. A high-temp polyurethane bushing mount, sound and thermal insulation pads, and the patented sound-dampening center shaft are standard on each shifter. Each shifter is crafted from CNC-machined type 3 anodized aluminum or 303 aircraft-grade stainless steel. (Photo Courtesy MGW Shifters)

CHAPTER 3

As any racer knows, an SFI bellhousing is required at nearly any ET by most sanctioning bodies, and for good reason. When a clutch or pressure plate comes apart, it typically comes right through the floorpan. So it's not the type of thing to skimp on. The only negative is cost. (Photo Courtesy Rockland Standard Gear)

Getting the balance between torque capacity and street manners can be difficult when engineering a clutch, but no one does that better than General Motors. That's why Lingenfelter sells a Corvette ZR1 clutch that is adapted for use in the Camaro (PN L360020105). Lingenfelter's billet steel six-bolt flange flywheel is made to OEM spec and mates to the GM twin-disc clutch and pressure plate for more than 700-hp capability. The special Lingenfelter slave/actuator spacer (PN L360031410) is needed to adapt the ZR1 slave cylinder for the Camaro. Expect nothing but quiet and smooth operation with stock-like pedal effort and feel. (Photo Courtesy Lingenfelter Performance Engineering)

This crazy-looking Optimum-RR clutch from Quarter Master was designed for road racing. It uses three 7.25-inch discs that combine strength with ultra-light weight and is derived from NASCAR. A few of its features include gear drive technology, optimized friction material, and slotted pressure and floater plates for cooling. This is certainly not a bolt-in application but can be made to work if you want the clutch response of NASCAR. (Photo Courtesy Quarter Master)

The Quarter Master Optimum-SR Two-Disc Clutch (PN 542004) uses two 10.4-inch marcel-type discs with organic rag-type friction and a sprung hub. The vented floater plate and grooved friction surfaces are designed with cooling in mind. Capable of holding 1,400 hp and 1,000 ft-lbs, this is no lightweight, but pedal effort is still minimal. This particular clutch is going into a 650-hp Racing Head Service (RHS) LS7-powered 2010 Camaro SS. Depending on driving style, the stock SS clutch holds up quite well until you add cubic inches or forced induction. The ZL1's twin-disc clutch is more capable but certainly not indestructible.

DRIVETRAIN

RPM Transmissions is one of only a few builders of TR6060 transmissions, which are quite stout from the factory. The TR6060 has nearly double the torque capacity as its T56 predecessor because it has thicker gears, larger input bearing, and larger synchros, to name a few. RPM's most basic rebuild includes bronze fork pads, micropolished gears, a bronze shifter bushing, and a ZR1 pickup tube for the pump. This is in addition to many other standard rebuild practices that are superior to the factory by virtue of RPM's battle-tested specs and tolerances. (Photo Courtesy RPM Transmissions)

Thankfully most other driveline considerations are well taken care of by the factory. For example, many of the hydraulic issues that plagued earlier manual transmissions have been resolved. In an ongoing effort to remove all noise vibration

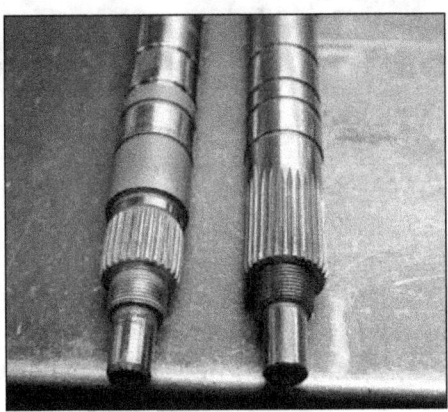

RPM upgrades its Level VI and VII transmissions with this billet 9310 main shaft (right), also known as the output shaft. Replacing the factory shaft (left) with this 30-spline unit makes power capability nearly infinite. The TR6060 came with an assortment of output shafts, including the early 27-spline units that were known to fail with stock or near-stock power levels. The later designs had better metallurgy, heat treating, and an improved chamfer but are still inferior to the 30-spline billet upgrade. (Photo Courtesy RPM Transmissions)

The bronze shifter bushing on the right is a simple yet effective upgrade over the plastic OEM bushing that is prone to wear and cracking.

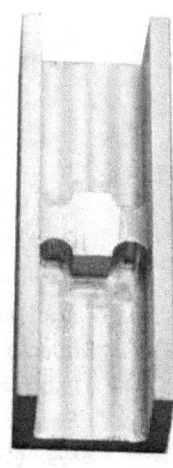

Bronze is the material of choice for fork pads. Have you ever had a transmission pop out of gear? That could have been a worn or broken fork pad, which is typically made of plastic. The shift forks move the sliders to engage the gears. (Photo Courtesy RPM Transmissions)

RPM upgrades the rear drive flange to billet (right), which attaches to the driveshaft. It is sometimes referred to as a flange yoke and slides over the output shaft. If the output shaft is changed to 30-spline, the yoke needs to match. (Photo Courtesy RPM Transmissions)

Carbon blocking rings are another upgrade on upper level transmissions (right) and optional on Level Vs. These are the friction material that the synchros use to synchronize the speed of the gear and collar when changing gears. If your transmission has trouble going into gear or grinds, the blocking rings could be worn out. (Photo Courtesy RPM Transmissions)

TCI offers a bolt-together convertor for the 6L80 and 6L90 with a triple-disc clutch, billet turbine, and stator. Previously bolt-together designs were used for racing applications only, but TCI allows street users to service their torque converter as well. Carbon frictions withstand the punishment needed for proper lock-up with increased torque. Three stall speeds are available. (Photo Courtesy TCI Auto)

harshness (NVH), General Motors used a two-piece driveshaft with rubber couplers instead of U-joints and slip yokes. Although these have proven to be surprisingly tough, most builders believe that past a certain power level it becomes necessary to switch to a one-piece aftermarket unit.

The Driveshaft Shop makes several variations, including 3½-inch aluminum and 3⅜-inch carbon-fiber units that use a 300M stub system mounted to a billet aluminum plate. When made properly, one-piece driveshafts with a billet plate instead of a pinion yoke should not have vibration issues according to The Driveshaft Shop. Past experience with NASCAR has shown that the runout on pinion yokes can vary greatly after they are removed and reinstalled to the point where it is beyond the acceptable tolerance. Conversely, the flanges retain a more concentric centerline no matter how many times they are remounted when they are machined properly.

Since its release, there has been many aftermarket shifter and knob options for the fifth-gen Camaro, starting with the not-so-aftermarket Chevrolet Performance ZL1 5:1-ratio shifter for the SS (PN 19299460). Unlike most other units on the market, it comes complete with the shift knob, boot, and surround. Of course, B&M and Hurst entered the action as the industry leaders in manual trans shifters.

Up-and-coming companies such as Barton Industries, MGW, and MTI

You can see how many working parts interact for just four forward gears. RPM hand-fits all of the sliders and hubs, assembled to exact specs. This attention to detail helps ensure you are using the TR6060 to the maximum of its potential. To that end, RPM offers micropolishing to reduce friction and cryogenic tempering for strength. (Photo Courtesy RPM Transmissions)

Circle D is in the custom torque converter market, building converters specific to your combination and needs. For the 6L80 and 6L90, Circle D offers a High Performance and Pro Series line of converters. (Photo Courtesy Circle D Specialties)

DRIVETRAIN

The High Performance line is for the budget-conscious street car with just a few mods. It is TIG welded by hand, uses a high-carbon spun-wound lock-up clutch lining and heavy-duty Torrington bearings. (Photo Courtesy Circle D Specialties)

The Pro Series meets higher horsepower needs, incorporating custom billet parts such as the front plate and piston, plus a flanged impeller hub (shown). It is available with either a single- or multidisk configuration, in multiple diameters (from 9¾ to 10½ inches) and for various GM transmissions. (Photo Courtesy Circle D Specialties)

The stock flexplate on virtually any vehicle looks as if it were made of recycled tin cans. TCI offers an SFI-approved 6L80 and 6L90 flexplate (PN 399757) made of high tensile-strength steel that is 33-percent thicker than stock. It is a good safety upgrade for any application. TCI's flexplate is dynamically balanced (internally), electro-coated, and precision ground with 168 teeth and dual bolt patterns (10.75 and 11.063 inches). A separate flexplate is available for the 4L80 (PN 399754) and other transmissions (PN 399753). LSA and LSX crate engines require an eight-bolt flange, and the LS9 has a nine-bolt flange (PN 399755). (Photo Courtesy TCI Auto)

Racing offer their own versions. Others on the market include the powertrain experts SLP Performance and the suspension gurus at LSR Performance. Each variation has its own feel and attributes, so choosing a shifter is entirely subjective.

The general principle is the same for all: reduce the throw of the shifter for faster shifts and improve the feel. MGW has perhaps the one approach that is significantly different, by offering a full replacement assembly made from CNC-machined and anodized aluminum. Although it comes at an additional cost, it offers an integral spring return to the 3-4 gate, polyurethane bushing mount, sound-dampening center shaft, and other improvements for any Camaro.

TCI and B&M are two of the most popular makers of transmission coolers. According to most 6L80 experts, you want the biggest cooler you can possibly get. Some even run two coolers. A basic kit includes the heat exchanger core with an inlet and outlet, high-pressure hose, clamps or fittings, and zip ties to thread through the radiator or condenser. For something more plug-and-play, ADM Performance, PCM of NC, and Flex-a-lite offer direct-fit kits for the Camaro. A cooler is a good upgrade for a stock Camaro but should be mandatory with a converter swap. (Photo Courtesy TCI Auto)

Century Transmission has some of the fastest ETs credited to its handiwork with the 6L80, not to mention its previous achievements with the 4L60, 4L80, and other GM trannies. Custom Power Packs upgrade the clutch discs with Alto Red Eagle and Raybestos HP frictions with Kolene-treated steel plates. By improving the friction material and number of clutch packs, Century increases the capacity. (Photo Courtesy Century Transmission)

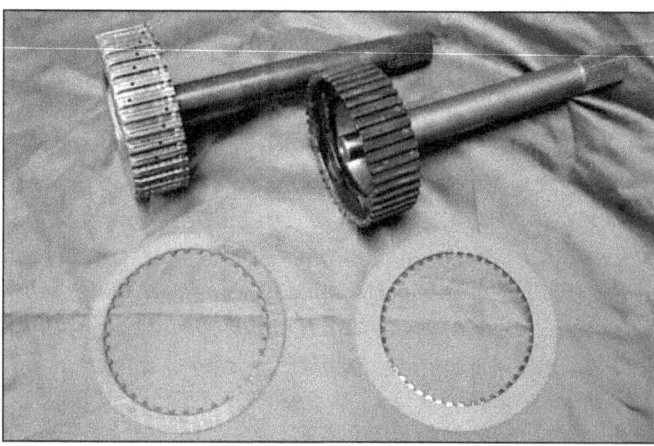

A 300M billet intermediate shaft replaces the powdered-metal OEM component. A Powerglide Powerpack hub and clutch kit allows the use of Red Eagle Powerglide frictions, twice as wide as the standard 4-5-6 friction for better power and RPM capability, as well as consistency. (Photo Courtesy Century Transmission)

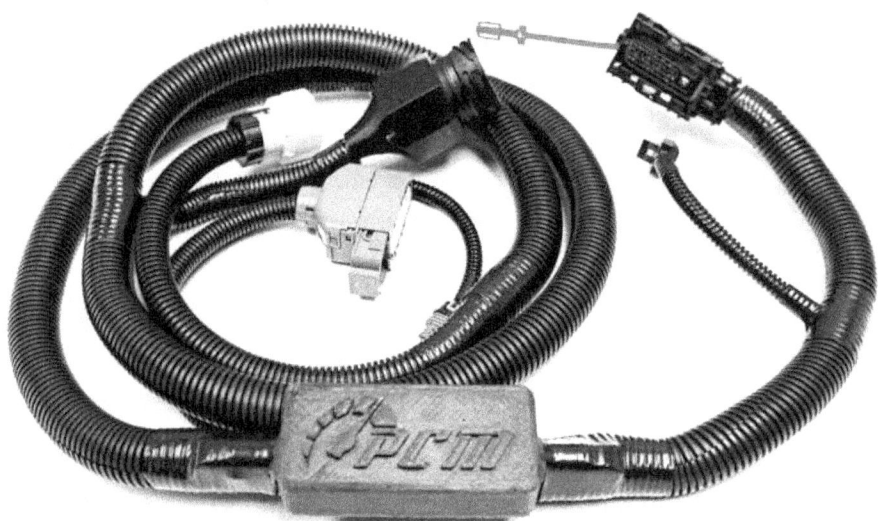

The 6L80 and 6L90 are great transmissions for the street but can be tricky for drag racing. Many prefer the 4-speeds, especially with forced induction. Luckily PCM of NC makes the swap easier with its conversion harness for the 4L60 and 4L80. This plug-and-play option includes an OEM GM Transmission Control Module that even operates the OEM trans temp gauge, and no programming is required. Although it does support cruise control, it's only downside is that it negates the paddle shifters. (Photo Courtesy PCM of NC)

Two of the OEM clutch hubs are TIG welded at the factory seams for increased reliability. A transmission tune is included with the package and is essential to making this trans live with high power. Packages are available for the larger 6L90, which are even more capable. Note: A 6L80 cannot be internally upgraded to 6L90 specs due to the larger drums, planetary, and case. (Photo Courtesy Century Transmission)

DRIVETRAIN

When switching from a manual trans to a 4L60 or 4L80, it can be easier to go the aftermarket route. TCI sells 4L80s and the EZ-TCU controller, which was recently redesigned to be even more user-friendly. Shift points, firmness, and speed can all be manipulated; however, it is fully configured right out of the box. Also available are custom options based on load, speed, and RPM. Powertrain Control Solutions is another transmission controller supplier frequently used by RPM Transmissions in conversions. (Photo Courtesy TCI Auto)

The 4L60 absorbs less power, so it is preferable to the 4L80 when possible. The 4L80, though, is much more durable and has a less steep gear set similar to a Turbo 400 but with overdrive. The non-electronic 2- and 3-speeds are best left to dedicated track cars. (Photo Courtesy TCI Auto)

Solid Axle Conversions

A solid axle is still the preferred choice for high-powered, dedicated drag racing cars when class rules allow. Chevrolet Performance engineers worked closely with MPR Race Cars to develop the NHRA-legal solid axle conversion for the COPO Camaro. MPR was intimately familiar with NHRA specs, having previously designed a similar conversion for the Dodge Challenger Drag Pak Stock Eliminator program. The end result was a five-link style suspension. Fixed-length lower control arms help locate the axle longitudinally and the adjustable upper control arms set the pinion angle. A panhard bar locates the axle laterally, and an anti-roll bar keeps the Camaro launching straight. It's no coincidence that this is the same style used by the Ford Mustang of the same era.

MPR used TIG-welded 4130 chrome-moly throughout the suspension with polyurethane bushings on the lower control arms and rod ends on the upper control arms and anti-roll bar. Rod ends actually secure the anti-roll bar to the chassis (rather than mounting to the frame rails), in addition to the rod ends that secure it to the axle housing. The axle itself

Strange Engineering produces this 9-inch rear for the COPO program, complete with a spool, 35-spline axles, 5/8-inch wheel studs, and drag brakes. (Photo Courtesy Chevrolet Performance)

CHAPTER 3

The COPO's anti-roll bar is secured to the chassis and solid axle, rather than to the cradle and lower control arms as is the OEM bar. Unlike the street car, the COPO's anti-roll bar is not concerned with cornering. Instead, its job is to counteract the twisting motion of the driveshaft as it delivers power to the axles off the starting line. The direction of the movement favors traction in the passenger-side rear, so the anti-roll bar acts to even that balance rather than twisting the body at launch. (Photo Courtesy Chevrolet Performance)

Fully installed, the COPO uses a five-link arrangement with a panhard bar, upper and lower control arms, an anti-roll bar, and Strange coil-overs. Because the axle assembly is no longer stationary, the clearance in this area is needed for suspension travel. This negates the factory fuel tank arrangement. Unlike with other solid axle conversions, though, it is not necessary to remove the floor. This is nearly a bolt-in installation, resembling the fourth-gen's setup. (Photo Courtesy Chevrolet Performance)

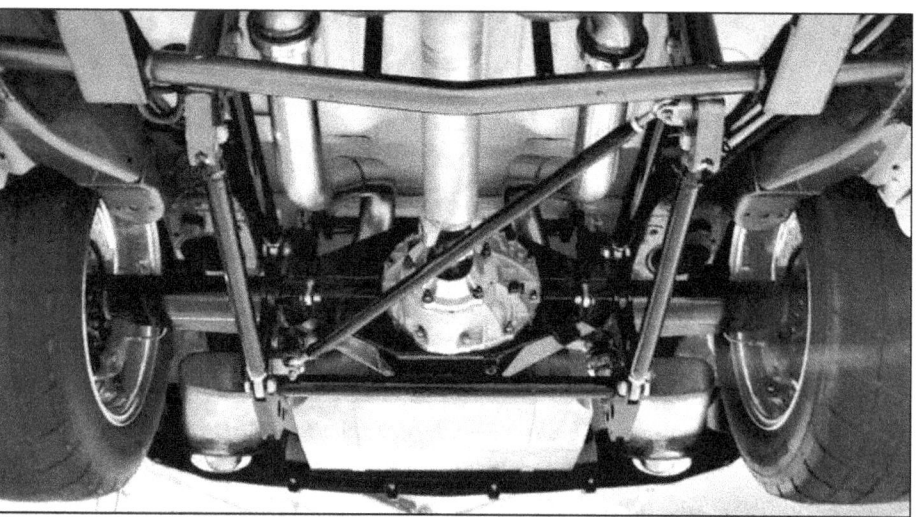

Xtreme Innovations' solid axle conversion is a bit more, well, extreme. Although you can work with whatever goals or class rules are needed, this trunk floor was modified to accommodate a fuel tank. Other versions completely remove the floor to tie into a full roll cage. (Photo Courtesy Xtreme Innovations)

DRIVETRAIN

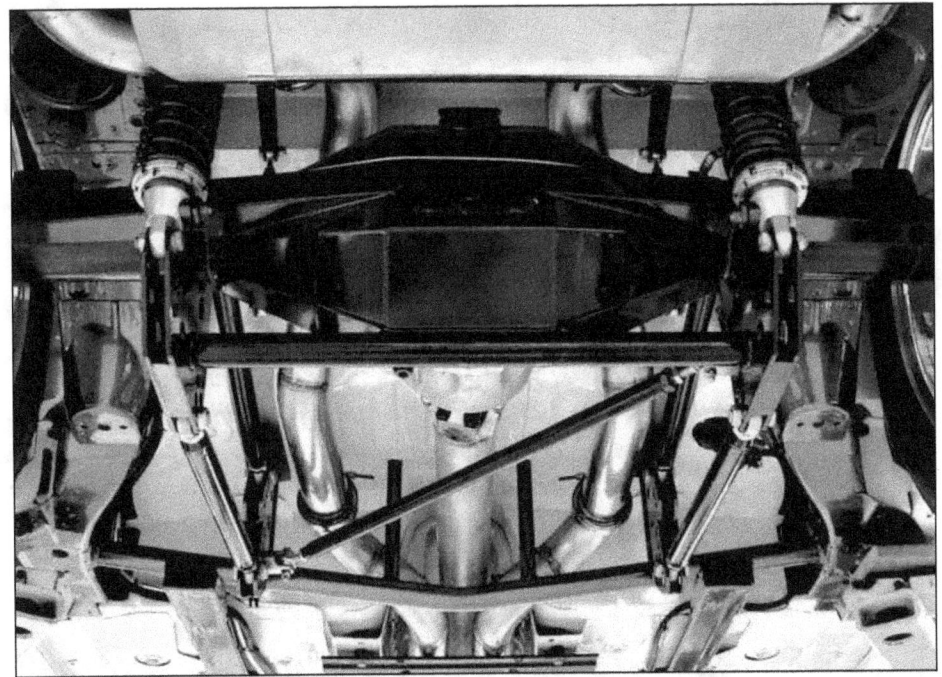

This is a tried-and-true traditional four-link arrangement that is not only for drag cars but for corner-carving ProTouring builds as well. The upper and lower control arms connect to a custom crossmember, and the coil-overs use a completely different mounting point (notice the empty spring pockets). Despite its use primarily in drag cars, a solid axle can be used in street cars with full exhaust and large fuel tanks. (Photo Courtesy Xtreme Innovations)

suspension is certainly much easier than a custom or back-half design. Instead of simply welding in brackets and drilling a few holes in the chassis, Outlaw Drag Radial and Outlaw 10.5 builders cut the frame rails and remove the floor. Because some drag radial classes allow IRS cars to use a factory-style suspension, one method is to use the fourth-gen Camaro's torque arm–style suspension.

The center of the floor must be cut out to make room for the torque arm, which mounts to the funny car-style roll cage. The frame rails must be modified because the spring pockets do not line up, and there is no mount for a panhard bar or anti-roll bar. The outside of the frame rails and wheelwells may also need to be cut for tire clearance.

The Outlaw 10.5 style is much more invasive. The reason these cars are often referred to as "back-halfs" is because you literally remove the entire back half of the car. Even the factory frame rails are chopped, replaced by fabricated frame rails that are welded in place to mount a solid axle with either a ladder bar or four-link suspension.

Pro Mods are the next step, which are basically a tube chassis with a factory body dropped over the top.

is a Strange Engineering 9-inch with 35-spline axles, 5/8-inch wheel studs, lightweight spool, and aluminum center section with Pro gear sets. Strange finishes the conversion with four-piston, 11.25-inch, lightweight drag brakes and coil-overs.

As part of the NHRA homologation, all of these parts are available through a COPO parts dealer (PN 22950665). Between the spool and the occupation of space where the factory fuel tank resides, this definitely isn't intended for a street car (in case you had any big ideas).

Any solid axle conversion is definitely not for the novice builder. However, the COPO's weld-in style

How-To Projects

Driveshaft Safety Loop Install

All photos for this project are courtesy of Joseph Potak.

The NHRA states that any vehicle running 12.99 or quicker must use a driveshaft safety loop. Given the Camaro's OEM two-piece driveshaft, a safety loop is recommended at any ET. Although the rubber couplers are ideal for NVH, they wear out just like rubber suspension bushings and can even tear when you exceed their capacity. It should come as no surprise that the ZL1 uses higher durometer couplers, but even those can give up the ghost with sticky tires and a shot of nitrous. BMR, among others, offers safety loops for the manual and automatic SS made of 1/4-inch steel. For this install, I ordered the manual version (PN DSL014) and put the Camaro on a lift.

CHAPTER 3

The NHRA states that any vehicle running 12.99 or quicker requires a driveshaft safety loop, which must be made to exact specs. BMR's version (PN DSL014) is designed for the OEM-style two-piece driveshaft and is made of 1/4-inch steel.

1 With a screw jack to support the transmission, use a 15-mm socket to remove the two nuts on the mount and four bolts holding the crossmember to the chassis.

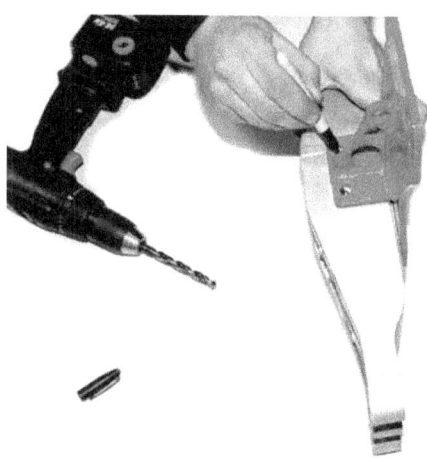

2 With the BMR mounting bracket lined up to the bolt holes for the trans mount (on the bottom of the crossmember), use the bracket as a template to mark holes for drilling.

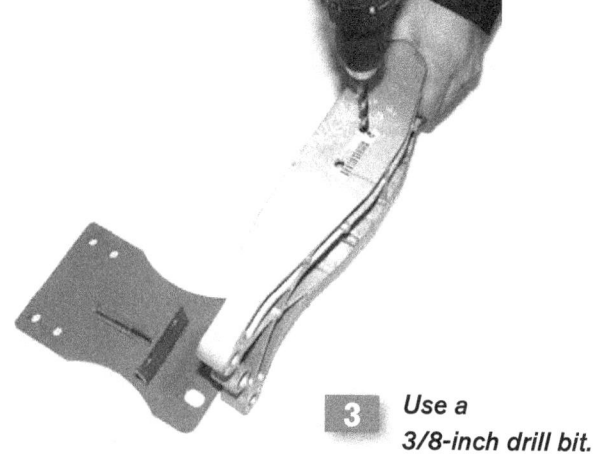

3 Use a 3/8-inch drill bit.

DRIVETRAIN

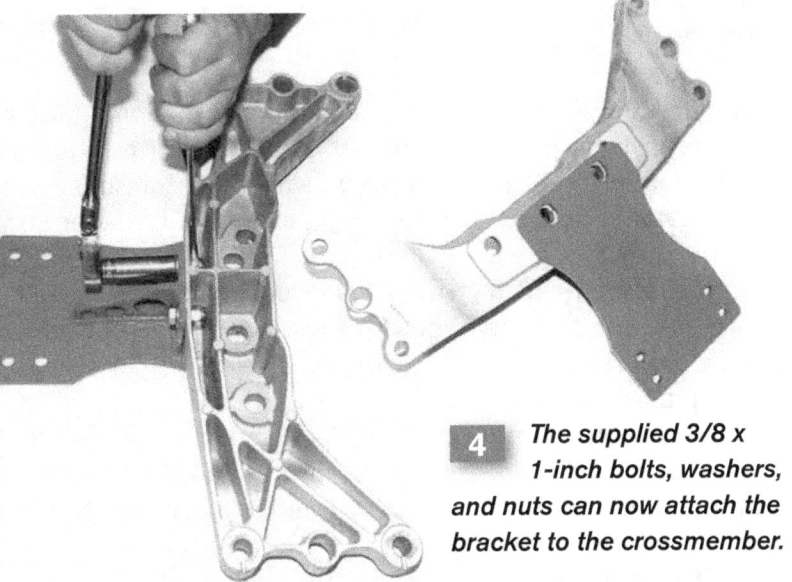

4 The supplied 3/8 x 1-inch bolts, washers, and nuts can now attach the bracket to the crossmember.

5 Bolt the crossmember to the trans and chassis. Because of this install, BMR now supplies spacers that drop the crossmember slightly for additional clearance.

6 Position the BMR loop over the driveshaft and line it up to the holes in the mounting bracket.

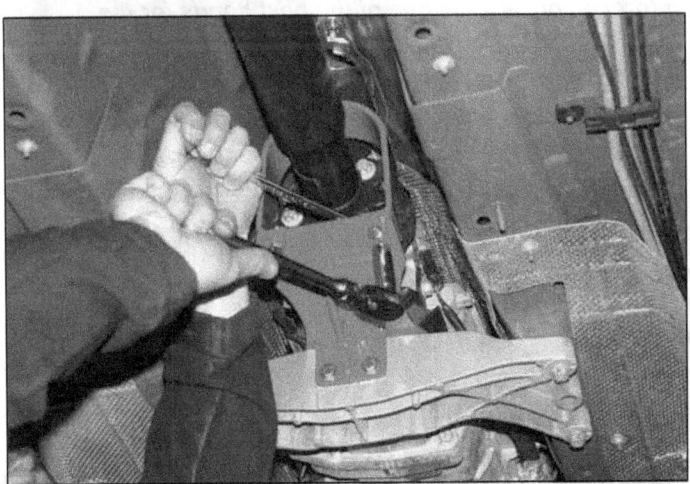

7 Use another set of 3/8 x 1-inch bolts and nuts to attach the loop to the bracket. Use two 9/16-inch wrenches to tighten it.

8 As per NHRA rules, the safety loop is within 6 inches of the front joint for a two-piece driveshaft. If you switch to a one-piece driveshaft, this is not within spec. Also note that due to the ZL1's larger exhaust, this loop does not clear.

CHAPTER 3

Torque Converter Install

All photos for this project are courtesy of Joseph Potak.

Out of the box, the fifth-gen Camaro is slower with an automatic, but an aftermarket torque converter changes all that. As they say, "spinnin' ain't winnin'." An aftermarket converter such as the Precision Industries Vigilante is lighter than stock, has a higher stall speed and better torque multiplication. Precision uses a forged steel front cover and a lock-up clutch designed to resist heat and increase fuel efficiency. Both 9.5- and 10.5-inch models are available for the 6L80 and 6L90 with stall speeds from 2,600 to 4,400 rpm and single- or triple-disk.

The torque converter bolts to the flexplate, which is bolted to the crankshaft, and transmits power from the engine to the transmission. It allows the engine to spin independently of the transmission, and also pressurizes the transmission fluid so that it can operate.

Inside, converter fluid dynamics are at work. A centrifugal pump (spun by the engine) flings fluid to the outside while creating a vacuum that draws more fluid into the center. Fluid hits the turbine blades, which start spinning. Because the turbine is connected to the transmission, it causes the trans to spin. A stator then redirects the fluid coming off the turbine before hitting the pump again, so it doesn't slow the engine.

This is an oversimplification, but you get the idea. The size, angle, and pitch of the turbine blades plus all of the other components can drastically change how a converter operates.

When engineering a converter, it is a gentle balance between efficiency and capacity. You want the converter to put the engine into its powerband, but also not slip excessively. Although a race car with a Turbo 400 or Powerglide tolerates some slippage for better 60-foot times, this can play havoc with the 6L80/6L90's internal design and calibration. Some builders use multidisk converters almost exclusively with these transmissions as the result, except for near-stock or bolt-on SSs.

When selecting the stall speed, you want to consider the operating range of the camshaft or any power adders, as well as the usage. A daily driver with concerns for fuel mileage is best on the low end, such as 2,800 or 3,000. You don't want the engine revving up to 4,400 rpm when you are trying to parallel park.

On the other hand, a weekend toy with a healthy camshaft really comes alive with a 3,600- to 3,800-rpm stall converter. Although it might not add power you can measure on the dyno, a torque converter (similar to rear gears on a stick car) is one of the simplest and most effective ways to dramatically improve how your Camaro responds. It really is a substantial improvement, and a great bang-for-the-buck modification.

A torque converter is one of the best bangs for the buck available on the Camaro, improving acceleration significantly by keeping the engine in its powerband. With the factory 6L90, it is extremely important to minimize converter slippage for transmission longevity. The torque-based calibration relies on precision clutch application timing.

1 *Begin the process with your Camaro on a lift. With the exhaust supported, you can unbolt and remove it. This is to give clearance so that the transmission can be lowered. You also want to remove the cats.*

DRIVETRAIN

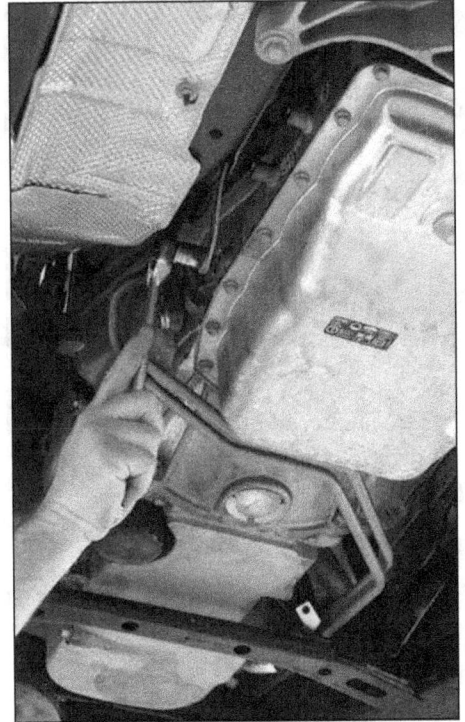

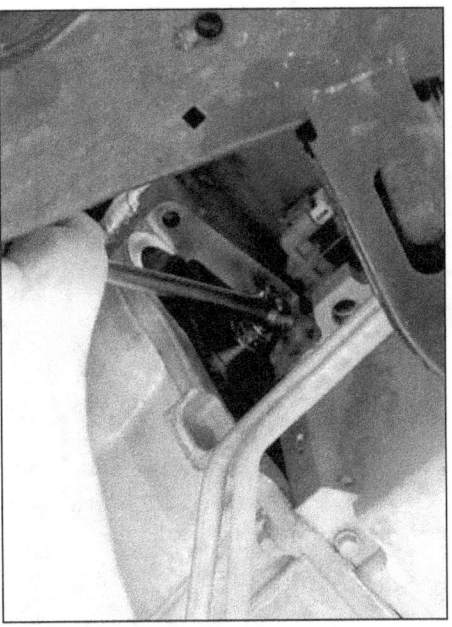

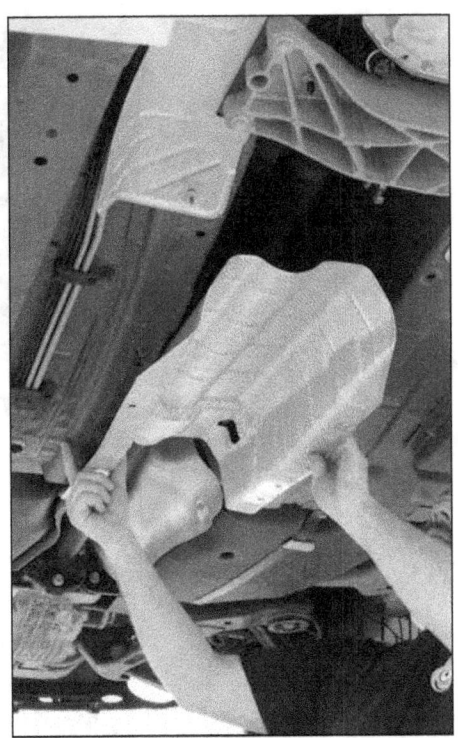

2 Disconnect the shift linkage and remove the vent hose from the retaining clips.

3 Remove the converter cover and remove the flexplate-to-converter bolts, rotating the flexplate by the engine's harmonic balancer bolt. Most likely this requires unbolting the starter.

4 The heat shield needs to come off so you can access the driveshaft.

5 Unbolt the driveshaft at the differential coupler, using a pry bar to keep it from spinning. You want to mark the coupler first so that you can reinstall it with the same orientation.

6 Unbolt the transmission cooler lines and use a drain pan to catch the fluid. You can also tie on a used latex glove or use plugs. The O-rings need to be replaced.

CHAPTER 3

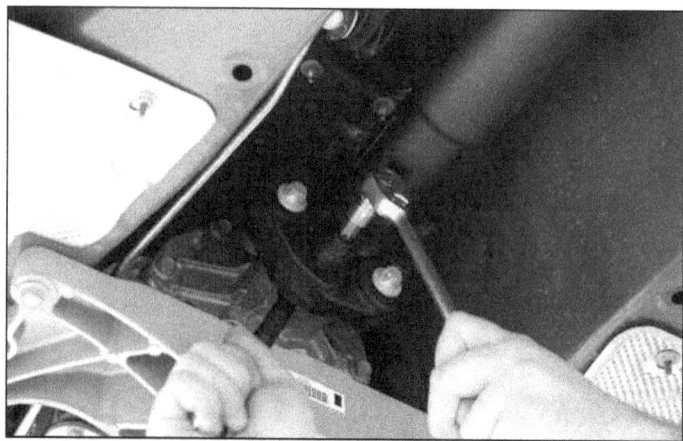

7 The driveshaft must then be unbolted from the transmission.

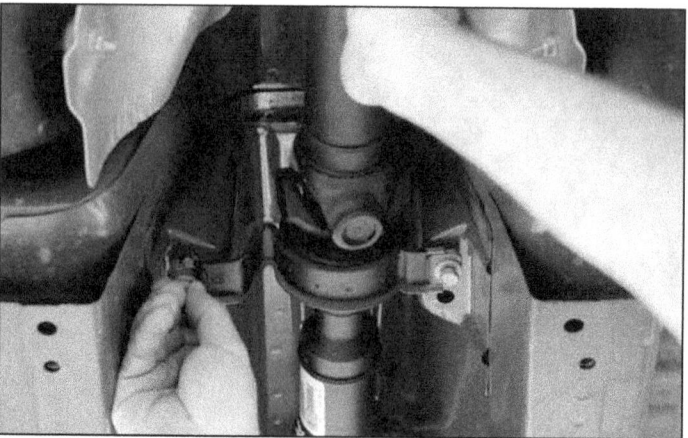

8 And finally the collar can be removed (and the driveshaft with it).

9 With the trans supported, unbolt the transmission crossmember from the chassis and transmission.

10 The lock on the wiring harness must be rotated to unplug.

DRIVETRAIN

11 *By tilting the transmission down you can access the top transmission bolts with a long extension. The others are considerably easier.*

12 *The transmission just needs to be pulled free of the dowels once the bolts are out.*

13 *Twist and pull off the old converter to unseat it.*

14 It's always good to pour at least a half quart of fluid into the converter prior to installation. The transmission itself has no dipstick, so you need to fill that, too, once it is back in the air using a mechanical or hand pump. You just keep filling until it comes out the full port.

15 It is important to twist the converter after sliding it onto the input shaft to seat it properly.

16 When putting the trans back into place, the dowels help align it.

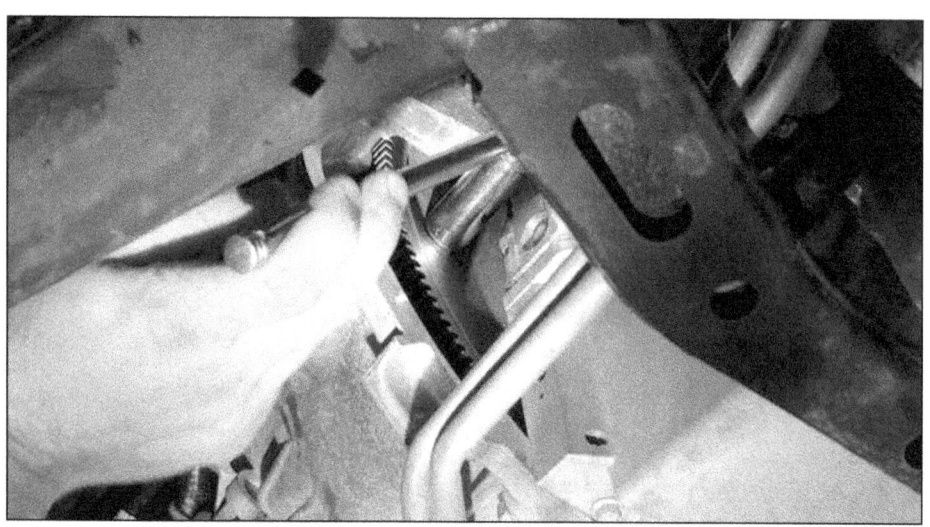

17 Brand-new torque converter bolts are provided from Precision. The stockers are torque-to-yield head bolts, which means they cannot be reused. The rest of the parts go back on as they came off.

Clutch Install

All photos for this project are courtesy of Joseph Potak.

The factory clutch in the Camaro SS and Z/28 is a single organic disc, identical to the 2006–2013 Corvette Z06's. Depending on driving style it holds up to some decent power levels, but with a high-compression stroker or forced induction, it is best to switch to a quality twin-disc clutch. Even the ZL1's twin, which was designed for low-pedal effort more than performance, is not exactly bulletproof.

The RAM Force 9.5 and 10.5 are excellent upgrade options. The Force 9.5 is even available for the V-6 Camaro. Upgrading from the stock single-disc organic clutch material to a metallic is no longer necessary, thanks to this multidisc design. As a result, not only is RAM able to keep the pedal effort light, but smooth as well.

Aftermarket clutches of only 10 or 11 years ago were known for being like an on/off switch, chattering like crazy and bucking whenever you tried to slip it. The twin discs allow enough friction to negate more aggressive materials and the right balance of weight to make a clutch equally at home at high RPM as at low speeds. The 300 Series Force 9.5 holds 700 ft-lbs comfortably, using two organic discs.

The Force 10.5 may be a better choice the closer you approach that threshold. The flywheel is billet steel, the floater plate uses three sets of straps to remain quiet at idle, a sprung hub on the top clutch prevents chatter, and the pressure plate is optimized for proper engagement with factory hydraulics. Also, aRAM slave is used in this build.

The RAM Force 9.5 dual-disc clutch is available for V-6 and V-8 models at nearly the cost of other aftermarket single-discs. This is a 300 Series, which uses two organic clutch discs for great street manners and 700 ft-lbs of torque capacity. More aggressive materials are also available for increased capacity and durability at the dragstrip. The RAM Force 10.5 uses a very similar design, except with another inch of diameter for better holding capacity. Some users report that the 10.5 has lighter pedal effort, but both have similar engagement.

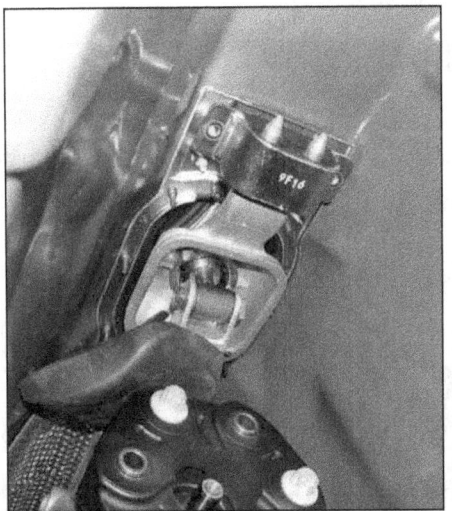

1 *During the initial prep, removing the TR6060 is almost no different than the 6L90 except for the different lines, wiring, and the two bolts that attach the shifter to the chassis.*

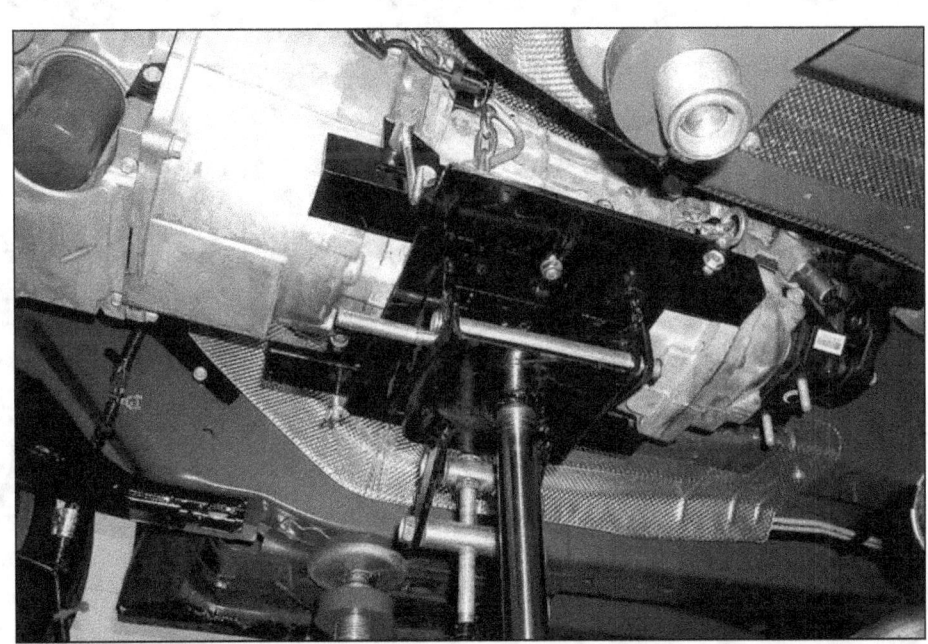

2 *With the trans supported, you can unbolt the bellhousing from the engine now that the driveshaft and all other items are out of the way.*

3 The factory LS3 clutch is identical to the C6 Corvette, including the Z06, though the spacing and hydraulics are slightly different. Unbolt the pressure plate from the flywheel before you remove the six bolts that attach the flywheel to the crankshaft.

4 A trans jack and a lift are pretty much essential to swapping a clutch in a fifth-gen.

5 Bolt up the RAM flywheel with the supplied 11-mm bolts using 80 to 85 ft-lbs of torque. Blue Loctite is recommended.

6 Here is a good look at the sprung organic clutch, which is aligned with the bottom clutch using the supplied tool. The three straps on the floater plate have already been torqued to 30 ft-lbs, and the plate sits between the two clutch discs.

7 The pressure plate goes on last, using the alignment tool, before you apply 30 ft-lbs to its bolts.

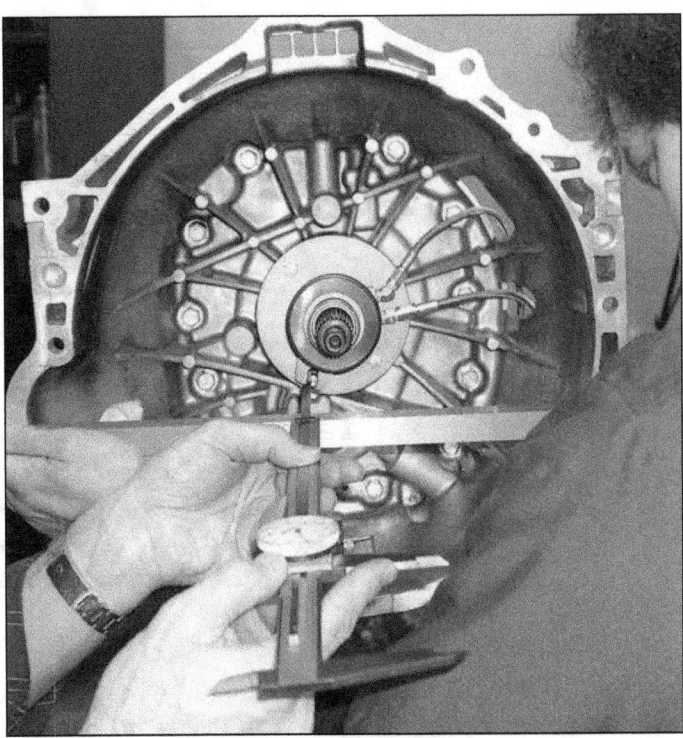

8 It is very important to check the clearance to ensure that the slave cylinder collapses and extends properly. Just .100 inch is enough to prevent premature wear with stock hydraulics.

9 RAM recommends upgrading the hydraulics with its T-56 Release Bearings (PN 78180) that increase the travel. It has the added benefit of accommodating a remote bleeder setup, so that you can bleed the system from outside the bellhousing.

10 The braided hydraulic lines simply run through the opening in the bellhousing, and then you are ready to bolt the transmission back into your Camaro. Installing the transmission is simply the reverse of the removal process.

CHAPTER 4

Basic Engine Performance Upgrades

From 300 to 580 hp, the Camaro can feel quite fast the first time you turn the key. With a few miles, it is easy to start getting the itch for more power. Depending on your budget and mechanical ability, many options yield significant results. V-8s are quite responsive to modifications, as are early (LLT) V-6s. Among the list of basic performance upgrades, these items are generally referred to as "bolt-on" upgrades.

Although the definition of a "bolt-on" varies greatly depending on whom you ask, in this context it refers to any nonfactory noninternal part that increases the engine's performance. This does not include the use of forced induction, but it does allow for modification to factory forced-induction components, such as on the ZL1's 1.9L Eaton supercharger. Ported stock or aftermarket cylinder heads, camshafts, and rocker arms fall under the umbrella of valvetrain upgrades. (Those items, as well as engine swaps, are covered in Chapter 5.)

V-6 Upgrades

V-6 upgrades are not nearly as plentiful as for the V-8, though the list of aftermarket components continues to increase. The most common modifications include the typical ported throttle body, cold-air intake, exhaust, and tuning. The direct-injection system makes tuning particularly challenging and should be left up to experienced EFI calibrators familiar with direct injection. Gains on mostly stock V-6s are generally in the 10- to 25-hp range.

Roto-Fab, Injen, Volant, CAI, Airaid, and K&N, as well as Camaro-specific manufacturers such as BBK and SLP Performance, offer cold-air intakes for the V-6. An intake with a quality reusable air filter and good MAF sensor placement, in a straight section of tubing 6 inches or more from throttle body, is ideal. Some kits go to great lengths to seal the air

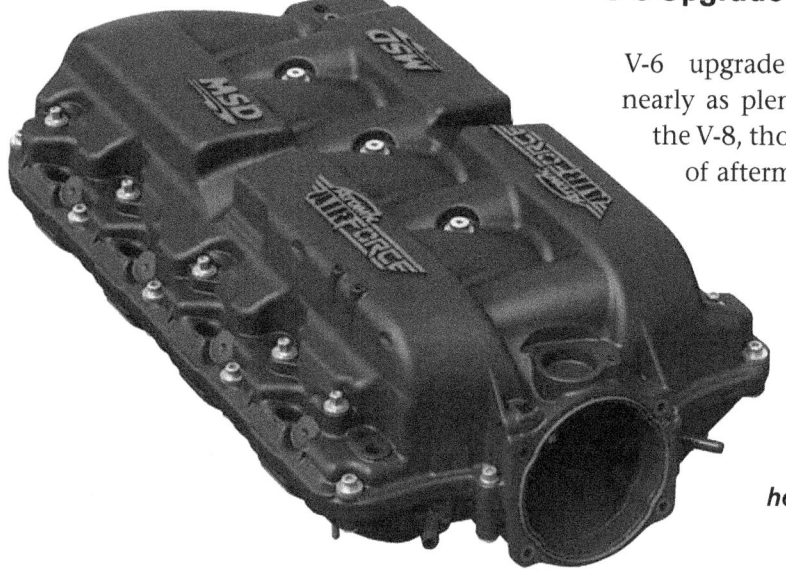

Bolt-on products such as this MSD Atomic AirForce intake manifold are a proven way to improve engine performance. The term "bolt-on" refers to the fact that it is not an internal engine part, and it simply bolts onto the exterior of the long-block. There is some debate about what is and is not a "bolt-on," but most agree cold-air intakes, intake manifolds, headers, exhaust, and throttle bodies make the grade. (Photo Courtesy MSD)

BASIC ENGINE PERFORMANCE UPGRADES

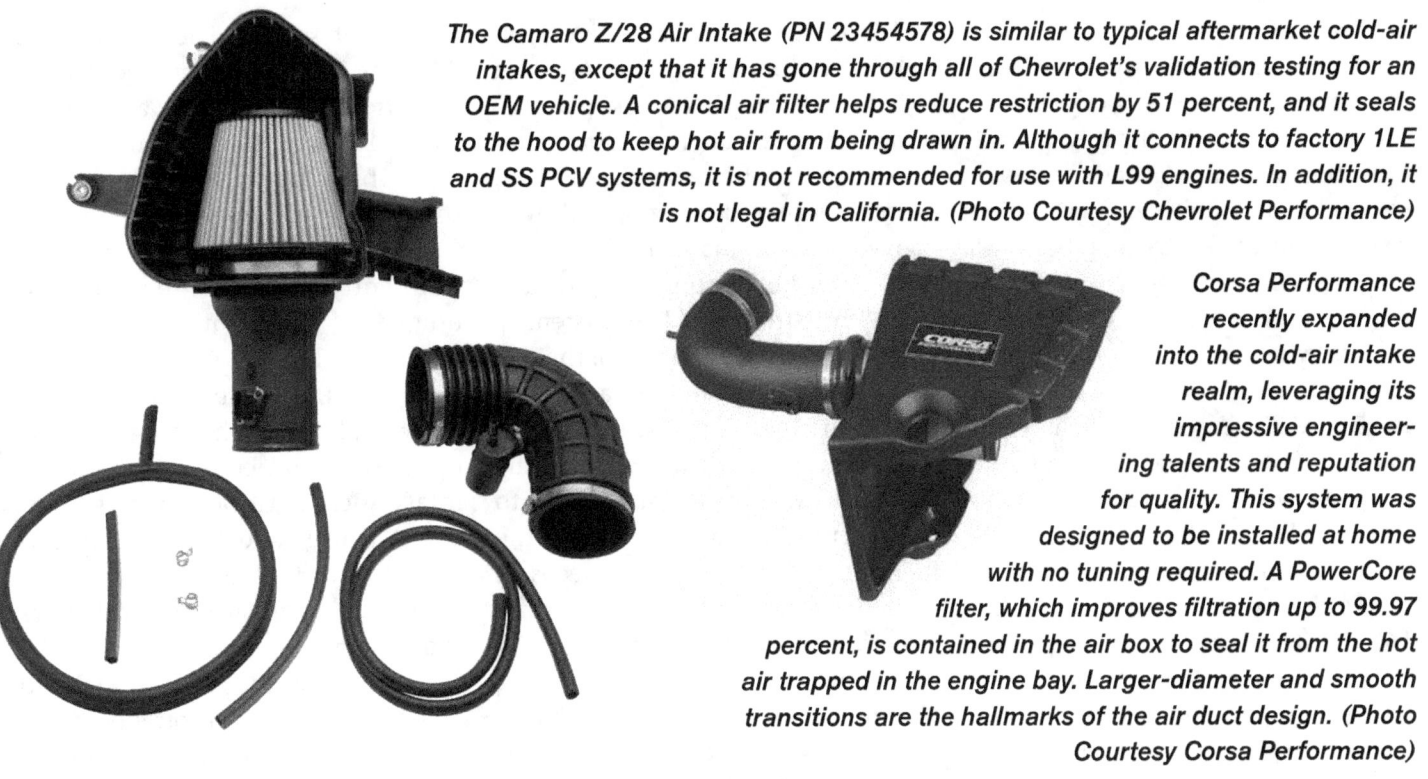

The Camaro Z/28 Air Intake (PN 23454578) is similar to typical aftermarket cold-air intakes, except that it has gone through all of Chevrolet's validation testing for an OEM vehicle. A conical air filter helps reduce restriction by 51 percent, and it seals to the hood to keep hot air from being drawn in. Although it connects to factory 1LE and SS PCV systems, it is not recommended for use with L99 engines. In addition, it is not legal in California. (Photo Courtesy Chevrolet Performance)

Corsa Performance recently expanded into the cold-air intake realm, leveraging its impressive engineering talents and reputation for quality. This system was designed to be installed at home with no tuning required. A PowerCore filter, which improves filtration up to 99.97 percent, is contained in the air box to seal it from the hot air trapped in the engine bay. Larger-diameter and smooth transitions are the hallmarks of the air duct design. (Photo Courtesy Corsa Performance)

filter to the hood and block out the heat from the rest of the engine bay. Plastic or composite is the preferred material for intakes because it does not transfer heat such as aluminum tubing that can increase IAT.

The majority of horsepower gains from cold-air intakes are accomplished through decreasing restriction. Manipulating the size and type of air filter as well as the diameter and shape of intake enhances the quality and quantity of air entering the throttle body.

On the exhaust side, gains tend to be minimal from an axle-back system, although many prefer the sound of aftermarket mufflers or even none at all.

MRT is one of the most reputable builders of V-6 Camaro exhausts, which come in the highest grade 304 stainless steel with various exhaust tip and two muffler options. Full exhaust systems with headers can have a significant effect on performance (more than 20 hp). Because the exhaust manifolds were integrated into the cylinder heads of the LFX (2012–2015 Camaro), headers are only available for the 2010–2011 models. BBK Performance, Stainless Works, American Racing, and JBA all offer V-6 headers.

Some lesser-known V-6 modifications include an intake manifold isolator, plenum spacer, and catch can. A product such as RX Speedworks' ICE-OLATOR stops some of the heat transfer from the engine to the intake manifold. It is essentially a heat-resistant plastic block that is CNC-cut to the intake pattern and mounts between the intake and cylinder heads. Plenum spacers are available from several companies to provide better air distribution to each cylinder.

Although there is a slight increase to plenum volume, Mace Engineering says the spacer's purpose is to slow the air speed. "There is less of a pressure drop inside the plenum chamber between cylinders, and less air momentum, resulting in better air distribution and power." More even air distribution also means less chance of having a lean cylinder that could potentially detonate and cause damage. Catch cans have the potential to increase performance by removing oil from the incoming air charge. Oil lowers the engine's resistance to knock, sort of like dumping lower octane gas in the tank. All three of these modifications pay even greater dividends with boosted applications that have more heat and cylinder pressure.

V-8 Upgrades

Because General Motors has tried to wring every last ounce of power out of its powertrain, there simply aren't as many quick, easy, and cheap wins as there used to be. Often enthusiasts jump right to a camshaft upgrade with a set of headers (or even forced induction), bypassing the usual first and second stop.

CHAPTER 4

Tuning

Tuning is less effective in extracting power from the V-8 than in the V-6 for stock vehicles. However, modifications such as camshafts and even some cold-air intakes require tuning to run properly. All LSx engines use a mass airflow–based system with two narrowband oxygen sensors to adjust fueling when in "open loop" operation. The incoming air is measured by the MAF sensor, which is compared to the air/fuel reading from the oxygen sensors in the exhaust manifolds. Fueling is adjusted accordingly at idle and part-throttle.

During wide-open throttle the ECM switches to "closed loop" and relies entirely on the fuel maps. This makes it especially crucial that the tuning is spot-on when you modify the engine with a camshaft or anything else that affects the airflow or the sensors' ability to read.

The Camaro uses two knock sensors on either side of the block as a safeguard. However, if the tune is off considerably, the ECM is not able to react quickly enough to the knock sensors' signal.

Intake air temperature and coolant temperature are two other sensors that can affect what fueling and timing the ECM commands and, consequently, the engine's performance.

The Camaro SS and Z/28 use the E38 ECM; the ZL1 uses the more sophisticated E67. Handheld tuners are sufficient for lesser modifications. Brands include DiabloSport, SCT, Superchips, and Hypertech. Speedometer recalibration for tire size, elimination of Skipshift, fan-activation temperature, and raising the speed limiter are just a few basic changes that can be made besides ignition timing and fueling. Laptop-based tuning software, such as HP Tuners or EFI Live, are typically used for custom tuning with aftermarket camshafts. Skilled custom tuners can alter camshaft timing (L99), delete AFM, delete VVT, change fuel injector sizes, and even convert the Camaro to Flex Fuel (E85) with the appropriate hardware.

With a true Flex Fuel system, a GM sensor is placed in-line of the fuel supply to measure the ethanol content of the fuel to adjust the fueling and timing as needed. E85 from the pump can vary by as much as 10 to 15 percent. The more ethanol in the fuel, the richer the air/fuel needs to be. More ethanol also means greater tolerance to knock, which typically means you can add more timing (for more power). Although ethanol is not measured like gasoline, E85 is said to have 100- to 105-octane.

Intake Manifolds

Because the intake manifold on the SS and Z/28 does not touch oil, it is typically considered a bolt-on. Given the efficiency of the stock LS3/L99 and LS7 intake manifolds, upgrading the intake only benefits more radical combinations. The FAST LSXR and MSD Atomic AirForce intake manifolds are the most applicable to street-going combinations, using a factory-style lower-profile design that is made of polymer to resist heat soak and reduce weight. Both products allow the use of stock and aftermarket fuel rails and have a larger 103-mm throttle body opening, which can also accommodate the stock 90-mm.

MSD's Atomic AirForce is a front-entry two-piece design with unique bell-mouthed runner entrances. The FAST LSXR intake is a front-entry modular design with individual runners housed under the upper shell and bolted to the lower intake shell. Mast Motorsports, Edelbrock, Holley, and Chevrolet Performance offer traditional single-plane aluminum intake manifolds that are available with injector bungs.

To use a factory-style 90- to 103-mm electronic throttle body, an intake elbow is needed to bolt to the intake's 4150 or 4500 flange. Sheet-metal elbows, as well as billet and cast elbows from Edelbrock and Wilson Manifolds, are common. This setup is best for high-boost high-RPM race applications. Custom sheet-metal and billet intakes are mostly used for race-only applications as well. Prices usually exceed $2,500. Wilson Manifolds, Precision Metalcraft, Procomp, RCI Performance, Late Model Engines, Marcella Manifolds, Hogan's Racing Manifolds, and Berry Motorsports all offer intakes for LSx applications.

FAST and Nick Williams manufacture aftermarket throttle bodies for the Camaro. Typically gains are only seen when stepping up to a 102-mm and an aftermarket intake with more radical combinations and forced induction. The LSA has the most to gain, though it requires significant porting of the blower snout to match the throttle body opening. (Photo Courtesy Fuel Air Spark Technologies)

BASIC ENGINE PERFORMANCE UPGRADES

The FAST LSXR is the go-to LS3 intake for street combinations, but unlike years past there is less to be gained from an intake manifold swap. The plenum volume is larger, as is the throttle body opening (102 mm), and the tapered runner design is nearly as good as it gets. It is a modular design with a base, cover, and individual runners that bolt in and can be removed for porting. A large-cube stroker or forced induction offers the most benefit. Stock cubic inches with bolt-ons and a camshaft or ported heads don't typically pick up power. The LSXR is also available in the LS7 version for the Z/28 and is extremely effective. (Photo Courtesy Fuel Air Spark Technologies)

After significant testing, MSD's Atomic AirForce intake was released for the LS7, as well as the older LS1/LS2 cathedral port (not the LS3). Early reports were excellent with modified LS7 engines thanks to its unique bell mouth runner entrances, which do not obstruct the opposing runners and maximize plenum space. Like the FAST, the AirForce uses a polymer two-piece design, accepts an OEM or 103-mm throttle body, and fits stock or aftermarket fuel rails. (Photo Courtesy MSD Performance)

For extreme applications, Holley offers Hi-Ram and Mid-Rise intakes that are modeled on custom sheet-metal manifolds. By casting them out of aluminum, it significantly cuts the cost for the end user. It uses a two-piece design, and the top can be swapped out. The top shown here, however, is perfect for mating to the electronic throttle body of your choosing and is favored in big-boost combos. The 92- or 105-mm throttle body openings are available in natural or black finish for the LS3/L99, LS7, and even LS1/LS2 heads. (Photo Courtesy Holley Performance)

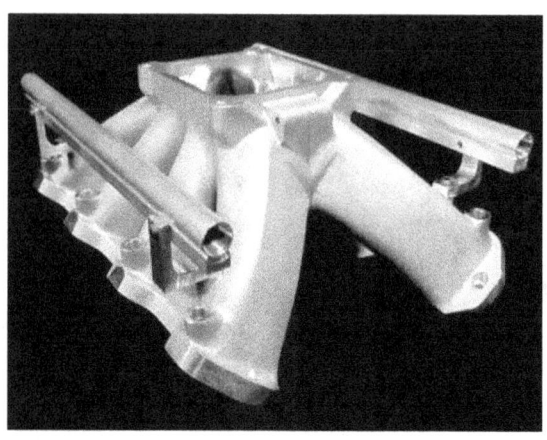

A single-plane carb-style manifold, such as this one from Mast Motorsports, is also an option for more extreme applications. A cast elbow from Wilson Manifolds or Edelbrock, as well as a custom sheet-metal piece can mate to an OEM-style throttle body. Owners of race cars with aftermarket EFI tend to do a cable throttle body conversion. Mast's two-piece intake has long runners that make it useful for a wide range of applications, with great average and peak power. It has a mirror-like finish from CNC porting and hand finishing. (Photo Courtesy Mast Motorsports)

The cast, two-piece Holley Hi-Ram (LS7) and Mid-Rise (LS3) intakes offer a similar front-entry design as its billet competitors, but at a fraction of the cost ($650 to $770 with fuel rails). Because the intake runner length and taper greatly affect the RPM range, the Hi-Ram and most custom intakes are intended for peak power in the 7,000- to 8,000-rpm range. The Mid-Rise is designed for hood clearance and a range of 1,500 to 6,500 rpm.

Throttle Bodies

Both the SS and Z/28 came with a fairly high-flowing 90-mm throttle body. Unlike previous generations, only minimal gains can be had with porting and aftermarket throttle bodies. In more radical combinations, a larger throttle body such as the Nick Williams 102-mm is helpful in extracting power from aftermarket intake manifolds such as the LSXR, AirForce, etc. Otherwise, a product such as the VMax Velocity Ring is needed to improve the transition from a stock or ported stock throttle body. Because the throttle body bolts to a supercharger on the ZL1's LSA, improvements in flow pay larger dividends, which is amplified by the fact that the LSA has a smaller throttle body than the LS3/L99 and the LS7. A ported 90-mm throttle body or a 102-mm is a noticeable improvement once other restrictions behind it are removed or reduced.

Front Dress

As with the throttle body, many other popular LSx bolt-ons are not nearly as effective as previous generations. Many of the "free mods" were eliminated by GM engineers, such as "de-screening the MAF." The fifth-gen Camaro not only has no MAF screen, it also uses a much different slot-style MAF.

Your typical underdrive pulleys and electric water pump do little to save accessory drag losses from an already efficient system. A quality balancer from ATI certainly improves harmonic dampening to protect the crankshaft and its bearings. And an electric water pump does have the benefit of allowing you to circulate coolant with the engine off, such as in the staging lanes of the dragstrip. It also allows you to completely negate the serpentine belt for 1/8- or 1/4-mile passes.

A 160-degree thermostat is one simple bolt-on that is still recommended for street/strip or all-out drag combinations. On the dyno its gains are minimal, but at the track it helps keep the engine cool prior to making a pass. Heat-soak can kill the elapsed time.

Exhaust

Long-tube headers are still one of the best bangs for your buck. A good set of long-tubes add 25 to 30 hp (or more) at the wheels in most applications. Contrary to some opinions, there is no sacrifice in low- or mid-range power, as even 1-7/8-inch primary headers make more power than stock exhaust manifolds at every RPM. The high-flowing LS3 and L99 heads need all the help they can get to relieve back pressure, which chokes the engine. A 4-into-1 style collector is most common, and some even have a velocity spike to improve scavenging. For ease of installation, a ball-and-socket or V-band flange is best. In terms of longevity, 304 stainless steel is the way to go.

Popular brands include Kooks Custom Headers, American Racing Headers, Stainless Works, Dynatech, BBK, SLP, JBA, Hooker, and LG Motorsports.

Shorty headers, such as the Camaro Z/28's Tri-Y, are not nearly as effective, though they usually carry 50-state legality. Hooker, BBK, ARH, JBA, Hedman, Doug Thorley, and Borla are a few brands to consider.

The rest of the stock exhaust system isn't nearly as restrictive. Behind the catalytic converters, the SS, ZL1, and Z/28 use a balance pipe. The balance pipe serves to even the exhaust flow, reduce back pressure, and also increase scavenging from the cylinders. Many experts believe that

BASIC ENGINE PERFORMANCE UPGRADES

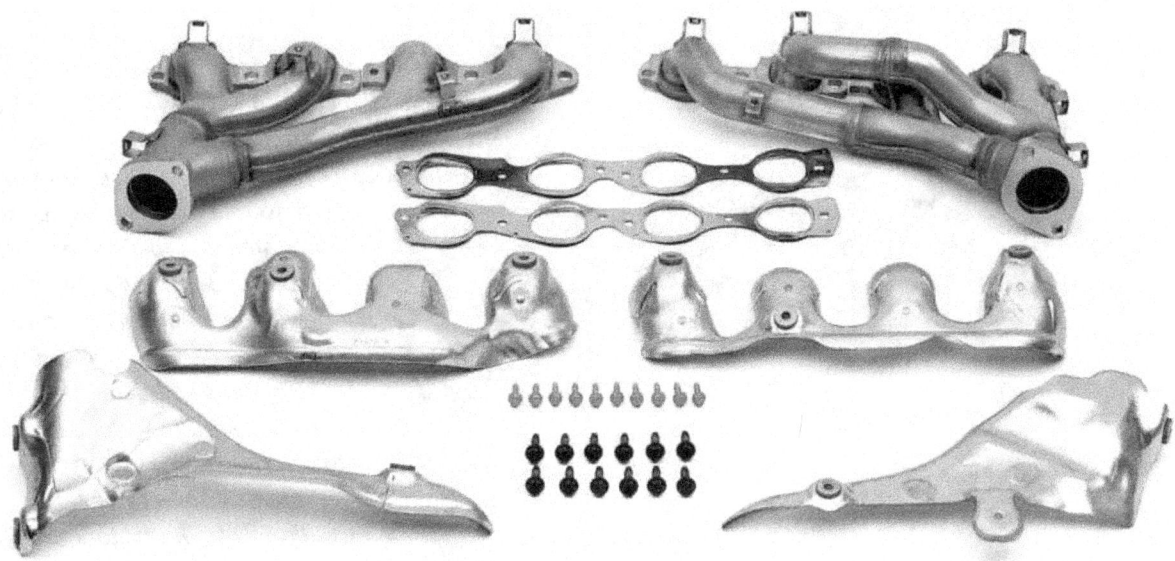

In the exhaust department, Chevrolet Performance offers the shorty Tri-Y headers from the Camaro Z/28. A Tri-Y design has a theoretical advantage in that it pairs specific cylinders together that use varying exhaust pulses to pull, or "scavenge," the spent fumes from the combustion chamber. The more efficiently that any set of headers or manifolds scavenge exhaust, the more power an engine can make. Many other factors besides the collector design affect this, from the primary tube and collector diameter, to the length of the primaries, and even the convergent angles. Because many factors go into making a set of headers fit into a production car, it is impossible to say that any one design is superior. (Photo Courtesy Chevrolet Performance)

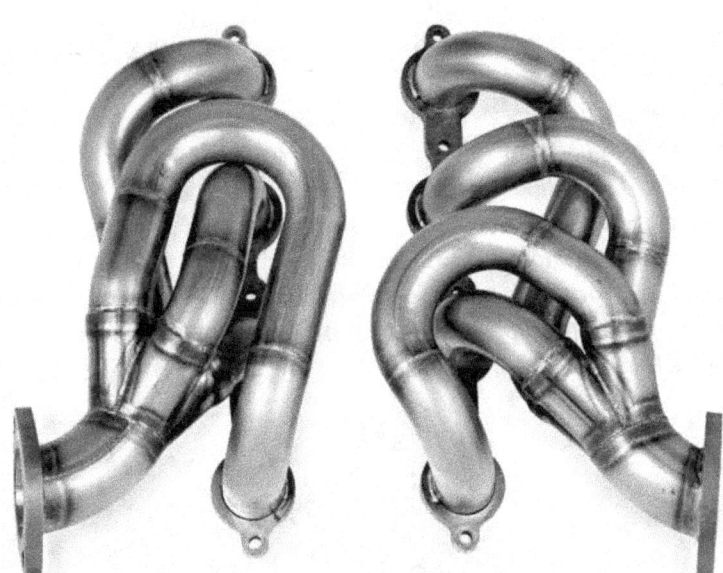

Shorty headers, such as Z/28s or these Hooker Blackheart headers, are typically easier to install and 50-state legal because they bolt to the stock cats and crossover. Although in many LS applications shorty headers don't typically make very much power, testing has shown these 1 7/8-inch primary, 4-into-1 style headers are worth the coin. American Racing makes a similar set that, like these, are made of 304 stainless steel and have 3/8-inch water jet cut flanges. (Photo Courtesy Holley Performance)

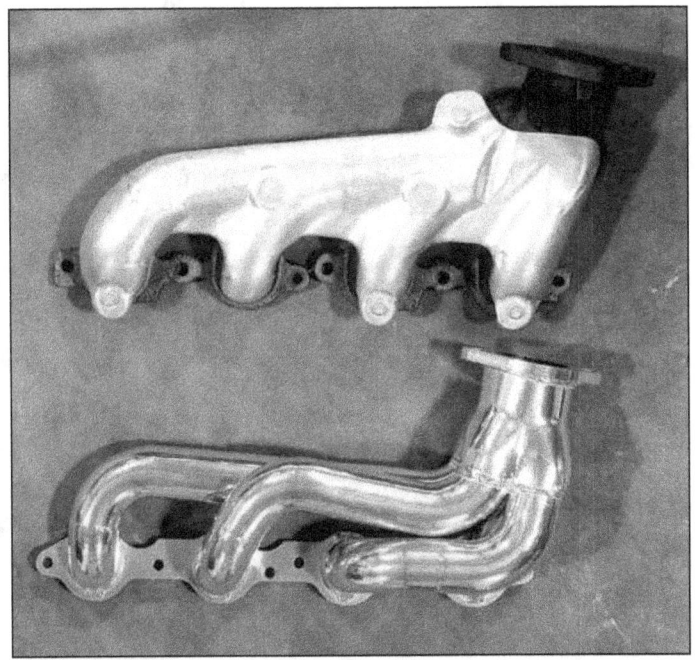

Next to a factory manifold (top), you can see how shorties (bottom) simply bolt in their place, right up to the factory cats. It is also evident how uneven the primary lengths are on a factory manifold. The log-style design has much more back pressure in the front cylinders as a result. Exhaust must overcome the flow of the other cylinders to exit the manifold. (Photo Courtesy Joseph Potak)

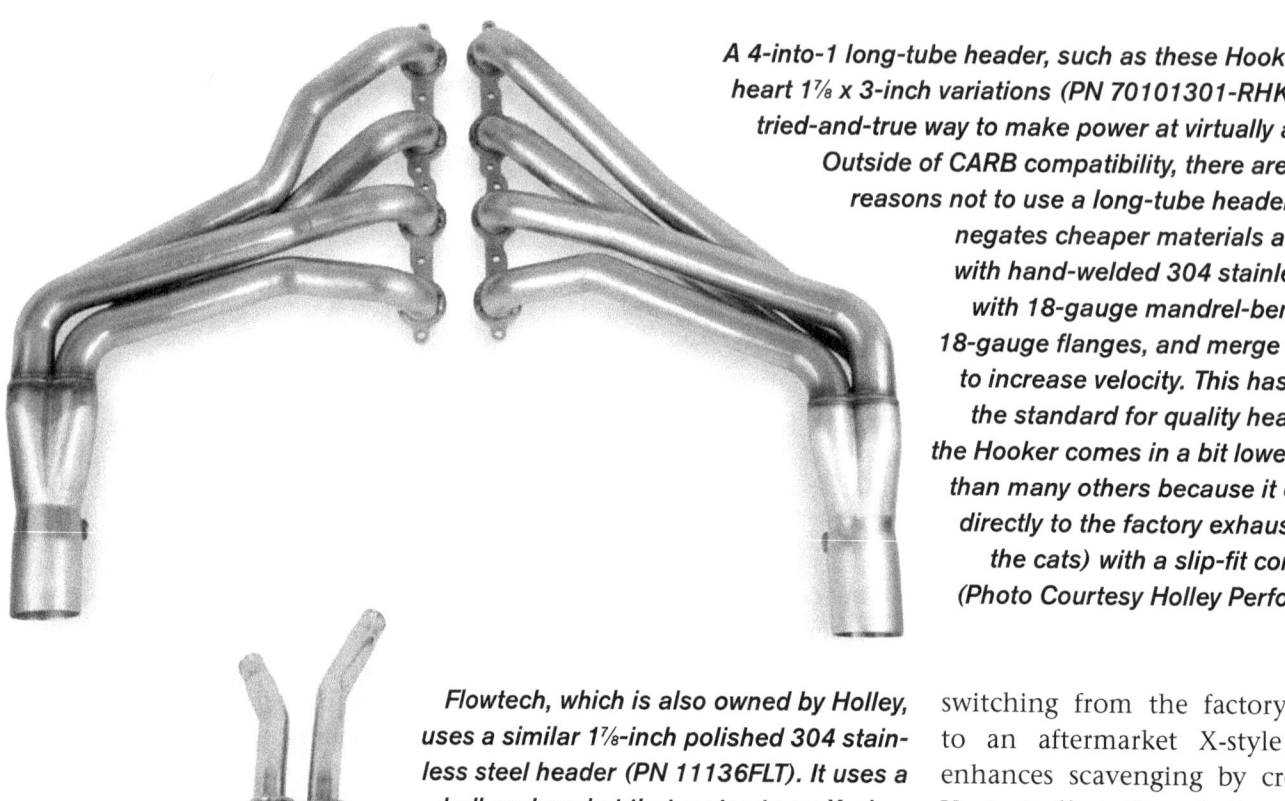

A 4-into-1 long-tube header, such as these Hooker Blackheart 1⅞ x 3-inch variations (PN 70101301-RHKR), are a tried-and-true way to make power at virtually any RPM. Outside of CARB compatibility, there are very few reasons not to use a long-tube header. Hooker negates cheaper materials and sticks with hand-welded 304 stainless steel, with 18-gauge mandrel-bent tubing, 18-gauge flanges, and merge "spears" to increase velocity. This has become the standard for quality headers, yet the Hooker comes in a bit lower in price than many others because it connects directly to the factory exhaust (minus the cats) with a slip-fit connection. (Photo Courtesy Holley Performance)

Flowtech, which is also owned by Holley, uses a similar 1⅞-inch polished 304 stainless steel header (PN 11136FLT). It uses a ball-and-socket that mates to an X-pipe, which connects to a factory or aftermarket exhaust at the axle. Like the Hooker, this is also an off-road design, which means there are no catalytic converters. Whenever you remove the cats, you have to account for that in the tune or it sets off diagnostic codes and warning lights. Some of the more expensive systems from American Racing, Kooks, and Stainless Works use high-flow aftermarket cats. (Photo Courtesy Holley Performance)

switching from the factory H-style to an aftermarket X-style further enhances scavenging by creating a Venturi effect, though the gains are small. The majority of the power lies in larger diameter pipes, such as the Z/28's 2.75-inch tubes, and freer flowing mufflers.

For SS owners looking for a slightly more rowdy sound, Chevrolet Performance offers the Z/28 exhaust (PN 22906768) and exhaust hook-up kit (PN 23454579). The improvement in flow is said to reduce backpressure by 26 percent. Typical

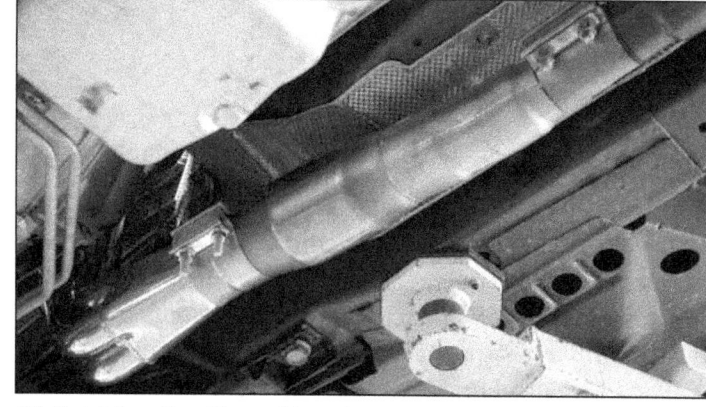

Wallet-friendly off-road headers, such as Blackhearts and these Pacesetter headers, use a connection pipe to mate to the stock cat-back exhaust. (Photo Courtesy Joseph Potak)

BASIC ENGINE PERFORMANCE UPGRADES

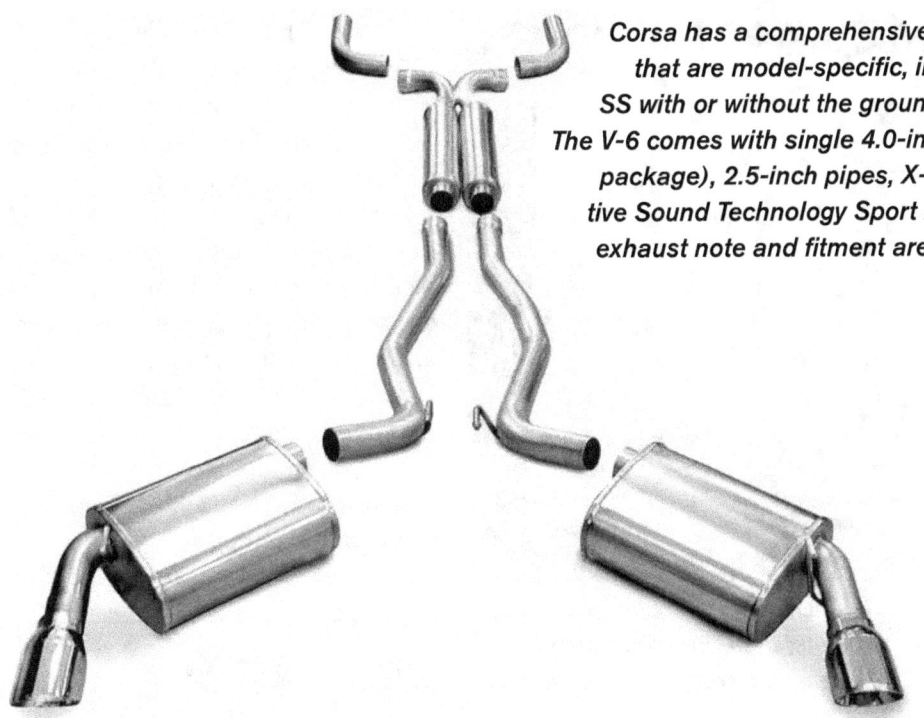

Corsa has a comprehensive list of exhaust systems for the fifth-gen that are model-specific, including the ZL1, manual and automatic SS with or without the ground effects package, and the V-6 (shown). The V-6 comes with single 4.0-inch tips (3.5-inch with the ground-effects package), 2.5-inch pipes, X-crossover, and Corsa's patented Reflective Sound Technology Sport mufflers. The perfectly tuned, drone-free exhaust note and fitment are what set Corsa's systems apart. (Photo Courtesy Corsa Performance)

aftermarket exhaust is available in an axle-back, such as the Z/28 option, or a full cat-back exhaust for even better flow. For SS model-specific, nearly every system on the market is a 2.5-inch with varying styles of mufflers (or even none). Magnaflow and Flowmaster are the exceptions.

Besides the sound and higher flowing mufflers, aftermarket exhaust usually adds the benefit of mandrel bending, which maintains the shape and diameter of the tube throughout the bend for better flow. Because the 2014–2015 models and ZL1 have a different rear fascia, do not take for granted that all systems are interchangeable. For example, the folks at Corsa offer a ZL1-specific 3-inch system that claims a 50-percent increase in flow.

The SS rear bumper can be modified to use the ZL1 diffuser and this system, should you choose to do so. The important thing to remember when choosing an exhaust system is that the pipes are supposed to become larger the closer the exhaust is to entering the atmosphere. So going from a set of long-tube headers with a 3- or 3.5-inch collector to a 2.5-inch exhaust is less than ideal and could limit performance. Of course, larger pipes are typically louder, so you have to weigh the benefits versus your personal taste.

Cold-Air Intakes

Just as with the V-6, a cold-air intake is typically among the first modifications for a V-8. However, substantial testing on several applications has shown that gains are minimal on stock vehicles (roughly 0 to 15 hp). A high-flowing air filter such as K&N's drop-in stock replacement yields nearly identical results at a fraction of the cost. In terms of aesthetics, however, many intakes on the market can vastly improve the look of your engine bay.

Phastek, BBK, K&N, CAI, Airaid, Rotor-Fab, Volant, and Chevrolet Performance, as well as shops such as Hennessey, LMR, ADM, New Era Performance, and Fastlane, offer intakes. Some require tuning while others do not. Of course, for every rule there is an exception. The ZL1's LSA engine does benefit significantly from a cold-air intake. A high-flowing filter and straighter intake path helps suck in more air for an increase in boost and typically more than 35 hp (with tuning).

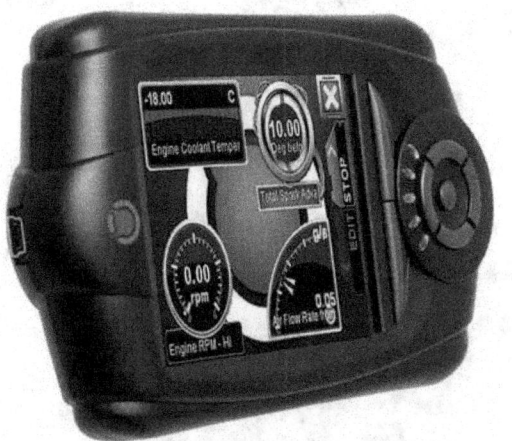

When it comes to tuning, you have two options: handheld or laptop based. For a stock or bolt-on Camaro, handhelds are sufficient and have many added useful features, including diagnostic code reading. The DiabloSport Trinity can even be used for data logging and testing by recording 0–60 mph, 0–100 mph, and 1/8- and 1/4-mile times. Handhelds can also be useful for uploading custom tunes done remotely, which are necessary with power adders, cams, and strokers. (Photo Courtesy DiabloSport)

CHAPTER 4

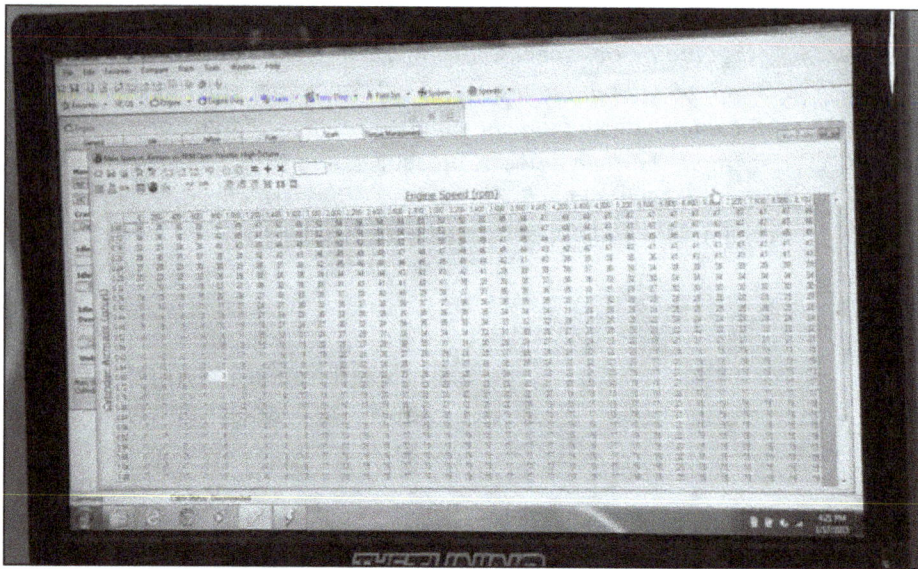

Tuning software from HP Tuners (shown) and EFI Live are the two most widely used. You purchase the interface and tuning credits, then download the software for free to your PC-based laptop. If all this data scares you, then it is best left up to a professional.

The Tuning School not only provides a learning resource for aspiring tuners, but also has a database of certified tuners who have passed their courses. This is the only way to get a truly custom tune, using the appropriate tools, such as a load-bearing dyno and quality wideband oxygen sensor. With more complicated installs (such as camshafts, crate engines, and power adders), it can really be the only option to have a properly tuned engine.

These programs can allow you to delete Active Fuel Management and Variable Valve Timing on L99 engines, add Flex Fuel capabilities, swap to a non-OE transmission, and much more.

The ZL1's supercharger also affords the opportunity for more bolt-on modifications that add significant power. The most obvious place to start is at the upper supercharger pulley. The factory pulley uses a rubber isolator coupler that is prone to wearing out and rattling. It is best to swap this out for a solid unit anyway, and in the process you can add more than 3 psi of boost with a smaller 2.55-inch pulley.

If you are looking for something less invasive, up to a 28-percent overdrive crank pulley is available from Lingenfelter. It uses an ATI balancer

Just as with a naturally aspirated engine, the first upgrade on a ZL1 is typically the air intake. Because the 1.9L Eaton supercharger sucks air through the throttle body before it generates pressure, intake restrictions are even more problematic. The factory intake chokes the engine, but the massive 6-inch washable filter uncorks the bottleneck. (Photo Courtesy Lingenfelter Performance Engineering)

The air box on the Lingefelter ZL1 intake seals to the hood to keep hot air from entering the filter and mounts the stock MAF. A heavy-duty black plastic intake duct keeps from collapsing at higher boost levels. (Photo Courtesy Lingenfelter Performance Engineering)

BASIC ENGINE PERFORMANCE UPGRADES

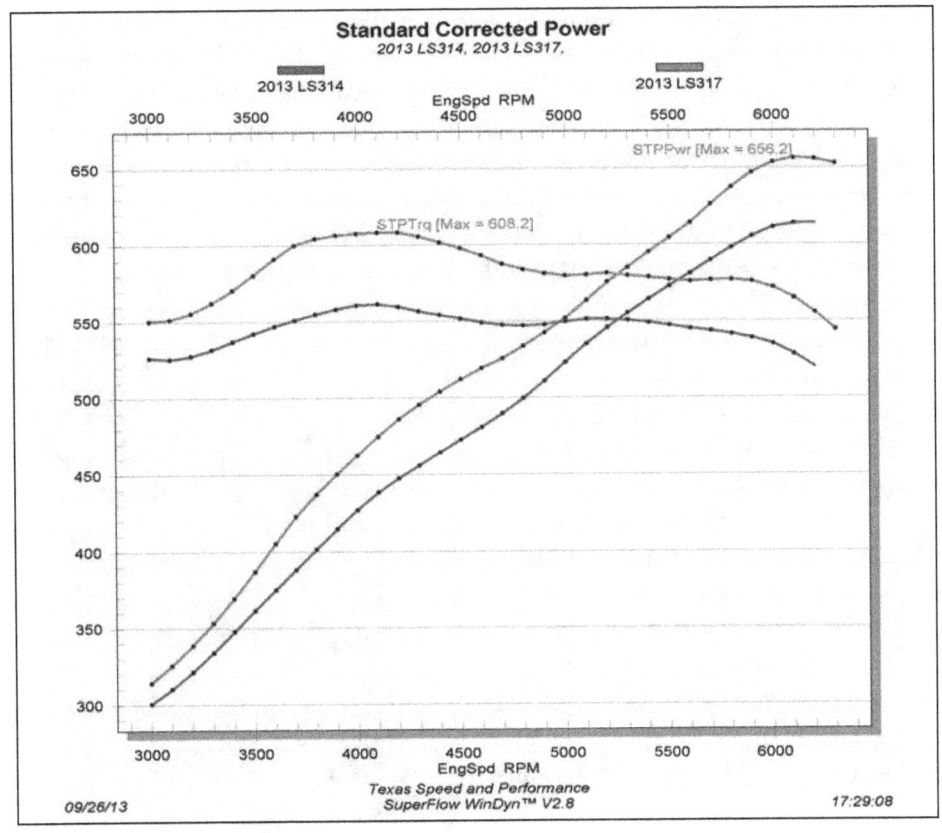

and a proprietary pulley. You can even combine a 5- or 10-percent overdrive crank pulley with the smaller blower pulley to max out the boost (around 15 psi). Note that spinning the blower higher than that could result in rotor failure.

Increased boost means increased heat, so you also want to add a heat exchanger reservoir or an aftermarket heat exchanger (or both). Because

The second upgrade is typically adding boost. With the ZL1's LSA, you must be careful not to overspin the supercharger by using the wrong combination of crank and supercharger pulley. This is from a 10-percent overdrive crank pulley, which simply bolts to the front of an aftermarket balancer. Although the 1.9L is small, it turns a modest boost increase into more power.

Lingenfelter offers a harmonic balancer kit with an overdrive crank pulley in five sizes: 5-, 10-, 18-, 22.5-, and 28-percent overdrive. The latter is 10 inches in diameter, uses the shortest belt, and generates the most boost. Levels vary, but the 10-percent overdrive is said to add 3.5 psi to an otherwise stock engine. The key component of the balancer kit is the ATI Performance Super Damper (PN L220050709). The improved harmonic dampening is better for engine longevity, especially in a supercharged application, which places greater strain on the crankshaft. (Photo Courtesy Lingenfelter Performance Engineering)

Lingenfelter also offers a full kit (PN L250466509), including a 2.55 supercharger pulley, 10-bolt stainless steel hub, solid supercharger isolator coupling, and 8-rib belt. With the air intake, LPE says it makes 630 hp. Installing a supercharger pulley requires removing the supercharger itself and the snout from the housing. While you are in there, the isolator coupling is prone to wear even in relatively low-mileage ZL1s, causing that familiar rattling sound. Replacing it with LPE's heavy-duty version (PN L960202012) has no downside other than potential labor cost. (Photo Courtesy Lingenfelter Performance Engineering)

nearly the entire supercharger casing is aluminum, porting is another option to maximize its efficiency. Porting the snout is very typical because it needs to be removed when installing a pulley anyway. A number of rough areas need smoothing and there is the potential to enlarge the throttle body opening as much as 106 mm, though this requires ditching the factory O-ring.

Weapon X Motorsports even goes into the intake manifold and other areas of the blower to free up as much as 40 hp. The ceiling is believed to be a little more than 700 hp with 93-octane pump gas before upgrading the camshaft or swapping the supercharger. Going to methanol injection, E85, or race gas is perhaps the only other option for pushing this even further. (I cover blower swaps, as well as methanol injection, in Chapter 6.)

With increased boost comes increased heat, and the solution is an intercooler coolant reservoir tank. There isn't one from the factory, so it simply recirculates hot coolant constantly. LPE offers a 4-liter plastic molded tank (PN L300152012) with an OEM-style cap, fittings, and hoses. It only fits with LPE's air intake (not stock or other brands), but many shops, such as KraftWorks, offer custom fabricated sheet-metal reservoirs as well to fit any intake. (Photo Courtesy Lingenfelter Performance Engineering)

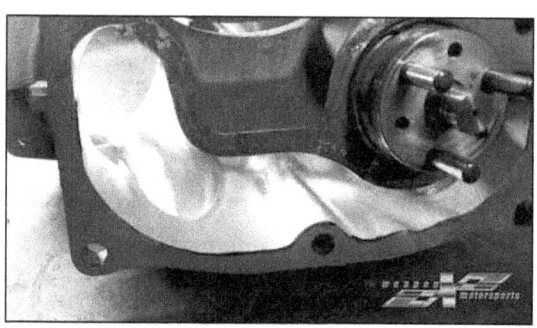

Porting and polishing can achieve a slick, mirror-like finish that increases horsepower. The fastest ZL1s in the world have used porting for low-10s with just bolt-ons and mid-9s with valvetrain upgrades (no nitrous). (Photo Courtesy Weapon X Motorsports)

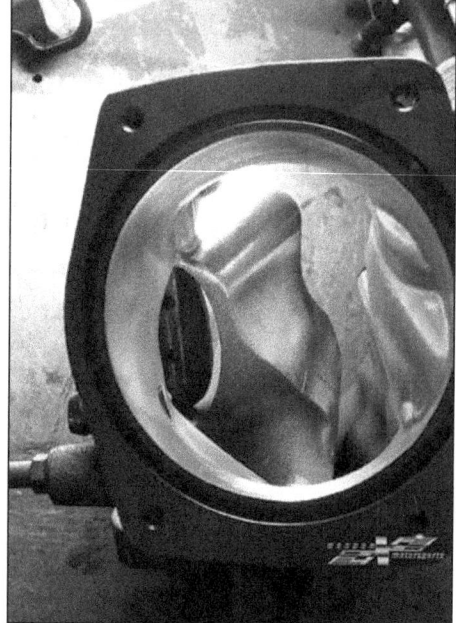

Weapon X Motorsports extracts the most it can from the 1.9L supercharger with porting. The snout entry and throttle body area typically offer gains by smoothing out the rough areas and enlarging the opening. The throttle body can be as large as 108 mm for an aftermarket throttle body. (Photo Courtesy Weapon X Motorsports)

Weapon X is one of the few companies that actually port the supercharger housing itself, the open plenum where the compressed air is funneled into the cylinder heads. The complete package improves airflow and Weapon X says it also affects the intake air temperature. A 30- to 40-hp improvement is typical across the entire RPM band. (Photo Courtesy Weapon X Motorsports)

How-To Projects

BASIC ENGINE PERFORMANCE UPGRADES

Cold-Air Induction Install

All photos for this project are courtesy of Joseph Potak.

Virtually every designer or engineer of cold-air induction kits attempts to straighten the intake tube's path and rid the Camaro of that flat OEM air filter. Whether or not these increases in flow are needed, however, is source for debate. Extensive testing on stock or near-stock fifth-gens typically yields limited gains. Nevertheless, it is often the first stop for anyone modifying their vehicle. Many designs use a sealed air box similar to OEMs, though the conical filter increases the surface area from which the intake can draw air. Some simply seal to the hood using weather-stripping as done with the radiator support.

Another method is to relocate the washer bottle and channel air from below to create a Ram Air effect. You want to be careful when traveling through deep puddles, so as not to suck up any water through the filter and hydro-lock the engine. All designs should have provisions for the factory MAF sensor; its location, as well as the diameter of the tube, largely affect whether tuning is needed with the intake. Because the MAF tells the engine how much air is entering the engine, a larger diameter tube, for example, could skew the data and lead to an air/fuel mixture that is lean, so lean that it could detonate.

Quality and materials are also concerns. A metal intake tube could increase intake air temperature (heat soak), a poor fitting system could have issues sealing properly, and a cheap or over-oiled filter could foul the MAF. With any modification you should proceed with caution, even one as docile as a cold-air intake.

This fully installed kit does away with the sealed air box and seals to the hood. The conical air filter increases surface area over the OEM flat filter. This has long been a great improvement for stock vehicles; it is only now that manufacturers have become better at leaving less on the table for the aftermarket.

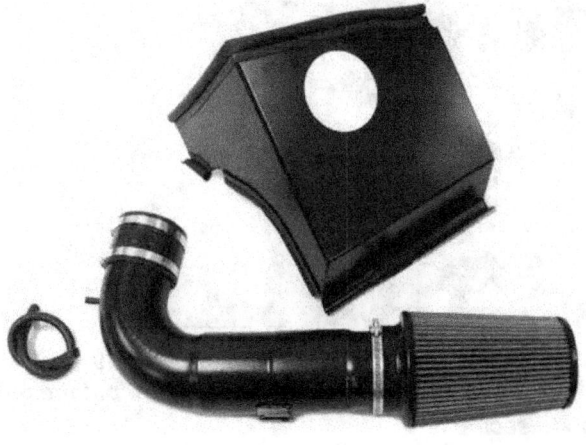

The basic elements of the kit include the air-intake tube, heat shield, K&N air filter, hose clamps, hose, and rubber tube for the PCV system. This is one of the easier intake systems to install as it does not require any relocating of factory components.

CHAPTER 4

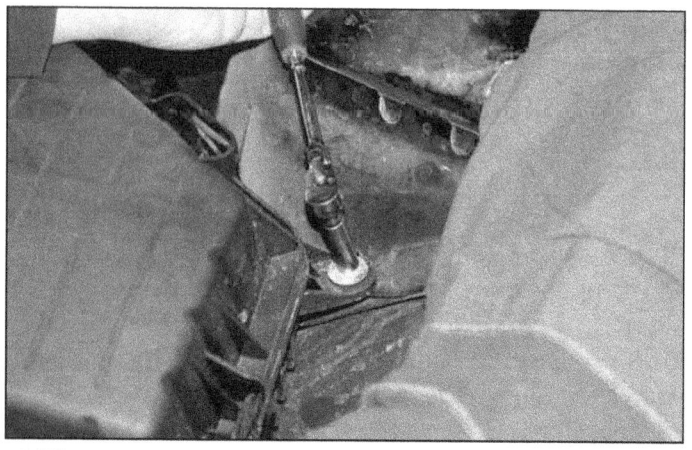
1 Remove the two OEM nuts on the air box with a deep 10-mm socket.

2 You can unplug the MAF from the air box by hand.

3 Remove the crankcase ventilation tube (PCV) by pulling straight out with a circular motion. Its connection on the valvecover requires a flat-head screwdriver for the locking clip.

4 Use a flat-head screwdriver or 8-mm socket on the hose clamps to the throttle body and air box.

5 The rubber elbow simply slides off the throttle body and air box. With that out of the way, remove the air box. Use both hands and give it a stiff pull.

6 Slide the heat shield into place, lining up the bolt hole. Using a 10-mm deep socket, put the nut back on to secure it.

BASIC ENGINE PERFORMANCE UPGRADES

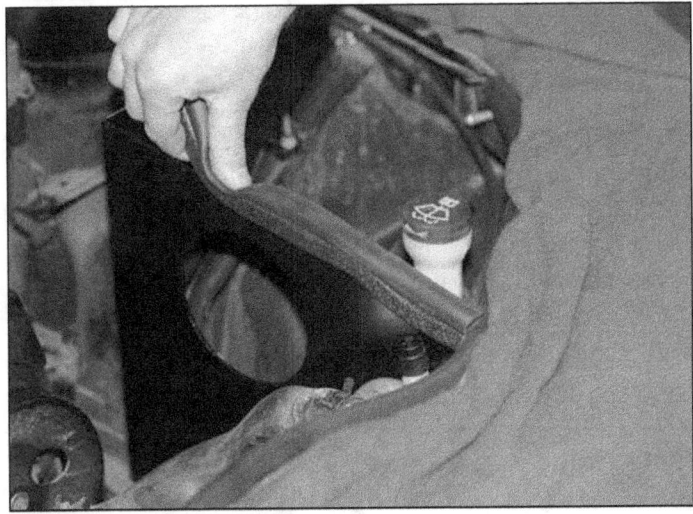

7 Pull the supplied weather stripping onto the edge of the heat shield.

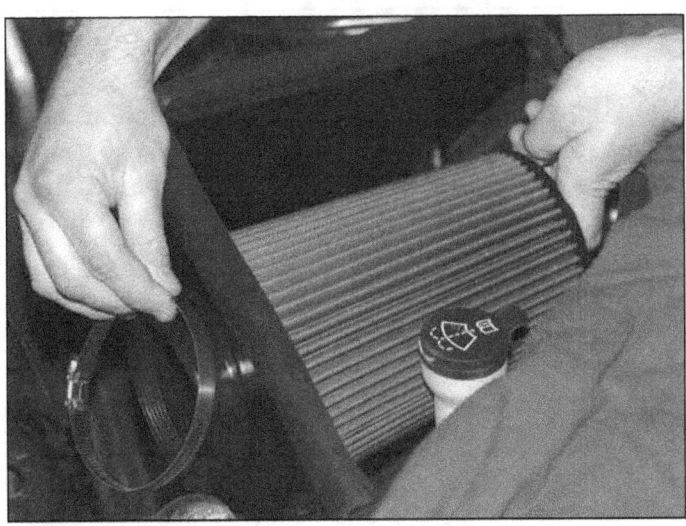

8 Drop in the air filter, feeding the end through the heat shield with a clamp on it.

9 Loosely tighten the supplied hose to the throttle body.

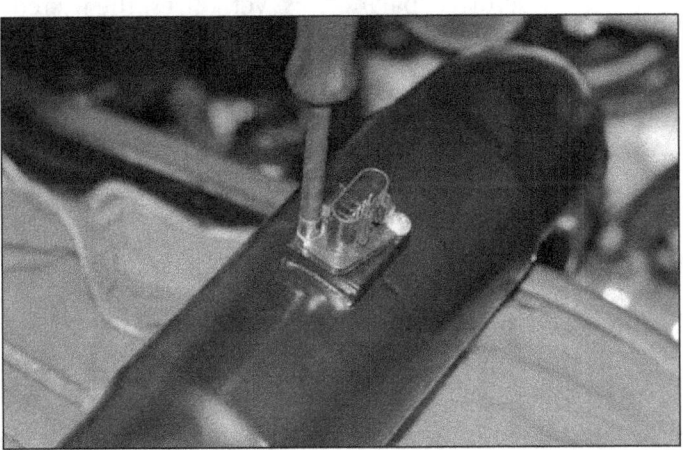

10 Unscrew the factory MAF sensor from the OEM air box with a 7-mm socket and delicately transfer it to the new intake tube.

11 Install the intake tube into the filter side first.

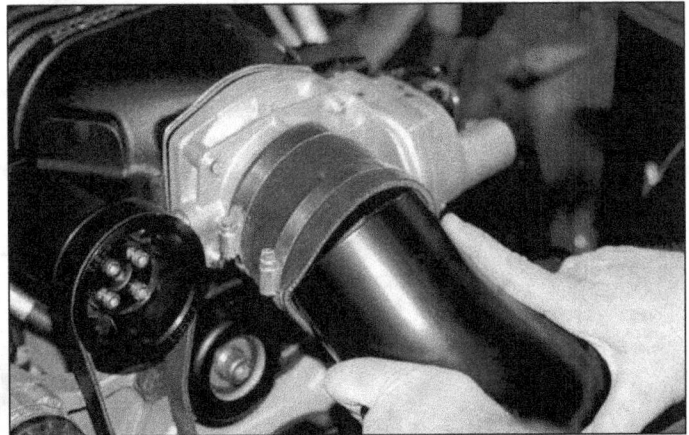

12 Once you have the tube into the hose on the throttle body, tighten all the clamps. Plug in the MAF sensor. The last step is hooking up the tube to the valvecover.

CHAPTER 4

160-Degree Thermostat Install

A thermostat is a much less talked about bolt-on, but can be quite effective, especially at the dragstrip. It acts as a door that opens only when hitting a specified temperature. OEM thermostats typically open at 180 degrees Fahrenheit, so even though the engine is running and the water pump is turning, coolant does not circulate through the radiator until the coolant reaches 180. Some drag racers remove the thermostat altogether, but this makes it more difficult to bring the engine up to temperature.

A 160-degree thermostat is a nice compromise, which helps keep the engine cooler between passes at the dragstrip or autocross. This can also work in tandem with a tune that turns the electric fans on at a lower temperature. In road racing or on the highway, it is most likely going to be open all the time and have less effect. But overall it is pretty cheap and easy to do, and requires only a 10-mm socket and a few gallons of Dexcool to replace what is lost.

Crank Pulley Install

All photos for this project are courtesy of Joseph Potak.

The underdrive balancer is yet another tried-and-true bolt-on modification to gain a few horsepower to the rear wheels by reducing parasitic loss. Just as with gears in a transmission or rear end, the diameter affects how hard the engine is working. An undersized harmonic balancer spins the accessories to the minimum speed needed, so that the engine only works as hard as it needs to spin them. This is just like riding a bicycle; in a low gear you put forth less effort to maintain speed, whereas with a high gear you pedal much faster.

Typically, balancers come in 10- or 25-percent underdrive, on naturally aspirated engines. With a supercharged engine, such as the ZL1's LSA, the diameter of the balancer plays a much different role. Because the supercharger is driven by the balancer, an overdrive balancer is sometimes used to increase boost. The increase in drag is more than overcome by the power increase with additional boost.

When selecting a harmonic balancer, there are a few other things to consider besides the diameter. The balancer bolts to the snout of the crankshaft and dampens torsional vibrations. As each cylinder fires, the incredible forces cause it to twist, vibrate, and resonate certain frequencies. A harmonic balancer uses rubber (elastomer) to dampen the vibrations and resonance. Without it, you couldn't expect much longevity from the crankshaft and the main bearings. As such, it is important to select a quality balancer that does its primary job

The difference in size between a factory balancer (bottom) and an underdrive balancer (top) is apparent. This ASP balancer is a 25-percent underdrive version. The smaller size helps reduce parasitic loss that results from turning the accessories, such as the water pump, A/C compressor, and power steering (on 2010–2012 models). Harmonic balancers use rubber to dampen crankshaft vibrations, and as such they are actually a wear item similar to bushings in the suspension.

1 *After disconnecting the negative battery terminal and air induction, you can remove the main accessory drive belt by applying pressure to the main belt tensioner using a 15-mm wrench (pushing toward the centerline of the engine). A smaller pulley means a longer belt, so this will not be reused.*

BASIC ENGINE PERFORMANCE UPGRADES

effectively. Finding a balancer with an SFI approval is a huge plus, which guarantees its safety amid catastrophic failure.

Another consideration is that most LS engines have no mechanism to keep the balancer from spinning on the crankshaft, instead of with the crankshaft. So replacing the balancer can be a good opportunity to pin the crank to prevent this, though it is not for the novice builder.

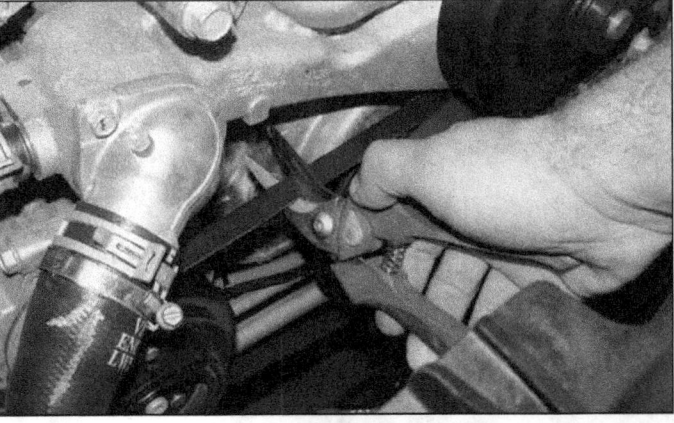

2 Notice that there is no tensioner on the A/C belt, unlike other LS engines, so it is best just to cut the belt to remove it.

3 With a 6-speed manual, it is best to put the car in 4th gear, set the parking brake, chock the tires, and use a breaker bar on your largest ratchet with a 15/16-inch socket to remove the crank bolt. With an automatic trans you can either use a heavy-duty impact gun or have a buddy keep the flexplate from turning with a pry-bar while you break the bolt free. You then need a three-jawed puller to remove the OEM balancer, each "jaw" grabbing a flat or notched surface. The hardest part is simply breaking the balancer free of the crank snout.

4 The new balancer should stay in place by itself while you thread the installation tool into the crank. The proper way to press on the balancer is to use an installation tool, which is essentially a long M16 x 2.0 threaded rod, nuts, and washers. By turning the nut, you press the balancer onto the crank until it is seated against the lower timing gear. You will know when it bottoms out. Just make sure it goes on square, not crooked.

5 To fully seat the balancer, use the old crankshaft bolt. Because these are torque-to-yield, they cannot be reused anyway. Torque it to 250 ft-lbs, remove, and discard. Here's a tip: the longer the breaker bar, the more leverage you have for applying such a high amount of torque. The new bolt requires a dollop of red Loctite (shown). The torque specs depend on whether it is another torque-to-yield GM bolt or a reusable ARP bolt.

6 I went with a GM bolt, which requires 37 ft-lbs of torque and then an additional 140 degrees of rotation. Once the 37 ft-lbs are applied, you mark the bolt and balancer as a reference point. Some electronic torque wrenches also have this measurement capability.

7 To install the new A/C belt, loop it behind the crankshaft pulley and then route it over the A/C compressor pulley. Starting at the top of the balancer, rotate the crankshaft clockwise as you hold the belt in place. Once it is stretched over the balancer, you keep rotating as the belt centers itself until it snaps into place. With a few more turns, the belt locks into its groove. Route the main belt by first putting it over the main tensioner, then down over the balancer, up to the smooth idler pulley, down to the alternator pulley, around the power steering, and laid in front of the water pump pulley. After you release the tensioner with a 15-mm wrench, you can slide the belt onto the water pump.

8 Before buttoning up the air induction and hooking up the battery, it is a good idea to make sure the belt is fully on and that the balancer lines up properly.

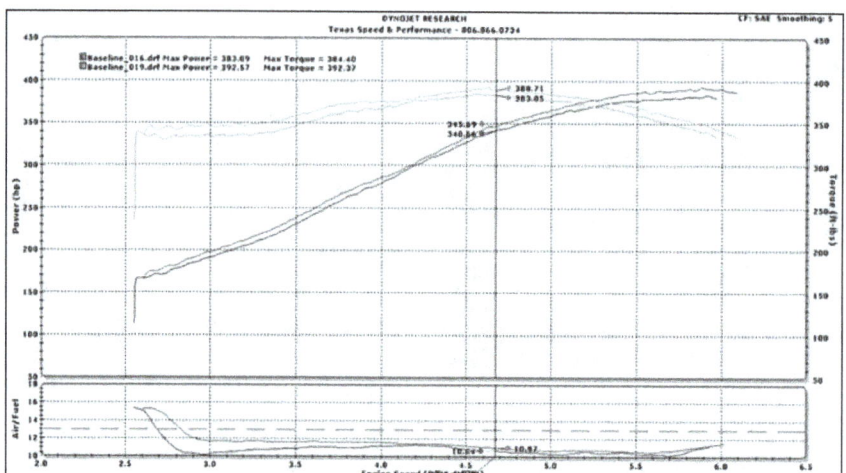

9 On the dyno you see how the pulley affects power, with a solid 9 hp and 8 ft-lbs of torque increase to the rear wheels across the entire RPM range.

Long-Tube Header Install

All photos for this project are courtesy of Joseph Potak.

Having the best of both worlds has never been easier with modern hot rodding and the fifth-gen Camaro. The factory dual exhaust is not nearly as much of a restriction as in previous years, so you can make plenty of power with long-tubes and stock exhaust. Many users appreciate this combo because it can be whisper quiet on the highway, but much more exaggerated when you hit the loud pedal. American Racing Headers makes a few kits that attach to the factory exhaust with either 1⅞- or 2-inch primary long tubes.

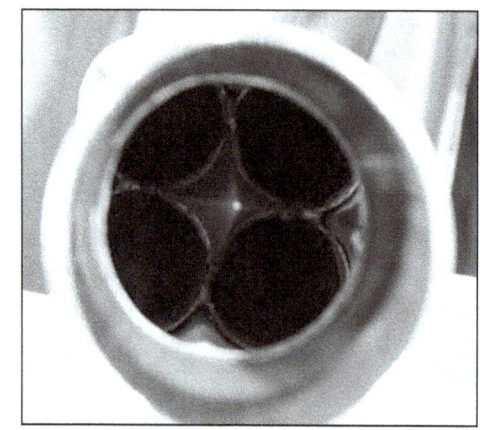

To those more familiar with older small-blocks (or, eek! Fords) this

American Racing Headers long-tubes feature a scavenger spike in the collector that helps smooth the transition as the four 1⅞-inch primaries merge into one. In doing so, it helps the exhaust gases from stalling out in the header. Some people think that exhaust is all about increasing the flow and decreasing back pressure. Not so. Velocity is every bit as important as flow, which is why you don't want to oversize the headers.

BASIC ENGINE PERFORMANCE UPGRADES

may seem quite large. Both sizes are appropriate for street-going Camaros in the proper application. Both use a 3-inch collector with a scavenger spike and are made entirely of 304 stainless steel, though larger collectors are available for race applications.

The install shown here uses 1⅞-inch headers with high-flow 200-cell metallic cats, which are suitable for most stock cubic-inch Camaros. A specific set of headers for the Z/28 clears the dry sump lines and other abnormalities to the platform. ARH also makes 1¾ x 2½-inch long-tubes for the 2010–2011 Camaro V-6.

1 Removing the stock manifolds and cats requires removing the spark plug wires, spark plugs, and manifold-to-cylinder head bolts, and unplugging the oxygen sensors and the clamps that connect to the cat-back exhaust.

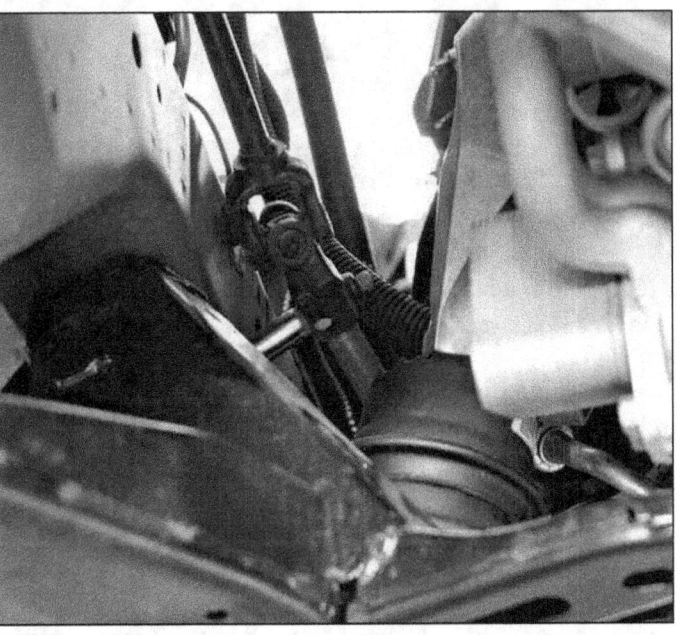

2 To get the drive side header in place, though, you need to unbolt the steering shaft with an 11-mm socket. Make sure you mark it for reference beforehand.

3 The header slides right in from the bottom on both sides.

4 The headers can be bolted to the heads with the factory hardware and provided gaskets. There is even enough room to use an air ratchet should you choose to do so.

CAMARO 5TH GEN 2010–2015: HOW TO BUILD AND MODIFY

CHAPTER 4

5 The spark plugs can go back into the heads at this time as well. I recommend replacing stock plugs with NGK TR55 in a bolt-on LS3, L99, or LS7. The colder TR6 plugs are ideal for the LSA or moderate level of boost or nitrous.

6 It is helpful to use the ARH X-pipe as a template to know where to cut the factory cat-back exhaust.

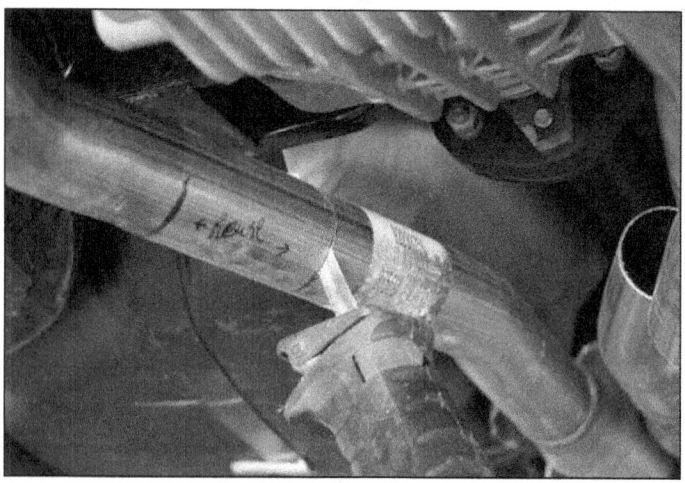

7 A reciprocating saw is the tool of choice for cutting the stock pipes.

8 Slide the X-pipe onto the headers and exhaust pipes with the clamps kept loose.

9 ARH uses a slip-fit collector, which requires a clamp to seal the cat pipes to the X-pipe. It is important to keep these loose until everything is lined up properly.

BASIC ENGINE PERFORMANCE UPGRADES

10 Once the exhaust is fitted, you can tighten the clamps.

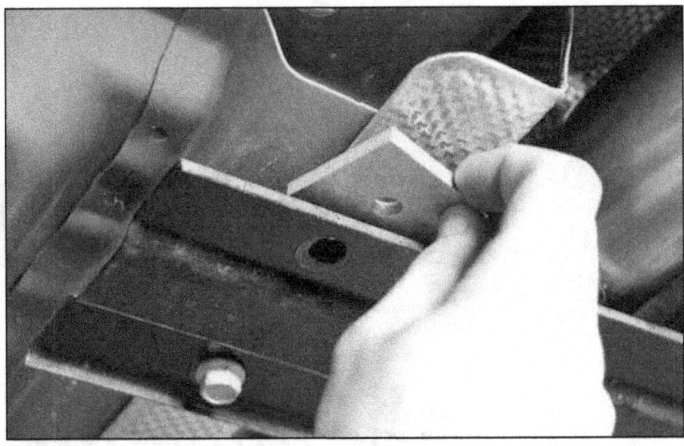

11 The factory transmission tunnel brace does need to be lowered slightly with these provided spacers to prevent the pipes from banging into it.

12 ARH mates the X-pipe to the exhaust system with this ball-and-socket flange. Although ARH also offers a full 3-inch kit, this transition necks down from 3 to 2.5 inches.

13 The transition pipe slips onto the 2.5-inch stock exhaust pipes, thanks to the previous handiwork with the saw, and seals with another clamp.

14 The rear oxygen sensors are in roughly the same place, but the front oxygen sensors are farther back. ARH supplies extension harnesses to accommodate this change.

CAMARO 5TH GEN 2010–2015: HOW TO BUILD AND MODIFY

CHAPTER 5

ENGINE BUILDS AND SWAPS

After exhausting (no pun intended) all possible bolt-on upgrades for your Camaro, the next logical step is to consider internal parts and full engine swaps. In this chapter, I cover these areas, although be warned that they will most certainly void the warranty and may not be emissions compliant. For many, these are not issues, but it is something to be aware of.

Some aftermarket companies offer warranties, such as crate engine builders, and some suppliers can help you figure out which parts are legal in your state. In California you need the approval sticker of the California Air Resource Board (CARB) to be emissions legal, which basically rules most things out, including an engine swap. In some states anything goes, and in others the vehicle needs to pass a tailpipe test.

Cylinder Heads

The familiar Gen IV architecture made many engine upgrades to the SS, ZL1, and Z/28 quite simple. CNC-porting programs for factory heads were available prior to the release of the 2010 Camaro, thanks to the Corvette. Soon after, full aftermarket castings hit the market from Mast Motorsports, Trick Flow, Edelbrock, Precision Race Components (PRC), Chevrolet Performance, and others.

For a naturally aspirated 6.2L LS3 or L99, the factory heads are hard to beat. A light CNC program yields some gains, particularly on the exhaust side, when used with a more radical camshaft. L99s also benefit from lighter LS3 valves. The LSA heads are a stepping-stone between the LS3 and the LS9, lacking the CNC porting and titanium valves of

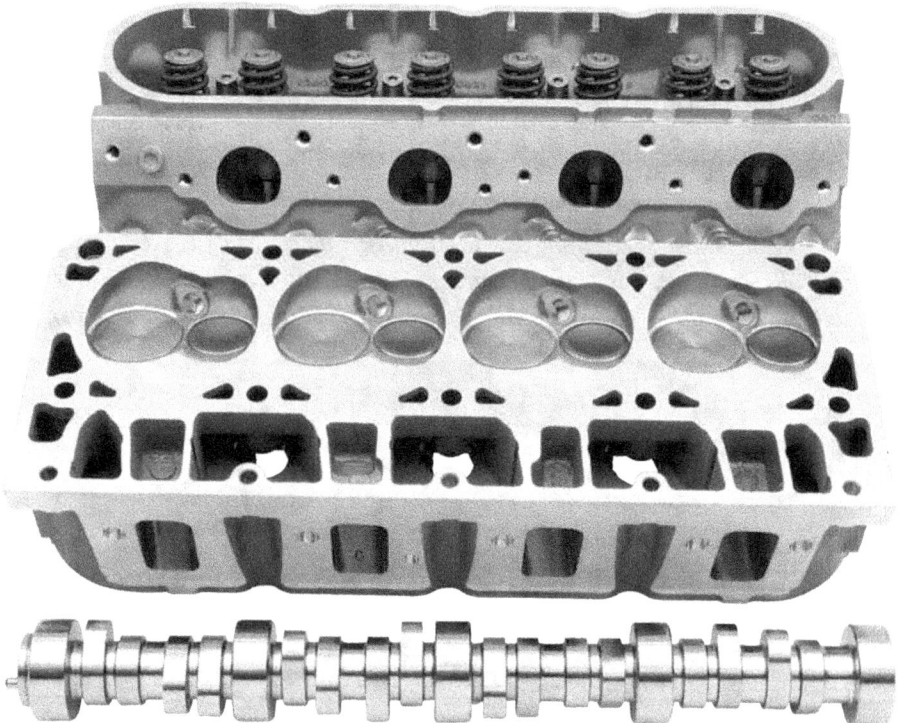

When simple bolt-on parts (such as exhaust and cold-air induction) aren't enough, the next logical step is a ported head and camshaft upgrade similar to this one from Chevrolet Performance (PN 19300535). Although not exactly 50-state legal, it adds 40 hp or more with CNC-ported LS3 heads and a 211/230 duration camshaft. (Photo Courtesy Chevrolet Performance)

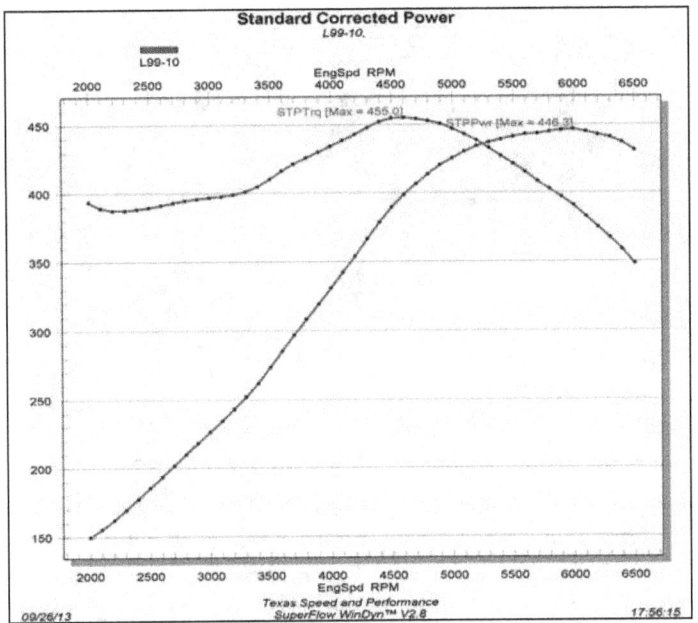

VVT on the L99 has the potential to maximize camshaft timing for peak torque and horsepower. In theory, a VVT camshaft always has better average power than a fixed camshaft (such as the LS3's). The L99 is severely limited by duration and lift. The stock cam specs, .500/.492-inch lift, and 198/201 duration are due to the limitations of the AFM lifters.

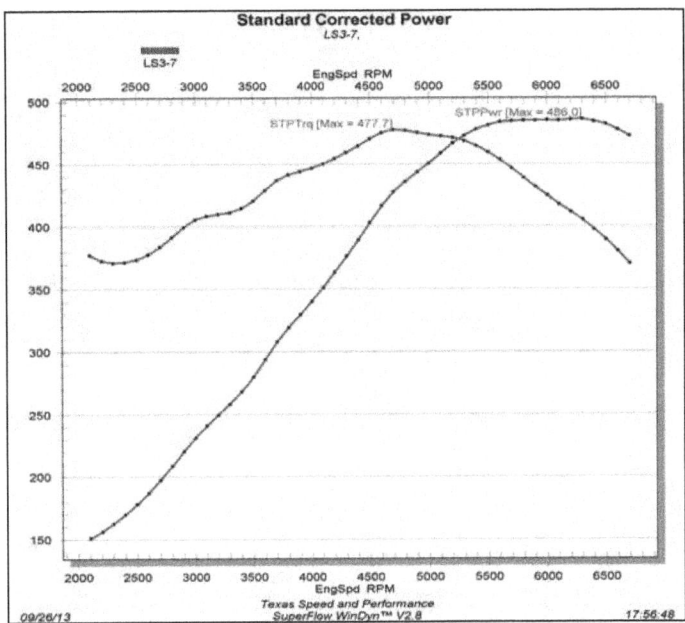

The LS3 camshaft has a more rowdy 204/211 duration with .551/.525-inch lift. Other than the camshaft and these other components, the LS3 is nearly identical to the L99, yet it makes a steady 22 hp and 20 ft-lbs more torque. If these power figures seem high given the factory rating, it's because they are tested without accessories and limiting factors needed for SAE testing. However, they are valuable for comparison to other crate engines on the market that are tested this way.

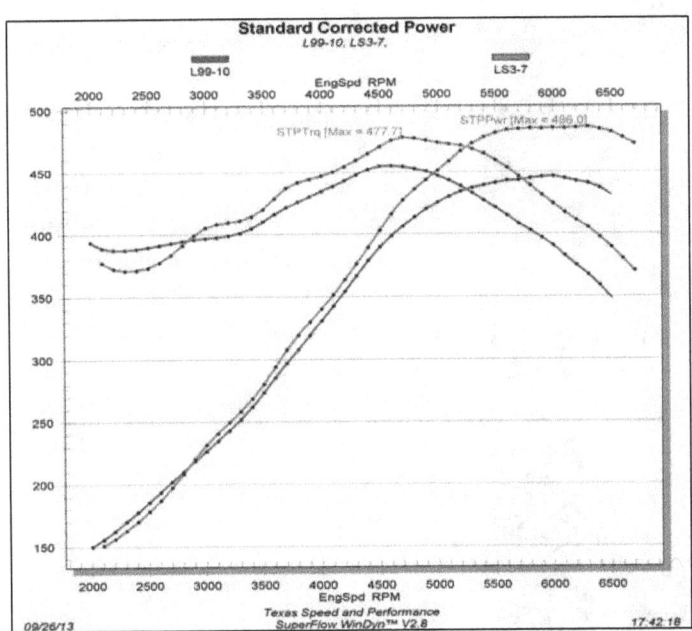

Here you can see the difference between the L99 and LS3. The LS3 is much more peaky, but the added duration and lift really take advantage of those high-flowing heads.

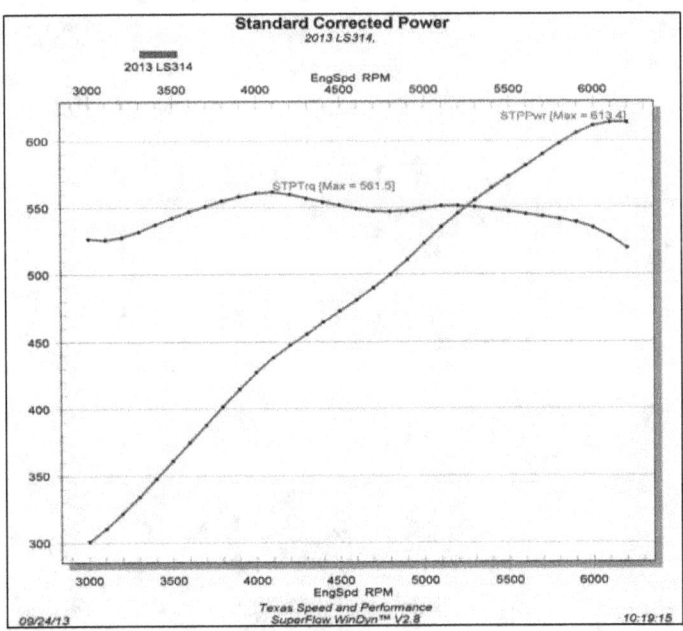

It's amazing what even a little 1.9L supercharger can do for a 6.2L engine. The LSA's camshaft is designed to be fairly mild with 198/216 duration and only .480-inch lift. Yet the instant boost of the hybrid Roots blower gives a nearly flat torque curve and power climbs until redline.

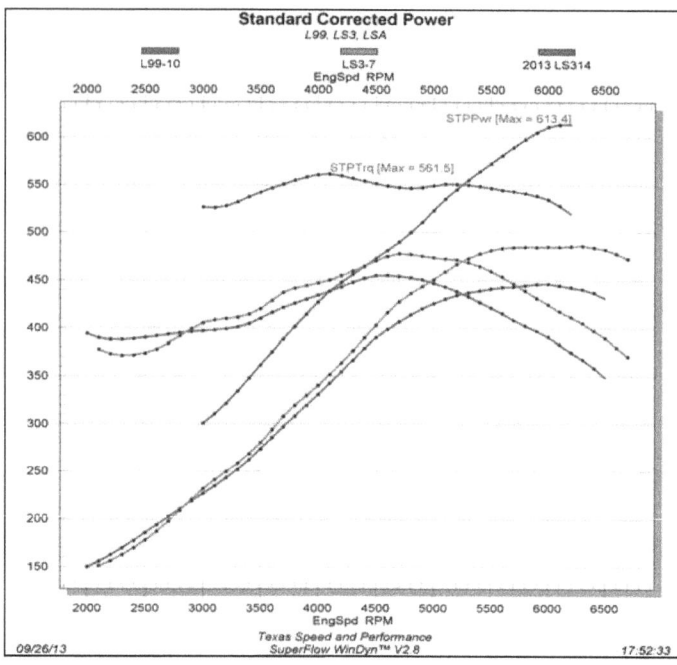

With data from all three, the differences in power delivery are even more obvious.

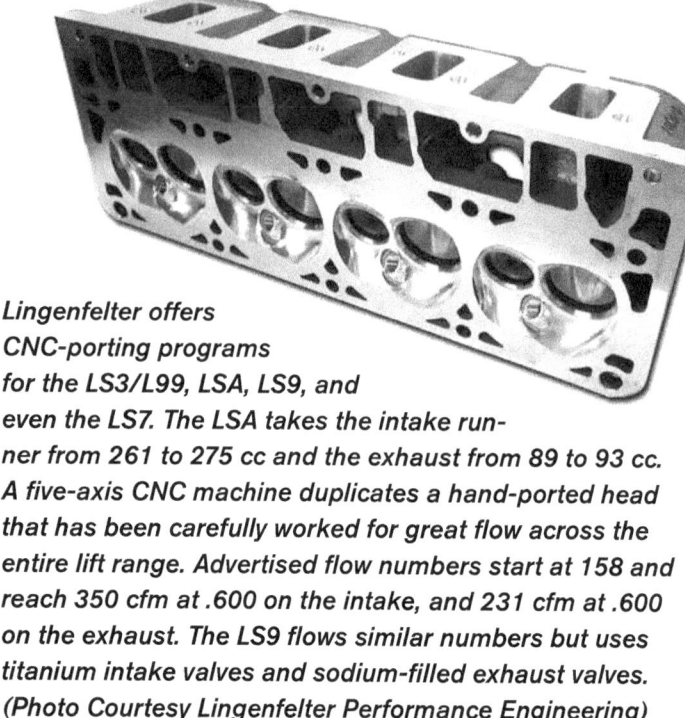

Lingenfelter offers CNC-porting programs for the LS3/L99, LSA, LS9, and even the LS7. The LSA takes the intake runner from 261 to 275 cc and the exhaust from 89 to 93 cc. A five-axis CNC machine duplicates a hand-ported head that has been carefully worked for great flow across the entire lift range. Advertised flow numbers start at 158 and reach 350 cfm at .600 on the intake, and 231 cfm at .600 on the exhaust. The LS9 flows similar numbers but uses titanium intake valves and sodium-filled exhaust valves. (Photo Courtesy Lingenfelter Performance Engineering)

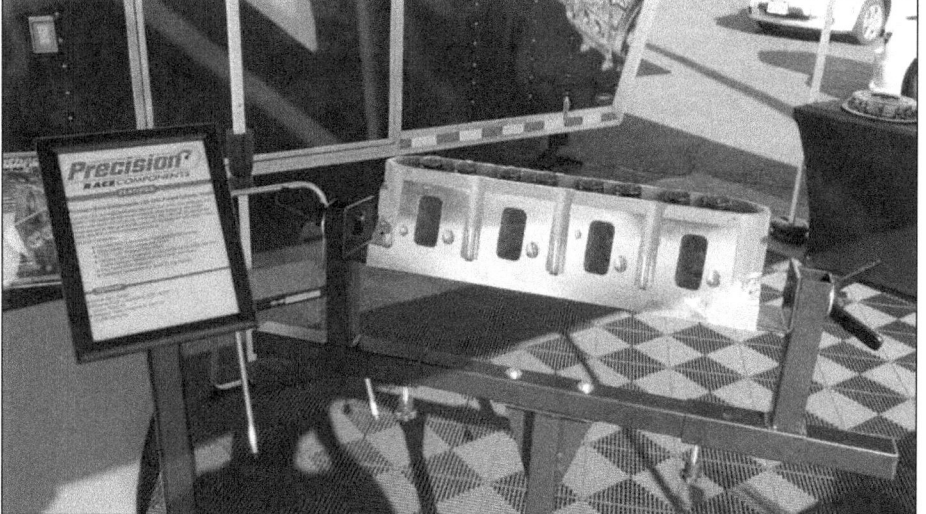

Although ported stock castings are plenty capable, an aftermarket casting has many benefits. For example, Precision Race Components (PRC) uses a smaller runner (250 cc) with higher flow. This increased efficiency in the port design translates into better velocity for more torque and better average power. PRC claims 60 cfm over stock. These heads, like most aftermarket castings, have the LSX six-bolt pattern to match up to an aftermarket block. This is a nice feature to ensure you won't outgrow them. (Photo Courtesy Joseph Potak)

PRC dual springs, titanium retainers, and stainless 2.165/1.59-inch valves come with the heads. Hollow-stem valves and higher lift springs are available. (Photo Courtesy Joseph Potak)

ENGINE BUILDS AND SWAPS

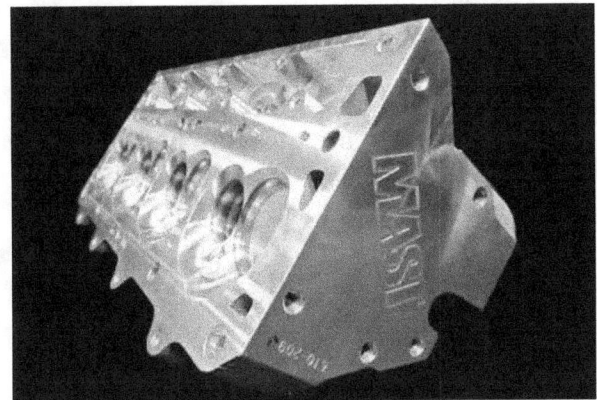

Mast Motorsports offers three variations on its LS3 heads, which all use an altered valve angle. For the stock LS3/L99 block, Mast offers a smaller than stock (255 cc) intake runner for better velocity, .750-inch-thick deck and 2.165/1.600-inch valves. The valve angle is rolled over from 15 to 11 degrees, which makes for a straighter intake path and increases piston-to-valve clearance. (Photo Courtesy Mast Motorsports)

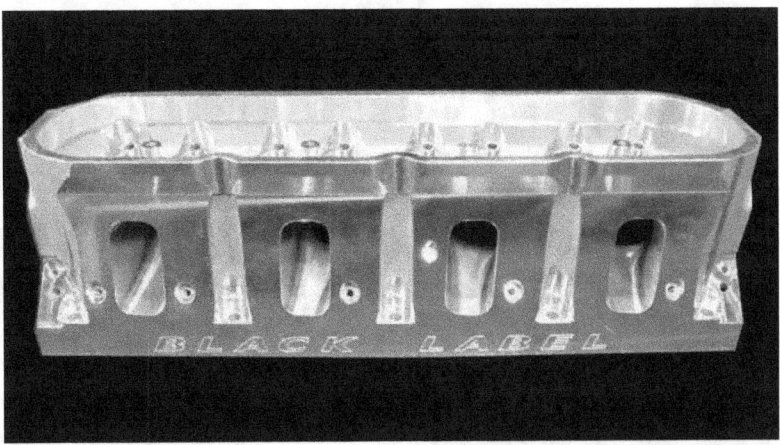

These heads are still compatible with all LS3 valvetrain and intake manifolds and flow an impressive 365/254 cfm at .650-inch lift. Mast also offers an 11-degree 265-cc LS7 head that fits stock LS3/L99 blocks and flows even better at .700- to .900-inch lift (race applications). Larger runner LS3 heads with LS7 valve angles (12 degrees) and valvetrain compatibility are available for large bores (4.125 inches), as are LS7 and special race heads with unique port configurations. (Photo Courtesy Mast Motorsports)

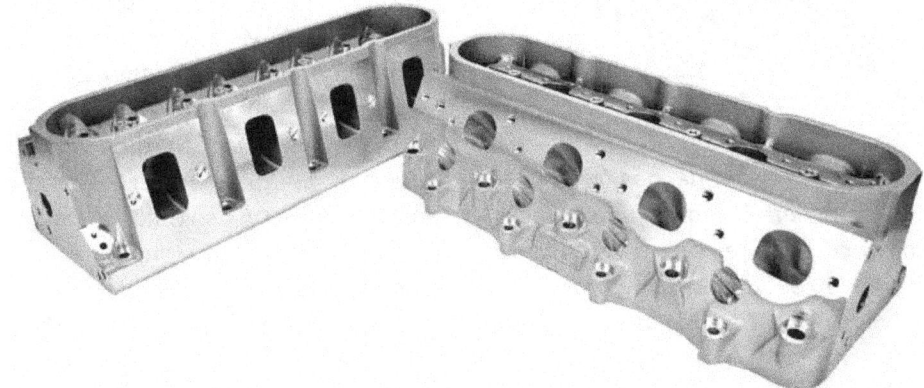

RHS LS7 Pro Elite 291-cc CNC-ported cylinder heads are available fully assembled with several spring, retainer, and valve options. These LS7 heads fit larger bores and are superior to the factory casting thanks to their .220-inch raised intake runners for better line of site into the cylinders. The runners are 100-percent CNC ported for optimized "volume, atomization, and velocity." Valve sizes are stock at 2.200 and 1.615 inches and, given the size, titanium is recommended for valvetrain stability and longevity. (Photo Courtesy Racing Head Service)

its big brother. Once the ZL1 supercharger upgrades are maxed out, CNC porting or an LS9 head swap yields more substantial gains on the LSA. Because the Z/28's LS7 heads are CNC ported from the factory and perhaps the highest flowing factory small-block heads ever made, further porting or aftermarket castings should be reserved for more radical combinations.

It is worth noting that all Gen III and IV heads are essentially cross-compatible, so long as the bore supports the size of the valves. The intake manifolds and rocker arms don't necessarily carry over, but the heads physically bolt onto the block.

Camshafts

Like the cylinder heads, aftermarket LS3 and LSA camshafts were available prior to the release of the Camaro. Most feature larger splits between the intake and exhaust duration than its cathedral-port predecessors (LS1, LS2, LS6, etc.) due to a substantial difference in intake and exhaust flow. The LS3 and LSA also use a single bolt to attach to the timing gear (unlike its predecessors, which had three bolts). Although manufacturers now have direct replacements, many choose to convert with an aftermarket timing set or factory three-bolt timing gear (PN 12586481).

Stiffer valvesprings and pushrods are another necessary upgrade with aftermarket cams; otherwise you could experience valve float or serious damage to the engine. High-lift

CHAPTER 5

The LS3 uses a traditional three-bolt LS camshaft. Comp Cams, Crane Cams, Lunati, Mast Motorsports, and Bullet are the most common aftermarket suppliers. Although many sell direct, you can also purchase through Summit Racing and other retailers. It is important to select a cam specific to LS3/L92-style ports because they need more exhaust duration to make up for a restrictive exhaust runner. (Photo Courtesy Comp Cams)

The L99 uses a single-bolt cam, which is where the phaser attaches for the VVT. The phaser uses oil pressure to alter the camshaft timing. Although it was mainly used for fuel efficiency, it can increase average power. With a fixed camshaft, engine builders use an adjustable timing set to advance or retard the timing to move the peak power up or down in RPM. This can also be ground into the camshaft. (Photo Courtesy Comp Cams)

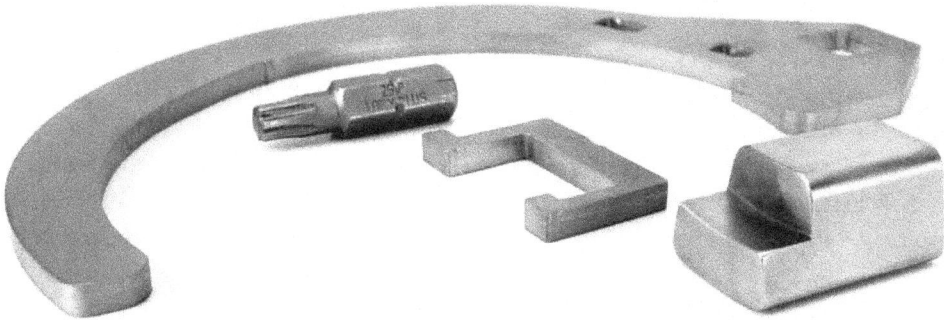

Because the factory phaser was not meant for longer duration and higher lift, it needs to be restricted when used with an aftermarket cam. Comp Cams and Mast Motorsports make such a limiter. Instead of the camshaft swinging 52 degrees, it is limited to just 22 degrees. This keeps the valves from unceremoniously meeting the pistons. Although more mild camshafts are compatible with AFM, the most gains require ditching AFM and its spring-loaded lifters. (Photo Courtesy Comp Cams)

camshafts require aftermarket roller rocker arms or a trunnion upgrade, which replaces the factory rockers' needle bearings (known to come apart and destroy engines) with captured roller bearings. Although either works in nearly any application, roller rockers apply more even pressure to the valve. This ultimately keeps the valveguides happy and prevents premature wear.

Valvetrains

The L99 is an entirely different animal when it comes to the valvetrain. Mast Motorsports was the first to embrace the challenge of VVT, and Comp Cams was right behind it. Both offer camshafts that are compatible with VVT and AFM. In performance applications AFM has proven to be unreliable, and severely limits camshaft design (hence why the L99 makes 26 hp less than the LS3). Nevertheless, with supporting components AFM-friendly cams can pick up significant power. By deleting the AFM system, though, there is the potential to pick up an additional 20 to 50 hp routinely. The high-flowing LS3 heads need higher lift cams to make use of their airflow.

Either way you go, a camshaft phaser limiter is needed to keep the valves from making contact with the pistons. A kit from Mast, Comp Cams, or Texas Speed & Performance includes this vital piece. Of course there is also the option to delete variable valve timing and negate the gains from altering the cam timing. Some people may prefer the simplicity, but only a dedicated race car truly needs to delete VVT.

When your basic valvetrain upgrades won't cut it, the LS platform has an abundance of options: from 500 ci, 2,000 hp, and beyond.

ENGINE BUILDS AND SWAPS

Preferences vary as to single or dual springs. These 918 beehive springs from Comp Cams are lightweight and certainly serve a purpose, but higher lift camshafts require dual springs. Ideally you want the lightest valvetrain possible, but durability is also crucial. Either way, don't even think about using an aftermarket cam with stock springs. (Photo Courtesy Comp Cams)

If a beehive is good for lower lift cams, and duals are good for higher lifts, these dual conical valvespring hybrids are for nearly everything else. This new design is capable of up to .800-inch lift in some applications, using a progressive frequency design for better valve control, less deflection, and less parasitic loss. (Photo Courtesy Comp Cams)

With higher lift camshafts, it is imperative that you upgrade the bearings on the factory rocker arms. The captured roller trunnions allow you to save money and keep the lightweight factory rockers without having to worry about whether the OEM needle bearings will come apart and ruin your expensive engine. This complete kit is available from Comp Cams (PN 13702-KIT). Some suppliers, such as Brian Tooley Racing, can install them for you and even micropolish or coat the rockers. (Photo Courtesy Comp Cams)

With high-RPM applications, switching to a shaft-mount rocker system is necessary. It completely changes the leverage point on the rocker and cylinder to give the stability necessary. In addition, switching to a roller tip reduces friction and more evenly pushes on the valve. Some have seen premature valve-guide wear from using stock rockers with very high-lift cams. The downside is cost. Not only do these Comp Cams LS3 rockers (PN 1521) cost more than $1,400, but shaft-mounts often need additional machining and setup. You have to pay to play with the big boys. With a solid roller race application, you definitely need a set of these. T&D and Jesel are two other popular suppliers. (Photo Courtesy Comp Cams)

One of the few limitations of the platform is the standard small-block Chevy 4.400-inch bore spacing. As a result, 4.185 inches is near the upper limit of bore size for aftermarket iron blocks such as the Chevrolet Performance LSX. Aluminum blocks are typically even smaller. Thankfully, even standard deck height blocks allow for a 4.125-inch stroke and more than 454 ci. Tall-deck blocks generally accept 4.600-inch-stroke cranks or larger with a custom deck height.

For a radical street car, this generally equates to more than 700 hp naturally aspirated, and more than 1,000 hp with forced induction.

Crate Engines

For those looking for the simplicity and reliability of a crate engine, Chevrolet Performance offers a num-

Chevrolet Performance offers two LSX376 crate engines as a boost-friendly replacement for the factory L99 or LS3. Both use a 211/230-duration cam with .560/.555-inch lift, LSX-LS3 heads, 9:1 compression, and (stock) 376 ci of displacement. The B15 variety (PN 19299306) comes with forged powdered-metal rods, forged eight-bolt crank, and forged pistons. The more cost-effective B8 (PN 19260831) comes with the standard powdered-metal rods and nodular-iron crank but upgraded forged pistons. Both are rated at 450 hp naturally aspirated. (Photo Courtesy Chevrolet Performance)

The LSX454 (PN 19244611) is meant for naturally aspirated combinations and makes 620 hp at 6,200 rpm out of the gate. Although it comes at a steeper price, it provides 454 ci and 11:1 compression thanks to the 4340 forged steel crank and rods, as well as big 4.185-inch forged slugs. The cam has a .648/.648-inch lift and 236/246 duration and is mated to LSX-LS7 heads with titanium intake and sodium-filled exhaust valves. (Photo Courtesy Chevrolet Performance)

The 6.2L LS9 (PN 19244099) is the ultimate engine swap, at 638 hp, and much more is just a pulley swap away. The OEM engine choice of the top dog Corvette ZR1 has a forged steel crank, forged pistons, and titanium rods. Titanium is also used for the intake valves, the exhaust is sodium-filled steel, and the 9:1-compression engine uses a 211/230-duration cam. A stronger alloy is used on the heads and block for durability with the Eaton TVS2300 supercharger. (Photo Courtesy Chevrolet Performance)

ber of mild to wild options. Starting with OEM-based options, the LS376/480 is ideal for a stock replacement LS3 with just a little more kick. A 219/228-duration hydraulic roller offers 50 hp and 70 ft-lbs of torque advantage with a nice, flat power curve. The LS376/525 takes this just a bit further, adding the high-RPM ASA camshaft developed for circle-track racing to make 525 hp. As you can imagine, this is a fairly radical cam that idles rough and peaks at 6,300 rpm. Although it makes nearly 500 ft-lbs of torque at 4,200 rpm, it is certainly a more peaky powerband. This same engine is available in a sealed version for drag racing competition in the National Muscle Car Association (NMCA) LS Stock class.

If you'd like to build your own version of the Z/28, the 505-horse LS7 is an easy drop-in. Swap out the dry-sump oil pan and pump for LS3 or L99 components, and away you go. The supplied exhaust manifolds, water pump, and balancer are of no use. If you intend to use the dry-sump oiling system, you need the Z/28's oil tank, lines, and so on to squeeze them into the engine bay (including the cooling fan).

Swaps

Swapping an LSA or LS9 into an SS or Z/28 is complicated. As mentioned in Chapter 4, these supercharged engines use the E67 engine controller in their OEM applications and place sensors in different locations. Because the LSA came in the ZL1, it is considerably easier to accomplish this swap using OEM ZL1 parts.

The 638-hp LS9, on the other hand, requires quite a bit of work to fit the Corvette accessory drive arrangement. Thankfully Lingenfelter's LSA

Fesler Built and Thomson Automotive both managed to perfect the art of the LS9 swap in a Camaro SS. Although the engine is mostly the same as an LS3 (minus the supercharger), a few hurdles to overcome include the dry-sump oiling system, wiring and ECM, fuel system, and pulleys. Thomson swaps the ECM for the LS9's E67, re-pins the harness, trades the dry-sump oiling for a stock LSA pump and pan, upgrades to a ZL1 fuel pump, and uses the Corvette ZR1 pulleys. That may seem simple, but it takes some relocating to get the accessories to fit, and rewiring the harness is not for the novice. In a ZL1, the LS9 is a much easier swap. (Photo Courtesy Joseph Potak)

to LS9 Supercharger Conversion Front Cover (PN L250406509) makes life a whole lot easier. This handy item makes the LS9, the most powerful factory LS engine ever offered, a fairly easy upgrade for ZL1s as well. A larger 2.3L supercharger, CNC-ported heads, forged rotating assembly, stronger block, and healthier camshaft make it the LSA's brawny big brother with a whopping 604 ft-lbs of torque.

For higher levels of boost or nitrous and maximum cubic inches, an aftermarket block such as the Chevrolet Performance LSX cast-iron block is ideal. The LSX block has been proven to hold more than 2,000 hp and features priority main oiling, billet main caps, and 5.575-inch-long cylinders with ample rod clearance. The 6.2-liter LSX376-B15 and LSX376-B8 are affordable, entry-level crate engines built with boost in mind using the LSX block. Both make 450 hp on engine and can provide a great foundation to build upon. They are nearly identical aside from the crankshaft and rods, which are upgraded to forged versions on the B15 to hold more boost.

These cost-effective 9:1 compression engines use LS3 heads (six-bolt version on the B15), making them a direct bolt-in for SS models. The cam is a smooth-idling 210/230-duration hydraulic roller very similar to the LS9.

The LSX454 is the modern equivalent of the venerable 454 big-block Chevy, except that it uses

Should you go the custom engine route, there are several noteworthy LS builders around the country, including Late Model Engines, Kurt Urban Performance, Bischoff Racing Engines, and Mast Motorsports. These four use the Chevrolet Performance LSX block in some of their builds, which is available in both standard and tall-deck varieties. The iron construction with billet six-bolt mains is sturdier than factory blocks for more boost, RPM, or nitrous. It also allows for more cubic inches; a maximum of 4.200-inch bores and extra-long cylinders allow for larger stroke cranks. LSX blocks are now available in semi-finished and finished with 4.065- or 4.185-inch bores. (Photo Courtesy Chevrolet Performance)

The RHS LS Race Block is also available in semi-finished and fully machined (3.90-, 4.125-, or 4.165-inch bores) with billet main caps and either standard or tall-deck. Its most obvious difference, though, is that it is made of A357-T6 aluminum with press-in spun cast-iron liners. The RHS block uses a raised cam location, which allows for larger camshafts without interference with the crank's stroke. This is especially important with the tall-deck. It also has provisions for piston oil squirters, similar to the LSA and LS9. Like the LSX, it has priority main oiling and better bay-to-bay breathing. (Photo Courtesy Racing Head Service)

Dart was last to the party with the LS Next, but the company made up for its tardiness with quality and a unique perspective. By going with a conventional four-bolt steel main cap, the LS Next reduces the windage issues that plague traditional LS engines. Ultimately this means more power and better lubrication. Available in both iron and aluminum, the LS Next accommodates long strokes and up to 4.220-inch bores (4.165 with aluminum) in either standard or tall-deck. Custom deck height is also available with the billet aluminum block. (Photo Courtesy Dart Machinery)

a standard-deck LSX block with 4.185-inch forged pistons and a 4.125-inch-stroke 4340 forged crankshaft. Using LSX-LS7 heads with titanium intake and sodium-filled exhaust valves and a 236/246 hydraulic roller camshaft, the LSX454 makes 580 hp and 600 ft-lbs of torque with a stock LS7 intake manifold. Unlike its street-friendly pump-gas-sipping cousin, the LSX454R comes complete with an intake manifold and carburetor.

The LSX454 is built for drag racing with a solid roller camshaft, race-gas-only 13:1 compression, and LSX-DR cylinder heads. This high-revving combo makes 770 hp at 7,000 rpm with plenty of piston and valvetrain stability thanks to the shaft-mounted rocker arms and tall-deck block. To run the LSX454R in a fifth-gen with a factory ECM, you need to drill the cast injector bosses in the intake manifold and use an elbow with a drive-by-wire throttle body.

All LSX crate engines require remote mounting of the ignition coils (or swapping to stock-style valve-covers) and an eight-bolt flexplate.

Cranks and Rods

The stock LS3, L99, and LSA blocks easily accommodate a 4.00-inch-stroke crankshaft from Callies, Scat, Lunati, Manley, or K1 Technologies, to name a few. A 4.100- and 4.125-inch stroke is also possible, but not recommended with forced induction. The LS7 is more forgiving of the longer stroke. A 58x reluctor wheel is essential for compatibility with the factory ECM, and generally speaking a 2.100-inch rod pin diameter is ideal (though not essential). Out-of-the-box 4340 forged steel cranks are sufficient for all but 1,800-hp combinations.

All-out high-RPM drag racing combinations typically go with a custom billet crank that is center counterweighted. A 6.100- or 6.125-inch connecting rod made from 4340 forged steel with ARP2000 rod bolts is plenty strong for most applications.

Depending on the RPM range and whether it is forced induction or naturally aspirated, an I-beam may be sufficient. An H-beam with ARP Custom Age 625 cap screws holds an awful lot of power, depending on the design. Billet and aluminum rods are typically used with 1,200 hp and/or 8,000 rpm.

Aluminum has a short fatigue life and is only suitable for dedicated drag racing applications. Titanium and other alloys (such as Carrillo's proprietary blend of chrome, nickel, moly, and vanadium) also have merit for being versatile, light, and strong, although the factory LS7 titanium rods are not recommended for forced induction.

Pistons

Piston design is crucial in any LS application, but especially with factory blocks. OEM blocks such as the LS3, which have just 5.460-inch-long cylinders, can experience piston rock with longer strokes. Excessive scuffing and wear is a recipe for disaster, which is exactly why the LS7 came with 5.900-inch-long cylinders. Piston manufacturers such as Diamond, Mahle, JE, and Wiseco emphasize offset pins and piston skirt design.

JE says its asymmetrical piston increases strength and minimizes weight due to designing the piston around where the thrust loads actually exist. JE is also one of the few companies to make a piston that clears the factory piston oil squirters in the LSA and LS9 engines.

Material is also another crucial consideration with LS pistons, which were known to have considerable piston slap from the factory (because of its inherent geometry). Only the LS9 was given forged pistons from the factory for this very reason.

Mahle offers mostly 4032 alloy because it creates a tighter seal, less noise, and has a longer life cycle. This high-silicon low-expansion alloy is less ductile than 2618, making it less forgiving to detonation. NASCAR and the American Le Mans Series (ALMS) as well as the drag racing world use 2618 as it's more ideal for extreme duty because of its high-expansion characteristics. Of course, the increased clearances needed cause piston slap after a cold start. My advice? if your Camaro sees more street than track time and low or no boost, stick with 4032.

Fuel Options and Compression Ratios

The efficiency of the LS platform as well as the emergence of new fueling options has changed the game when it comes to developing combinations. More traditional and conservative compression ratios, for example, have gone by the wayside. With 93-octane pump gas, 11.5 and even 12:1 is certainly possible with naturally aspirated and nitrous combinations. E85 and race gas blends allow even more compression for street combos. Dedicated drag cars are seeing 15:1 or higher when running a quality race gas such as VP Racing Q16. Boosted combos seem to be happy around 9 or 9.5:1 with pump gas, though higher boost levels require methanol injection. With E85 or race gas and moderate to high boost, 10:1 is extremely common.

Keep in mind, though, that the cylinder head and cam design, as well as other factors that affect the overall cylinder pressure, have a huge effect on the optimum compression. With boost and nitrous, cylinder head clamping is a large concern. Higher compression can exacerbate an inadequacy, resulting in blown head gaskets or pushing fluid out of the cooling system. High-boost drag racing combinations frequently use various methods such as copper head gaskets, O-rings on the heads or block, and even a solid deck.

Past experience is the best determinant of optimum compression, so try to find someone with a similar combo or speak with an experienced builder. Sometimes bargain hunting can get you in trouble, by putting a bunch of parts together that don't jive. For example, stock rocker arms and solid L99 valves might be fine with one cam, but on another can result in broken valvesprings or dropping needle bearings into your engine. That's a recipe for a bad day.

When putting an engine together, it is important to have a holistic mindset, understanding how each piece fits with the others. For a street/strip or handling setup with factory ABS brakes, you want to make sure the camshaft has optimum vacuum for the power assist. On a road course you also want good throttle response and a broader power curve, so that you'll be in it when you exit the corner, not watching other cars pass you. The compression ratio can exaggerate or hide these inherent tendencies; low compression with a big cam makes it sluggish, and at low RPM it's possible that it can even stumble.

With a lighter weight drag car, a smaller powerband with the highest peak power is usually preferred when you are able to use supporting components such as gear ratios and/or a torque converter to keep the engine within the powerband. When it comes to street cars, some owners are simply less tolerant of certain things, such as a rough idle or NVH.

A Pro Stock cam with a gear drive might be fine for one driver, but a nightmare for another. When power adders are used, special consideration needs to be taken for the cam design, compression, and other parts used. For example, a Roots supercharger with a less efficient intercooler may need a 9.0 or even 8.5:1 compression; whereas, a centrifugal blower might be comfortable at the same boost level with 9.5 or 10:1. Similarly an LS9 cam might be perfect with a Roots, but a centrifugal needs a cam that accelerates the engine into boost quicker (better low-end torque).

One common thread is that all power adders require beefier components that are more tolerant, or that help resist, detonation. Thicker piston crowns, coatings, larger wrist pins, stronger rods and cranks, head and main studs (in contrast to bolts), stainless or Inconel exhaust valves, and aftermarket head gaskets are just a few things to consider.

Oiling Systems

When putting together an LS engine, the oiling system is typically the last thing that most builders think about. Factory systems are typically very good compared to their predecessors. However, some improvements can be made. Porting a factory LS3 or L99 oil pump can help increase the flow and keep the engine better lubricated. Aftermarket pumps from Melling or Moroso can actually help increase the pressure (up to 10 psi) as well as the flow, depending on the model.

Although the Melling 10295 has a stock volume with a 10-percent increase in flow, the 10296 offers an 18-percent increase in volume and the 10355 offers a 33-percent increase (similar to that of the factory LSA pump). The latter is usually reserved for engines with AFM or piston oil squirters. These can also be ported to add to its flow thanks to longer steel gears and enlarged inlets and outlets.

Some builders also laud the Melling pump for its sturdier cast cover, which is more reliable at maintaining oil pressure. Running these pumps with a double-roller timing chain requires spacers and additional clearance to the timing cover.

Fear not Z/28 owners, many options are available for the dry-sump system as well. Katech offers a factory-style scavenge pump with 30-percent greater capacity with standard or a 20-percent increase in pressure. External pumps are also available from Aviaid and others, which require a separate timing belt to drive. These are best suited for dedicated track cars and can be used on SS or ZL1 models with other retrofit components.

External wet-sump setups can also offer improved scavenging to eliminate oil starvation without having to deal with a separate oil tank.

Unlike the previous generations of small-blocks, the deep-skirted LS engine block does not offer any power advantages over aftermarket oil pans. Aftermarket pans are more effective in keeping the oil pump pickup submerged in oil, which ultimately keeps the bearings happy.

ENGINE BUILDS AND SWAPS

Moroso is the only company offering a fifth-gen wet-sump pan designed for drag racing and built for the COPO Camaro program. Improved Racing offers a baffle for the stock pan that is ideal for road racing, autocross, and other forms of racing. The trapdoor baffling keeps the pickup submerged at high Gs, and the data proves it thanks to Improved's oil sensor block.

Crank scraper and oil cooler kits are also available. With the standard LS block, a crank scraper is perhaps the only way to actually increase power through windage improvements.

Of course, the Dart LS Next block is an entirely different animal, which trades the skirted six-bolt main caps for a traditional SBC four-bolt splayed caps. A special oil pan from Moroso and Canton is needed for these blocks. Z/28s have the benefit of aftermarket pans from many companies such as ARE, as well as oil pan inserts for the stock dry-sump pan from Aviaid and inserts for the tank itself.

Typical bolt-on replacement setups go as high as three stages, though companies such as Dailey Engineering offer up to five stages of scavenging with cast aluminum vented and baffled tanks. Some retain the A/C; others do not.

Custom Engine Builders

Several reputable LS engine builders are pushing the factory components harder and offering even wilder aftermarket variations.

Mast Motorsports is one of the largest builders of LS crate engines, shipping 550- to 1,000-hp combinations all over the world daily. LS3- and L99-based packages use a forged rotating assembly with a 4.00-inch stroke to increase the displacement to 416 ci. LS7-based engines range from 630 to 675 hp with 427 ci; LSX engines make 640 to 685 hp with 440 cubes.

A line of Whipple supercharged engines range from 750 to 1,000 hp using an LS3, LSX, LS7, or Racing Head Service (RHS) block.

Lingenfelter is another big player in the market, which puts together LS3, LS7, LS9, and LSA crate engines. The naturally aspirated 417-cube LS3 makes 605 hp; the supercharged version makes 700 hp with a Magnuson TVS2300. The LS7 versions make 650 hp naturally aspirated and 750 hp supercharged. The stock-cube LS9 crate engine also makes 750 hp.

The top dog is a Kenne Bell blown (stock) LSA making 900 hp. Both Lingenfelter and Kenne Bell offer short-blocks and long-blocks separately if you plan to reuse many of the stock components.

Turnkey Engine Supply is known for offering complete "turnkey" engines from the oil pan to the air filter, fuel system, ECM, and wiring harness. Although this might not be ideal for a fifth-gen, Turnkey offers plenty of long-block assemblies more appropriate with various LS3, LS9, LS7, and LSX combinations. The 427-ci LS3 offers 580 hp at a reasonable price tag thanks to the 4.125-inch-stroke crankshaft and stock cylinders. A more traditional 4.125-inch bore and 4.00-inch stroke are offered with the LS7 combo, capable of 630 hp. Stock-cube LS3s are also offered with forged pistons and rods.

Golen Engine Service offers 416-cube LS3 strokers, as well as LS7 and LSX-based big-cube engines from 605 hp to 725 hp that are dyno tested and custom built to order. A separate line of engines is available for boosted applications with lower compression and beefier components. A 427-ci combo with an aluminum RHS block and heads is available to hold 20 to 30 psi and more than 1,000 hp.

Texas Speed is known for have a great bang for the buck and simple online ordering. Packages are offered from stock cube to 429 ci using either an LS3/L99 block or an LSA for an additional charge. The 427- and 441-cube LS7 short-blocks and long-blocks are also offered, as well as 408- to 454-cube LSX engines, with ported stock or PRC aftermarket heads.

Building Yourself

Whether you have a custom engine builder in mind or plan on assembling the engine yourself, you have quite a few things to consider. The LS3, L99, and LSA tolerate only a .005-inch hone to the cylinders, which limits bore size to a max of 4.070 inches. The LS7 is only moderately better, with up to .010 inch, though its 4.125-inch bore is already sizeable. Larger bore sizes are possible with aftermarket cylinder sleeves from Darton or ERL Performance, which requires considerable machine work.

ERL has also developed an aluminum truss system that can substantially increase the strength of the stock engine block for forced induction. The sleeves themselves are also an upgrade over the spun cast iron. ERL uses ductile iron that is three times stronger than stock, which becomes extremely important with larger bore sizes and forced induction. The LS7 is a poor choice for forced-induction builds due to its extremely thin cylinder walls. An ERL block with the same bore size can hold more than 2,000 hp with additional options such as billet main caps, main girdle, 1/2-inch head studs, and six head bolts per cylinder à la the Chevrolet Performance LSX block.

The cast-iron LSX block is the next step up if you require even more cubic inches and strength. The standard-deck provides a little more than 454 ci of available displacement, more than sufficient for most builds. The tall-deck is more suited for race applications that need greater piston stability. Although the cylinder length is sufficient for much longer strokes, the standard cam position limits cam size and cubic inches to around 468 using a 4.25-inch-stroke crank. The World Products Warhawk block has the same issue, though it benefits from the weight savings of aluminum along with RHS and certain Dart offerings.

The RHS LS Race Block, Dart Billet, and LS Next blocks' raised cam height accommodates up to 502 cubes, as well as larger cam cores. The RHS even has piston oil squirter provisions similar to the LSA and LS9 blocks, except that it does not have clearance issues with longer stroke cranks.

How-To Projects

Heads and Cam Install

All photos for this project are courtesy of Joseph Potak.

Thanks to the magnificent flow of the LS3 and L99 heads, it has become all too common for fifth-gen Camaro SSs to hit 500-rwhp when equipped with only the necessary valvetrain upgrades and supporting bolt-ons. With the previous generation, you were lucky to make more than 440-rwhp without race gas and a serious set of aftermarket heads. But even with a light CNC program, it is all too easy to exceed 340 cfm of intake flow from the "821" castings. The real gains are on the exhaust side, where the head typically makes only around 200-cfm stock (at peak) but can gain more than 30 cfm through porting. The power gains in head flow pale in comparison, though, to what can be accomplished with an aftermarket cam.

This install is a standard LS3 heads/cam swap. Things become quite a bit more complicated when you throw VVT and AFM equipment into the equation. On an LS3, the key points to keep in mind are to always use a set of valvesprings matched to the camshaft, upgrade the pushrods, and make sure that the cam is a single-bolt style or switch to a three-bolt cam sprocket. This install is the latter because the older three-bolt-style cams are much more common. Other than that, it is basically a simple remove-and-replace job. Although, at the end, you will most likely need to have the engine custom tuned. A recalibration is required for nearly all aftermarket camshafts.

1 To remove the heads and camshaft, you must first unbolt the intake, valvecovers, rocker arms, and the headers (or exhaust manifolds). You also want to drain the radiator and oil, as well as disconnect the battery while you are at it.

ENGINE BUILDS AND SWAPS

2 Significant gains can be had from a heads and camshaft upgrade to an L99 or LS3, just as with any other LS engine. Best of all, these upgrades do not have to affect the reliability or fuel mileage of your Camaro, making them friendly for daily driving duties.

3 The front accessory drive system must also be removed, including the idlers, power steering, A/C compressor, water pump, and balancer.

4 Thankfully the fifth-gen's engine bay allows for a decent amount of room when removing the cylinder heads. You can even access the back bolts with air tools. Because the head bolts are torque to yield (as is the crank bolt), they must be discarded and cannot be reused.

5 The heads simply lift off the dowels and can be carefully placed out of harm's way. Most places that CNC port the factory heads do so with a core exchange, so you need to package these up for shipping. This is also a good time to unbolt the lifter buckets and set them aside.

6 As with the head bolts, the head gaskets cannot be reused. For most heads/cam installs, a factory LS3 gasket is perfectly fine. General Motors did a really great job with the MLS design. With boost, nitrous, and aftermarket blocks, however, other options should be considered.

7 Believe it or not, cleaning up is one of the most crucial parts of the install. You want to scrape the excess gasket material off the surface of the block for a good seal. But, perhaps more important, make sure to vacuum/blow out any coolant or debris from the head bolt holes. Not only does it prevent you from getting a good, even torque on the bolts, but you may crack the block.

8 Now that everything is clean, use a 10-mm socket to remove all 10 of the timing cover bolts.

9 Use a 24-mm socket to remove the single bolt that connects the timing gear to the cam.

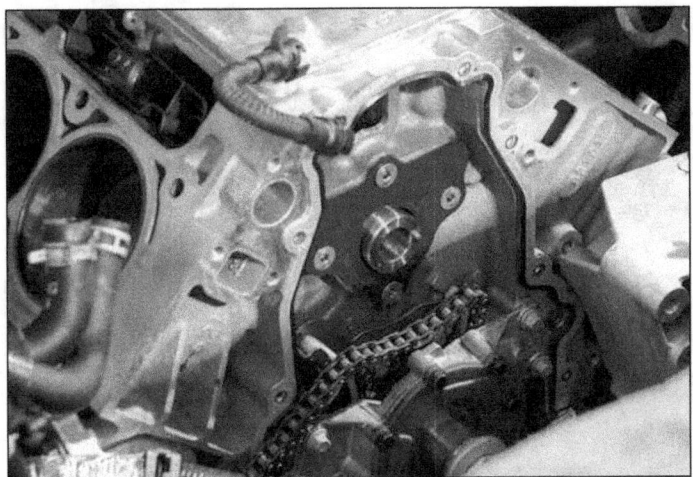

10 I hope you've got some Torx sockets in your box because the cam retainer plate requires a T-40.

11 Unbolt the radiator and pull it out of the way to provide enough clearance to remove the cam.

12 For this install I used a Texas Speed & Performance camshaft, which was lubed thoroughly with Comp Cams Pro Cam Lube before carefully inserting it into the block. It is important to find a grind that best suits your needs and tastes, so consult with a professional before purchasing.

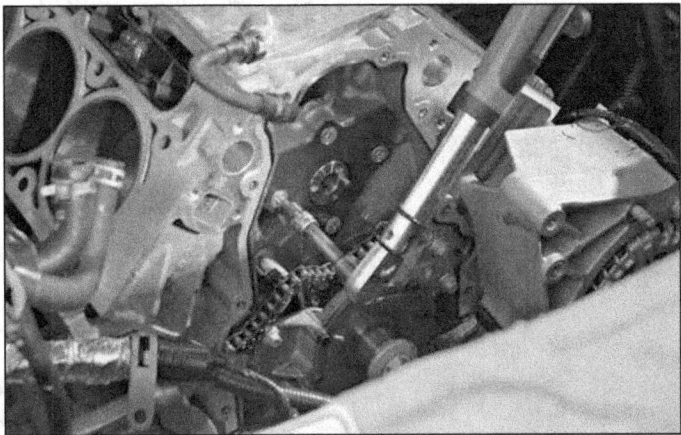

13 Treat the cam retainer bolts to some red Loctite and torque to 18 ft-lbs. Many DIY installers either forget to Loctite the bolts or over-torque them, so be warned.

14 The Texas Speed cam came as a kit with the three-bolt cam sprocket, which requires 26 ft-lbs of torque. Again, Loctite is recommended. After the cam is installed, you can drop the lifter buckets back into place and secure them with just 9 ft-lbs.

15 One neat trick is to use Permatex Copper Spray-A-Gasket on the new head gaskets and the exhaust gaskets. You need to do this ahead of time, so it has a few minutes to dry. High-boost race engines use copper head gaskets because it is stronger but still malleable for a better seal. The spray helps provide the best of both worlds on a street engine to fill surface irregularities and hot spots.

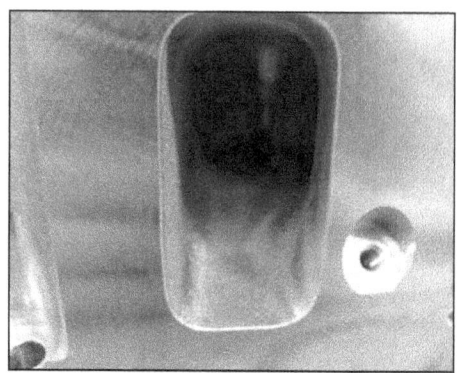

16 Because you are basically just paying for labor, porting your stock heads is a fraction of the cost of aftermarket heads. Although it is hard to beat a set of hand-ported heads from a master at the craft, CNC porting is replicable and cost-effective. Typically the CNC program is designed from a hand-ported prototype head. The intake runners on these PRC-ported heads flow 351 cfm at .600-inch.

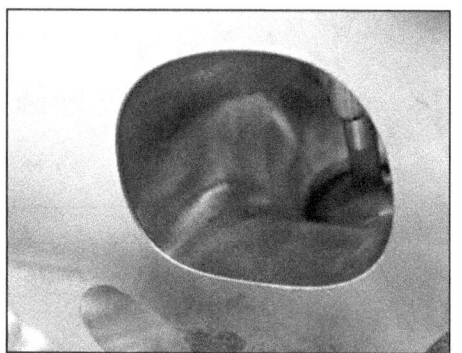

17 The exhaust runners hit 228 cfm at the same lift and hit 198 cfm at just .400-inch.

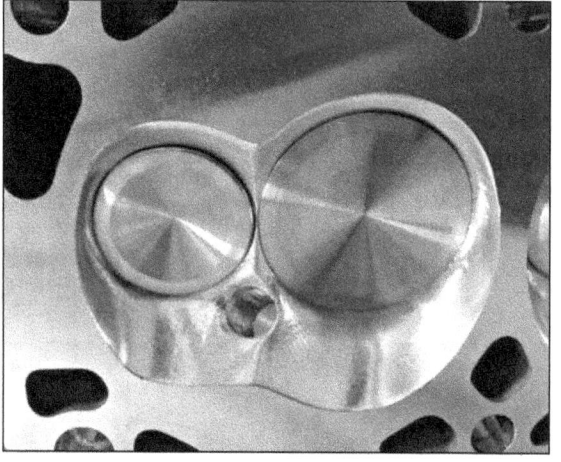

18 Although the heads are apart, you can upgrade to lighter or stronger valves. The factory valves are already plenty big enough at 2.165 and 1.59 inches. The stock LS3 valves have hollow stems to save weight, yet aftermarket hollow stems are even a bit lighter (91 versus 106 grams). For higher RPM, these are ideal for valve-spring stability and longevity.

19 Speaking of valvesprings, PRC has two sets of dual-spring kits, depending on the cam lift. Dual springs generally support more lift than single beehive springs and add an element of safety. If a beehive breaks there is nothing to prevent the valve from dropping into the cylinder, which can be catastrophic.

ENGINE BUILDS AND SWAPS

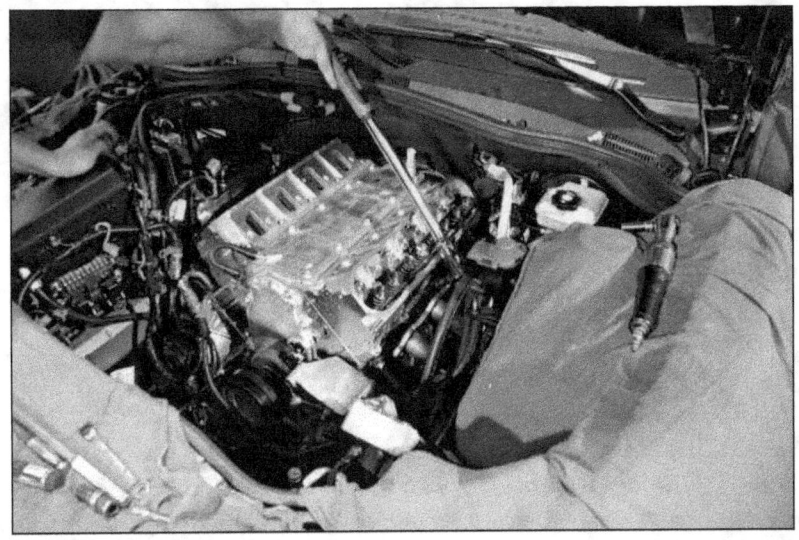

20 Texas Speed has a Basic Heads & Camshaft Bolt & Gasket Kit that includes new stock head bolts. You can upgrade to ARP bolts or studs, but the stock ones are fine for naturally aspirated street cars. The downside, though, is that they use a more complicated torque procedure.

On the first pass, apply 22 ft-lbs in a specific sequence from the middle out to the M11 bolts. On the second pass turn the bolts 90 degrees (electronic torque wrenches are available with degree indicators) in the same sequence. Then another 70 degrees on step three, and finally apply 22 ft-lbs to the M8 bolts on the intake runner flange. ARP hardware uses only torque (not degrees) to install and is reusable.

21 Torque the rocker arm bolts to 26 ft-lbs on the closed valves; make the open valves only snug. You need to turn the engine over to move the valves into position. After that, it is just a matter of reinstalling things as you removed them.

VVT Cam Swap and AFM Delete

All photos for this project are courtesy of Joseph Potak.

For the L99 crowd, it looks quite a bit different under the timing cover. The camshaft phaser, which alters the cam timing, sits in place of the camshaft sprocket. Instead of a regular bolt, it has a valve that feeds a number of holes in the phaser. Oil pressure is controlled by pulse-width modulation, which in turn causes the cam to retard. With no pressure it locks to full advance. An electromagnet with a pin in the timing cover pushes the cam phaser valve to control the pressure. With a factory camshaft, the L99 can advance the cam 7 degrees and retard it up to 45 degrees. The danger in altering the cam timing is that you run the risk of piston and valve interference.

From the factory, L99s have valve reliefs in the pistons and cams with very mild lift and duration as a result. Although it does boast advantages in fuel economy and average power, it lacks in peak power and overall performance compared to what can be done with a larger camshaft. To add a larger cam, the phaser must be restricted in its motion. Thankfully Comp Cams and Mast Motorsports offer kits to do just that.

In addition, the AFM system does wonders for fuel economy, but it also has some severe limitations when it comes to performance. In fact, trying to run an AFM-friendly cam means fairly low lift. For maximum performance, your best bet is to use a conventional lifter. And just as with an LS3 cam swap, making these changes requires custom tuning. Tuning the VVT system requires an experienced tuner, too.

CHAPTER 5

The L99 has a rather small camshaft to accommodate the variable cam timing and AFM systems. By going the aftermarket route, you can really wake up the engine. Just be sure to match your camshaft specs with the torque converter and rear-end gears. If you plan to keep both stock, then be sure to pick a more docile cam meant to be compatible.

The AFM lifters work with the circuitry in the valley cover to deactivate cylinders under light-load conditions, turning the V-8 into a V-4. The downside is that these spring-loaded lifters do not tolerate very much lift, duration, or boost. Swapping these for stock LS3 or LS7 lifters and trays is a wise decision for optimum performance.

1 A cam phaser is connected to the timing sprocket on the L99, which is the modus operandi for the variable valve timing system. It advances or retards the camshaft via this valve that controls oil pressure and screws into the camshaft to connect the cam to the phaser and timing sprocket. It is important that the engine be at TDC before beginning this process.

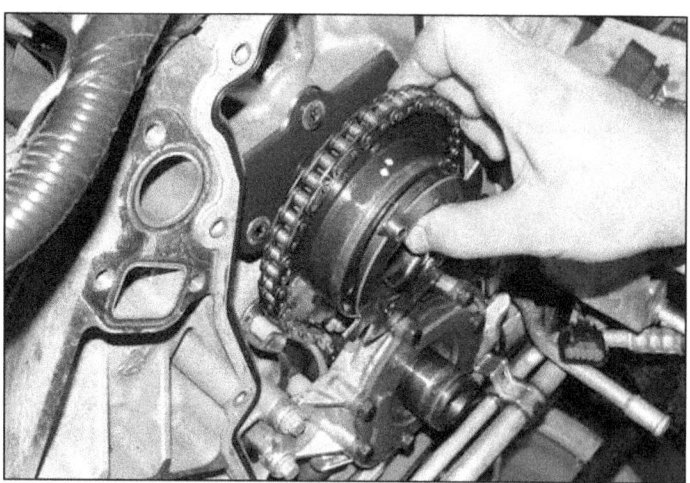

2 Once you unscrew the valve with a 24-mm socket, pull the phaser off the cam and timing chain. Behind the phaser, the L99 cam looks similar to an LS3 with a matching retainer plate.

3 The Texas Speed phaser limiter kit is needed for any aftermarket cam. Essentially it limits the phaser's ability to advance or retard the camshaft timing, so as not to cause any catastrophic piston-to-valve events. Most of what you see here are tools to open the phaser, aside from the block.

ENGINE BUILDS AND SWAPS

4 Out the phaser into a vice, with a piece of cloth to protect the sprocket. The spring tool hooks around the phaser, allowing the spring to pull away from the pin.

5 There is a spot where a 3/8-inch ratchet drive slips into the hook to help you apply enough torque. When the spring is pulled away, you can see the hole on each side of the cam position sensor.

6 Insert the musical note into the holes in the hook, which locks it in position to hold the spring away from the pin.

7 On the other side, use a Torx 4.5 for the bolts.

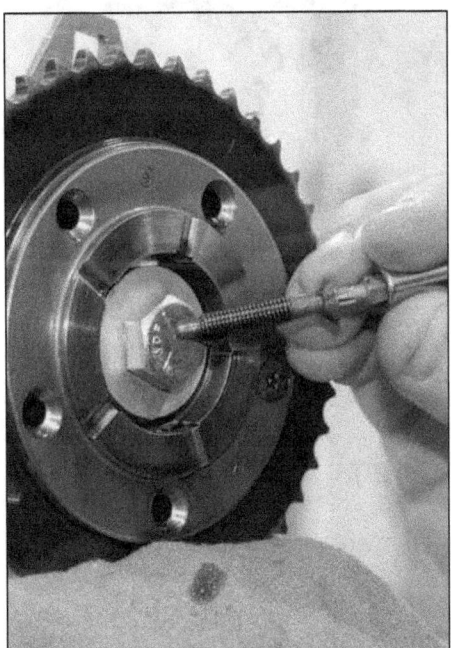

8 Remove all but the one with the pin, which is hidden by the spring. Just loosen this one to keep the cover attached yet able to pivot.

9 With the cover pivoted out of the way, slip the block into the phaser. The notch goes on the inside and top, facing the center of the phaser so that the oil can still flow outward.

CAMARO 5TH GEN 2010-2015: HOW TO BUILD AND MODIFY

CHAPTER 5

10 Apply just 8 ft-lbs with the Torx socket to seal the phaser back up. And then remove the other installation tools.

11 Getting the pin on the cam inserted into the phaser can be a little tricky because you are working blind. Putting a mark on the front of the phaser can help as a reference point. General Motors recommends using a new bolt every time the phaser is installed, which should be torqued with 48 ft-lbs plus 90 degrees.

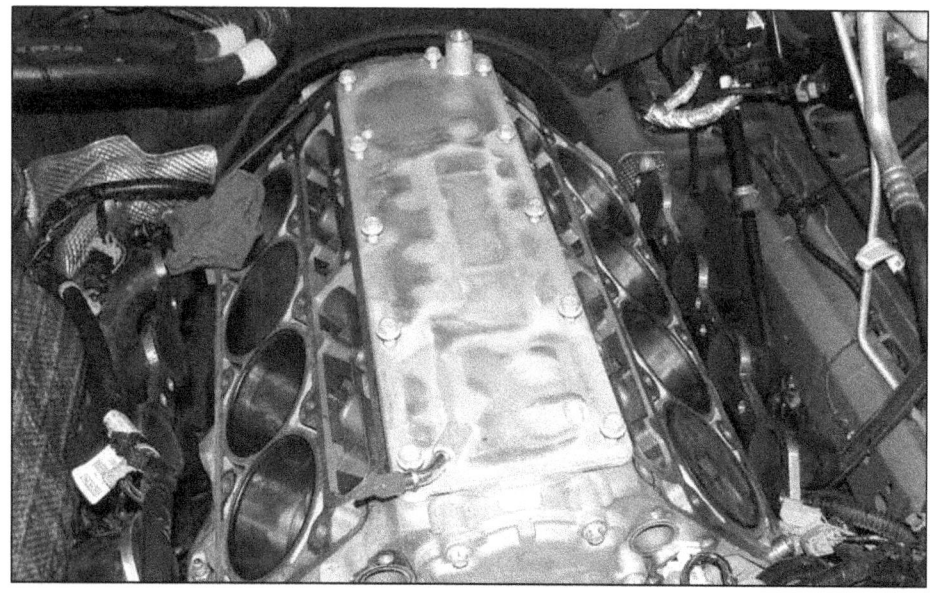

12 Last but not least, the valley cover needs to be switched over to an LS3 style. After reinstalling the heads and intake, tuning can begin.

Camshaft Degree and Piston-to-Valve Clearance

All photos for this project are courtesy of Joseph Potak.

There is an old saying: look before you leap. Here's another: measure twice, cut once. Even the best aftermarket camshaft manufacturers have been known to make mistakes. After all, there are humans operating those machines and punching numbers into the computers (at least for now). You should degree the camshaft whenever possible and check piston-to-valve clearance on any new combo. The extra time you spend could pay dividends down the road.

If you are new to these concepts, remember the "VVT Cam Swap and AFM Delete" install.

The phaser mounted to the front of the cam on L99 engines alters the camshaft timing. In doing so, it can have benefits in fuel efficiency, but from a performance standpoint, the cam timing moves the power curve up or down. When you degree the camshaft, you are first checking to make sure the cam is in phase with

130   CAMARO 5TH GEN 2010–2015: HOW TO BUILD AND MODIFY

ENGINE BUILDS AND SWAPS

the crankshaft. This is even more crucial with VVT. The crankshaft keyway and camshaft dowel orientation, as well as the lifter location, timing chain slack and gear machining, and camshaft machining can all affect cam timing.

If you have an LS3, LS7, or other LSx combo you can use an adjustable aftermarket timing set to retard or advance the cam, depending on the combination. You need a dial indicator, degree wheel, pointer, and the usual hand tools.

Piston-to-valve clearance is even more straightforward. You are basically just ensuring that the valves do not make contact with the pistons when the engine turns over. An adjustable length pushrod, dial indicator, test spring, and hand tools are needed to complete this task.

1 Camshaft degree and piston-to-valve clearance are two of the most fundamental procedures that you should do on just about every camshaft install. I say "just about" because if you use the same cam, heads, and pistons all the time, most likely the piston-to-valve clearance is going to be the same. But this is not the case with the camshaft degree.

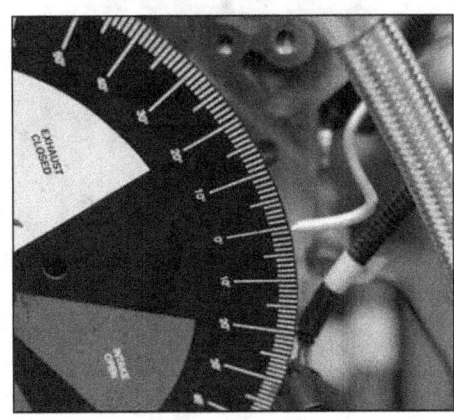

2 Ideally you degree the cam with the heads off to find true top dead center (TDC); however, simply lining up the timing chain marks gets you close to TDC on cylinder 1 and you can set the wheel to zero. I chose this method because I was just swapping cams instead of building an engine, as you may be inclined to do.

3 Install the test springs and pushrods on cylinder 1.

4 Bolt down the rocker arms as usual, removing the slack from the valvetrain (zero out the lash). Place the dial indicator atop the retainer on the test spring and zero it out.

5 The dial indicator measures valve lift as you turn over the engine by hand (via the crank bolt). Using the cam card, you know the open and closing times at .050-inch cam lift. When the dial hits .050, you stop rotating the engine and record the number that the pointer is indicating on the degree wheel (140 degrees in this case).

6 Now that you have the opening number, you need to rotate the engine until you hit .050 again to get the closing number (79 degrees in this case). These numbers should be within 1 degree of what the cam card says.

7 If you add the intake opening before TDC plus 180 degrees of crank rotation and the intake closing point, you get the degrees of duration at .050. After comparing this to the cam card, you can check the centerline. If you divide 260 degrees by 2 less than the intake opening (as calculated in Step 5), it should give you the centerline, which matches the cam card (109.75 in this case). Repeat the same process on the other valve, so that you have both intake and exhaust numbers.

8 To determine piston-to-valve clearance, start at 15 degrees before top dead center (BTDC) and push the valve until it hits the piston, then zero out the dial indicator. Ideally you use a solid lifter or an old set of lifters that are converted to solid when doing this to get a more accurate reading.

ENGINE BUILDS AND SWAPS

9 When you release the valve, you have a clearance measurement. Move at 5-degree increments until you hit 15 degrees after top dead center (ATDC). Repeat the same process on the exhaust valve.

Rocker Trunnion Upgrade

All photos for this project are courtesy of Joseph Potak.

Perhaps by now you have heard about rocker trunnions but are not quite sure what they are or why you need them. The term "trunnion" actually is derived from French and was used to describe the pivoting mechanism on a cannon. On a rocker arm, it is also the pivot point.

The body pivots on the trunnion as it is being pushed by the pushrod to, in turn, push on the valvespring. As such, with high RPM and high spring pressure, factory trunnions are prone to failure. Worse yet, OEM needle bearings are loose within the powdered-metal trunnion. When they do fail, the needle bearings get into the oil and circulate through the engine. The damage can be catastrophic. Comp Cams offers an upgrade to factory trunnions with an 8620 steel alloy and caged roller bearings (PN 13702-KIT).

Thus you can reduce cost while taking advantage of the light yet stiff factory rocker arm bodies, even with a high-lift cam. This may have been unthinkable on previous generations of the small-block Chevy, but the Gen III, IV, and even V all come well equipped from the factory. It just takes a little massaging and they can work perfectly well on even a 7-second drag car.

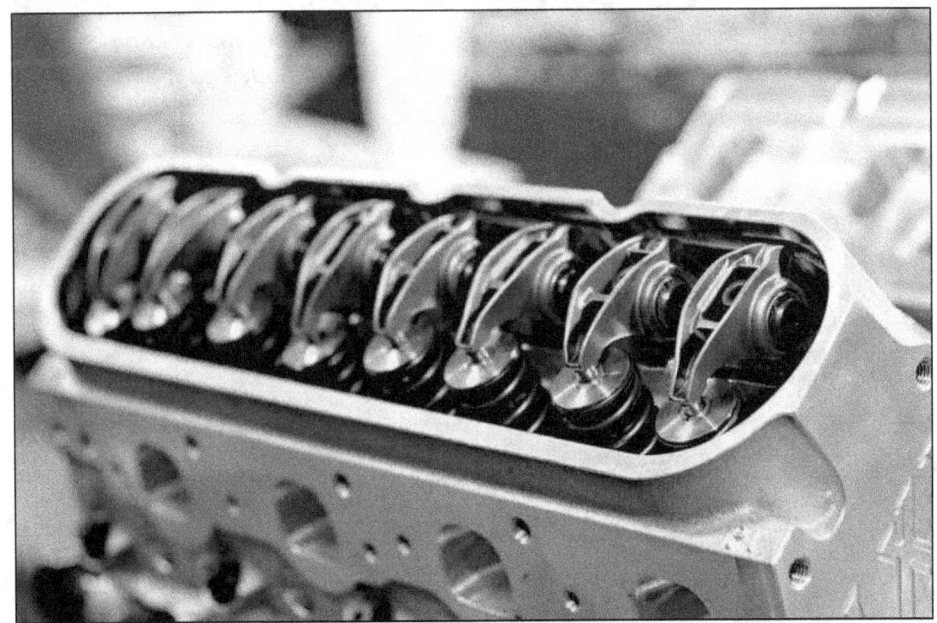

Rocker trunnions are sometimes an overlooked detail of LS engines but a major liability that can cost you thousands. Opinions vary on the amount of lobe lift that requires a trunnion upgrade, but it is great insurance on any LS engine with an aftermarket camshaft.

CHAPTER 5

2 OEM trunnions have loose needles inside the bearings, instead of a captured roller bearing such as with the Comp Cams versions. The trunnion shaft also has a smaller diameter and uses a cap to secure it, rather than a snap ring. The Comp version is superior in every way, including the material, 8620 steel alloy versus powdered metal.

1 Step one is to remove the OEM trunnion. A hydraulic press is the optimum method. Use a drift to push on the trunnion shaft and the bearing pops out on one side, then flips over. Insert the trunnion shaft again to punch out the second bearing.

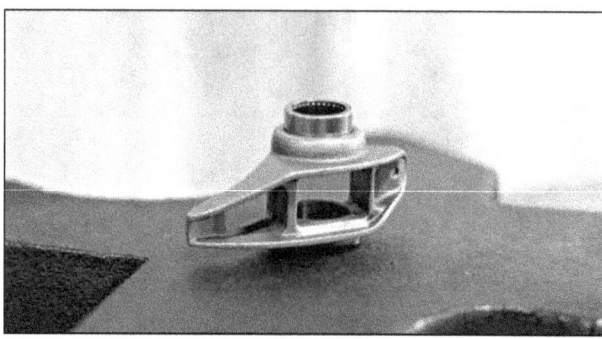

3 To install the Comp Cams rocker trunnions, set the bearings in place.

4 Use a hydraulic press to set the bearing into the rocker body.

5 Flip over the rocker and slide the trunnion shaft into place.

6 Set the second bearing atop the rocker body and then press it in.

7 Finally use the snap rings to secure the trunnion shaft.

ENGINE BUILDS AND SWAPS

The finished product is a reliable and affordable alternative that fits any LS rocker body from the LS3/L99 to the LS7, LSA, and LS9. Kits are already available for the Gen V LT1/LT4 if you're looking forward to the Gen 6.

In time for the 2015 SEMA Show, Powerhouse Products (a Comp Cams subsidiary) came out with this Rocker Arm Trunnion Upgrade Tool (PN 54702-TL) to simplify the installation. Powerhouse says you can upgrade a rocker in less than 30 minutes, and it only costs about $35. The tool is designed to work with an arbor press, bench vise, and C-clamp.

RHS LS7 Build

Using OEM components such as an LS7 block and heads, you can make upward of 650 hp naturally aspirated. However, it does require a quality CNC program for the cylinder heads, a properly selected camshaft, and all the supporting components, such as intake manifold, headers, and cold-air intake. AntiVenom Racing demonstrated just such a build for its own 2010 Camaro SS project car.

The LS3 had previously been upgraded with RHS LS7 heads, GM LS7 intake, Futral Motorsports camshaft, American Racing 1-7/8-inch headers, Fastlane cold-air intake, and ATI Performance underdrive balancer. AntiVenom had planned to use a re-sleeved LS7 block and Scat rotating assembly for a 430-ci bottom end for Phase 2 of the build. However, after assembly it became apparent that the block had a hairline crack and it was decided to upgrade to an RHS block.

In the process it gave me the opportunity to show an OEM-based approach, as well as a full aftermarket with all the bells and whistles. If a smoother idle and quiet valvetrain is your style, stick with the former rather than the latter.

AntiVenom chose the RHS block for its 2010 Camaro SS after discovering a leak in the freshly built LS7. The leak turned out to be a cracked head, but the upgrade helps achieve the desired goal of 600 rwhp naturally aspirated. It is hard to imagine such a feat 10 years ago with a street-going small-block of this size and manner.

If you intend to use an LS7 block with your factory oil pan, you need to drill through the side of the block for a dipstick hole. This guide plate from Tech AFX bolts up to the oil pan rail, so that you drill in the exact right spot. The stock dipstick and oil pan, as well as other oiling components, bolt right up.

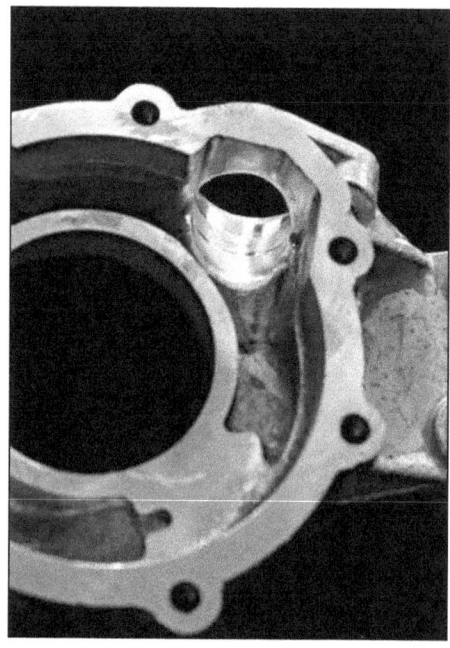

If you plan to purchase a new oil pump, you have a few options. The Chevrolet Performance High Volume Oil Pump (PN 17801830) shown here, is very cost effective, at less than $90, and can be ported to increase flow. The entrance is where you want to pay the most attention with porting and polishing. For a forced-induction build, the LSA pump or Melling high-volume pump might be a better option.

For a max-effort street engine, as well as many race engines, a double-roller timing set is essential. The factory single-roller type stretches and wears out over time. Add in higher RPM and you are inviting slop between the camshaft and crank, which can throw off the timing. This Comp Cams piece (PN 7106) is adjustable, too, in 2-degree increments for a total of 8 degrees advance/retard. The only downside to using a beefy timing set is that it requires additional clearance to the timing cover, which can be done with basic porting tools.

1 *The OEM lower timing chain gear can be used to press on the double-roller gear. With a few blows of a mallet, you can finish it off. When it is properly seated, the sound changes to something more metallic. Afterward, shims provided in the kit are needed for the oil pump.*

ENGINE BUILDS AND SWAPS

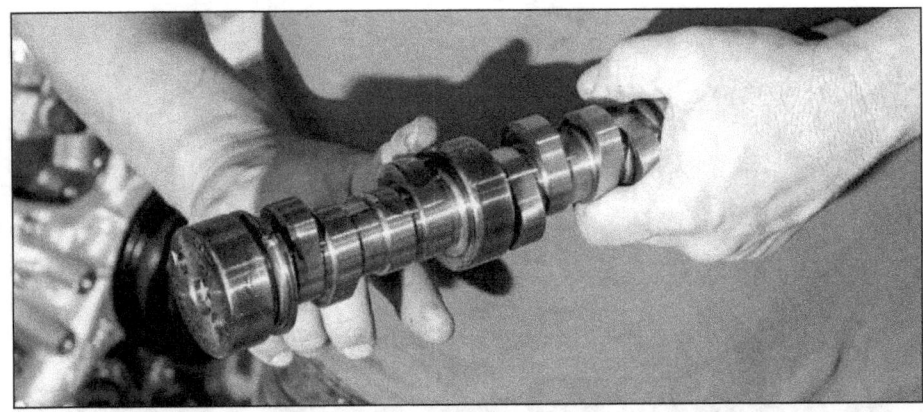

2 This cam came from Brian Tooley Racing and was treated to Comp Cams assembly lube prior to installation. The camshaft is one of the most crucial things to consider in any build. It ultimately determines the street manners and the overall power capability.

3 After the cam is carefully inserted into the block, it is torqued down the retainer plate with 18 ft-lbs.

4 Install the factory timing chain dampener (PN 1258860) after the cam gear and chain, which you also torque with 18 ft-lbs. The sprocket on the camshaft is typically 26 ft-lbs, but it depends on the fastener and timing set. Red Loctite is essential on the cam sprocket.

5 Line up the partially disassembled oil pump on the crank snout, using the shims to space it correctly. On the main caps you can see that this engine was assembled with ARP studs, and nearly the whole engine uses ARP fasteners. They are reusable and have greater tensile strength than OEM counterparts.

6 Because this engine uses Brian Tooley's Stage IV Naturally Aspirated LS7 camshaft, Comp Cams Short-Travel Race Hydraulic Lifters (PN 15956-16) were chosen for the ultimate high-RPM capability. These lifters are sort of like a stopgap between a typical hydraulic roller lifter and a solid roller. By minimizing the internal piston movement, these lifters have more reliable positioning as they "pump up" to enable greater RPM capability and more power. You may also notice that these use a link-bar instead of the factory plastic lifter guides.

7 After you bolt the clearanced timing cover and a new rear cover in place, transfer the oil pan, ATI balancer, RHS LS7 heads, and LS7 rockers from the LS3 to the new short-block. Using ARP moly lube to apply an even torque, give the head studs 25 ft-lbs, then 50 ft-lbs, then 70 ft-lbs from the middle out. ARP bolts eliminate the clumsy torque-to-yield procedure.

8 The easiest way to install an engine into the fifth-gen is from the bottom, placing the K-member and front suspension on a mobile yet heavy-duty metal cart. The engine mounts bolt up to the engine, which you can lower onto the K-member with a cherry picker.

9 It is important to consider clutch choice when dropping in a stroker. This car needed to upgrade from an aftermarket single-disc to this Quarter Master dual-disc. Thankfully this engine had a traditional LS crankshaft, but if this were an LSX or LS9 crate engine, a different flywheel would be needed. Pay close attention to the clearance from the fingers of the pressure plate to the edge of the bellhousing so you have optimum clearance for the slave cylinder to collapse and extend properly.

ENGINE BUILDS AND SWAPS

10 With the clutch, transmission, headers, and all accessories bolted-up, use a lift to lower the chassis carefully. This process requires constant checking at all areas to make sure something isn't caught or being pinched. With a handful of small alignment adjustments, bolt the K-member to the frame rails and the struts to the spindles.

For Phase 2, I chose an RHS LS Race Block. The A357-T6 aluminum block is quite a bit beefier in all the right places and made to accommodate a variety of applications, such as wet- or dry-sump, Gen III or IV, etc. Although it can be purchased fully machined for a 4.125- or 4.165-inch bore, AntiVenom elected to have the block machined locally in order to reuse the Scat rotating assembly for a 4.135-inch bore.

This Ampco 45 bronze cam thrust plate is one of many really nice features of the RHS block. Obviously the cam does quite a bit of rotating, so having a material that is designed specifically for abrasive wear is more ideal. Another is a raised cam centerline, which requires two extra links on the timing chain (available through Comp) and better accommodates longer stroke cranks.

The RHS block has provisions for piston oil squirters cast into the block, which do not interfere with longer strokes either (unlike the factory LSA and LS9 blocks). The press-in spun cast-iron cylinder liners are also quite a bit longer than factory blocks, topping out at 5.87 inches with the standard deck.

The main caps are a huge upgrade, which are made of billet steel and have improved windage over even the LS7 and LSX block. The main cap surface area has been maximized at the mating surface, with large fillets to support the cross-bolts. RHS chills the main bearing bulkheads for additional strength.

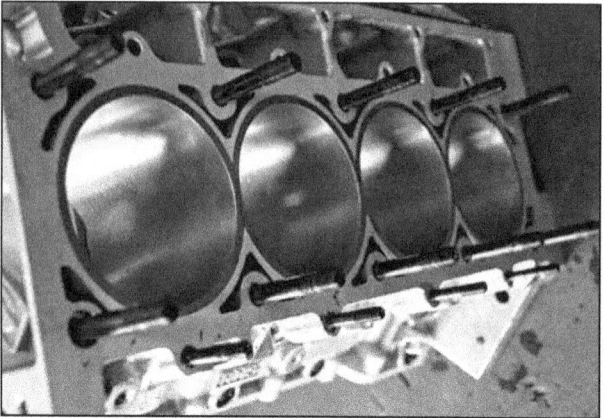

The RHS block has Siamese-cast bore walls, such as the LS7, which was originally started on the C5R and allows for such a large bore. The more obvious difference when looking at the top of the block is the extra head bolts. You can see an outer bolt in the center of the cylinder, plus an inner one you can't see. The increased clamping is essential with boost or nitrous.

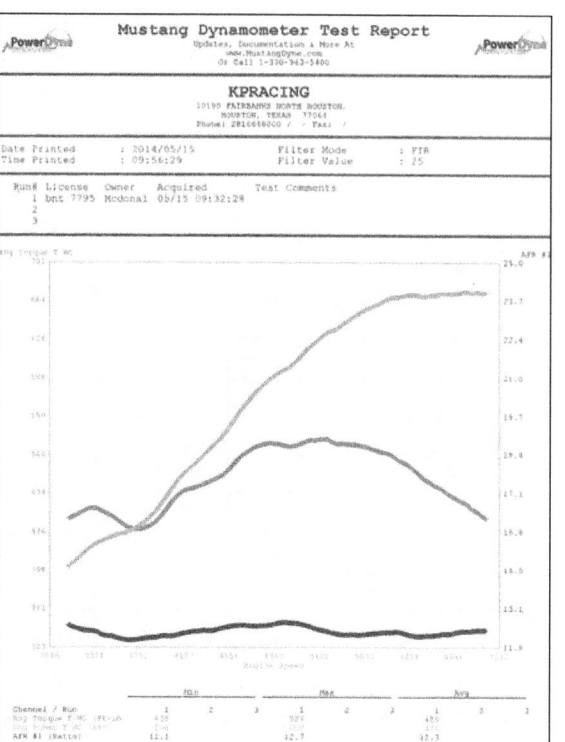

The Camaro did not make it on the dyno by press time; however, this graph is from a Corvette Z06 built by KP Racing with the same cam and otherwise similar combo. Although the Corvette has a more efficient drivetrain, it is still sporting a stock intake manifold, throttle body, and bottom end. AntiVenom hopes to achieve the same 600-rwhp on pump gas using BTR's 246/254-duration cam with a 111 LSA. This cam is not for those who want a smooth idle and low-end torque. It requires a hefty spring package, too, with .652/.630-inch lift and peaks around 7,000 rpm. It's definitely a screamer.

If you don't mind a little extra valvetrain noise, a gear drive is superior to even a double chain timing set. There is no chain flutter or backlash to affect valve timing. The gears simply mesh together to turn. This one is specific to the RHS LS Race Block (PN 5494); however, there is a version for standard LS blocks. Both are based on the award-winning LS Sprint Car Gear Drive.

CHAPTER 6

POWER ADDERS

In Chapter 5, I touched on some of the engine upgrades often needed for power adders. The stock LS3, L99, ZL1, and (to a lesser extent) even the LS7 can handle moderate levels of forced induction. As boost and nitrous levels increase, various components, such as pistons and rods, must be replaced accordingly. As I discuss various forced-induction methods, I also discuss what is and is not appropriate for a stock engine. Keep in mind, though, that these estimations are not foolproof. A bad tune, bad tank of gas, bad fuel pump, or other failures could easily result in severe carnage.

Conservative ignition timing and air/fuel ratios that are a full point or more rich are recommended when switching from naturally aspirated to forced induction such as nitrous, supercharger, or turbocharger systems. The basic principle with any forced-induction method is to increase the amount of oxygen in the combustion chamber, which then needs to be combined with an appropriate level of fuel and spark (with the correct timing) to produce more power. In other words, increasing the amount of oxygen allows you to burn more fuel, which results in more horsepower and torque.

Nitrous

As early as 1914, scientists have known about nitrous oxide's potential to enhance gasoline burning mechanisms such as a rocket or internal combustion engine. The Luftwaffe aircraft used during World War II, for example, injected nitrous to improve high-altitude performance. If you've been to the dragstrip, you know that nitrous can increase the altitude of your car as well, with sufficient traction.

Two parts nitrogen and one part oxygen make up a nitrous oxide molecule, which is not flammable at low pressure and temperature. In a 5-, 10-, 12-, or 15-pound bottle typically stowed in the trunk, nitrous is a compressed liquid. As the solenoids open, nitrous flows throw the orifice (limited by the jets), evaporates, and expands. The change of phase from

Forced induction offers many advantages over naturally aspirated. Whether you choose a supercharger, turbocharger, or nitrous, you have the potential to make more power and with a more docile, livable combination. (Photo Courtesy Joseph Potak)

CHAPTER 6

Nitrous oxide is typically thought to be the cheapest form of forced induction, though that is not necessarily the case as the initial cost savings is negated with every bottle fill-up. For typical street cars, a wet kit that uses a plate between the throttle body and intake is ideal. A plate is not only easy to install, but it provides excellent atomization and distribution to all cylinders. This NOS wet kit (PN 05169NOS) comes with a 10-pound bottle, nitrous plate, fuel and nitrous solenoids, jetting for 100/125/150 hp, braided stainless steel lines, micro-switch, and a blow-down tube. (Photo Courtesy Nitrous Oxide Systems)

The original ZEX 2010-Current V8 Camaro Blackout Nitrous System (PN 82380B) uses a nozzle to spray the wet nitrous mixture but can be upgraded with the plate. The advantage of the nozzle is that it keeps cost down and works with a larger aftermarket throttle body. The downside is that it adds complication to the installation, requiring a hard intake tube for plumbing the nozzle; the closer to the throttle body the better. (Photo Courtesy ZEX)

a liquid to a gas causes a drop in air temperature within the intake manifold and intake runner that results in a denser, more oxygen-packed charge of air entering the chamber. After it enters the chamber, nitrous oxide breaks down at 565 to 575 degrees, releasing the oxygen (36 percent of its weight) that allows the engine to burn more fuel and increasing the cylinder pressure during the compression stroke, causing the piston to return faster.

The essential parts of any nitrous system include a bottle, braided stainless steel lines with fittings, a solenoid, a nozzle of some type with jets to limit the flow, and some method of activating the solenoid. Two types of systems are available: wet and dry.

A dry system injects nitrous only, whereas a wet system has solenoids and nozzles for fuel enrichment as well. On a dedicated drag car, a dry system is typically preferred to be used with an EFI system for more precise fueling. There are many drawbacks to running a dry system on a street car, which is why you find few if any vehicle-specific kits. Nitrous would have to be injected prior to the MAF sensor to get a reliable reading on the added fuel needed, which has its limitations. Otherwise, a separate tune would need to be uploaded prior to spraying nitrous to account for the extra fuel as well as the retarded ignition timing.

A wet kit is generally more reliable in providing the fuel enrichment required, which means you need only modify the ignition timing prior to spraying. A product such as Lingenfelter's LNC-2000 allows you to drive around on the regular naturally aspirated tune and retard the timing by simply turning a knob when you arrive at the track. A

ZEX recently released a GM LS Perimeter Plate Conversion Kit (PN 82039). The benefits of this design include multiple injection points that fire the atomized mixture into the center of the intake plenum at an optimized angle and an engineered shape that creates a low-pressure area to enhance airflow. ZEX also says the design of the internal passages helps use the -127 degree temperature to cool the incoming air. (Photo Courtesy ZEX)

If you have upgraded to an aftermarket throttle body, you may want to check out one of Nitrous Outlet's kits. Because this company is a true plug-and-play manufacturer, it offers kits for every variation, including 102-mm FAST LSXR and MSD Atomic AirForce intakes, as well as standard Camaro SS 90-mm, ZL1, and even Magnuson supercharged 90-mm. The 2010 and later Camaro 102-mm FAST Intake Plate System (PN 00-10119-102) comes with everything you need to add 50 to 200 hp, connect to stock fuel rails, and even mount the solenoids. (Photo Courtesy Nitrous Outlet)

In a nitrous system, the solenoid basically stops the flow of nitrous (or enrichment fuel) to the engine until it is activated electronically. Each manufacturer typically has a proprietary design with varying features. This NOS Pro-Shot uses a PTFE plug puck with a 1/8-inch orifice, 1/4-inch inlet, and 1/8-inch outlet to support up to 400 hp. For the high-powered solenoids, including the Super Big Shot and Pro-Bigshot, the orifice jumps to 5/32 and 1/4 inch, respectively. (Photo Courtesy Nitrous Oxide Systems)

These stainless steel NOS jets aren't necessarily compatible with nozzles or plates from other brands. In fact, many others use brass jets. Most kits come with all the jets you need, but if you have a custom system, a pack with various sizes is a good investment. (Photo Courtesy Nitrous Oxide Systems)

100- to 175-shot requires a minimal amount of ignition retard (2 degrees for every 50 hp), which is not optimum but certainly acceptable for normal driving. So you could easily get away with driving around with the nitrous tune, whereas with a dry kit the car would be pig-rich and possibly do damage to the rings. Wet kits also do not tax the fuel injectors, so there is no concern for injector sizing and duty cycle.

Nitrous oxide has gotten a bad rap over the years for being dangerous. It is no more dangerous than any other power adder when used appropriately. Secondhand parts (in poor condition), lack of safety equipment, improper tuning, and greedy users are among the most frequent causes of nitrous mishaps. Too much ignition timing, not enough fuel, and too much nitrous can all result in a very bad day. An application-specific kit from Nitrous Outlet, for example, comes with jets for a 50- to 200-shot, which is the most nitrous recommended with an SS.

CHAPTER 6

A blow-down tube is required to be NHRA legal. Should there be excessive pressure in the bottle, the valve can relieve it without filling the cockpit with flammable gas thanks to this handy little piece of tubing. The downside is that you have to drill a hole in the floor. (Photo Courtesy Nitrous Oxide Systems)

Bottle heaters are a wise investment to maintain optimum bottle pressure no matter what climate you live. Most (such as NOS PN 14164NOS) are basically an electronic blanket; however, some offer a bottle bracket with a heater built in. These have a much cleaner look, but opinions vary on whether they are as effective. (Photo Courtesy Nitrous Oxide Systems]

Nitrous bottles are available in various sizes from 2-pound inexpensive bottles up to 20 pounders. These are 10- and 15-pound bottles next to each other. The weight refers to the quantity of nitrous oxide the bottle can contain, not the dry weight of the bottle. Each bottle has a limited lifespan, specified by the certification. Nitrous Outlet has a bottle exchange program to rid the industry of old, unsafe bottles still being used. Having seen too many injuries and even deaths as the result, the company offers credit on the purchase of a new bottle. (Photo Courtesy Nitrous Outlet)

The V-6, Z/28, and ZL1 are best limited to 150 or lower. You may be wondering why someone would use nitrous on a factory supercharged car. Rather than spending thousands to modify the ZL1's TVS1900 or replace it altogether with a larger supercharger, many have used nitrous to provide additional cooling. Most nitrous kits on the market for fifth-gen applications use a plate that is sandwiched between the throttle body and intake manifold.

Manufacturers include ZEX, Nitrous Outlet, Nitrous Express, Ny-Trex, and NOS. Their kits offer easy installation and excellent atomization on average. Both factory-sized throttle bodies, as well as aftermarket 102-mm openings, are supported.

For larger shots of nitrous, a direct-port system can be more

Purge kits are usually available separately; they are a nice upgrade. In addition to letting everyone know that your car has nitrous, a purge kit clears the nitrous line of air so that you have a more immediate hit. It is also a handy way to ensure that the system is working when testing the switches. (Photo Courtesy Nitrous Oxide Systems)

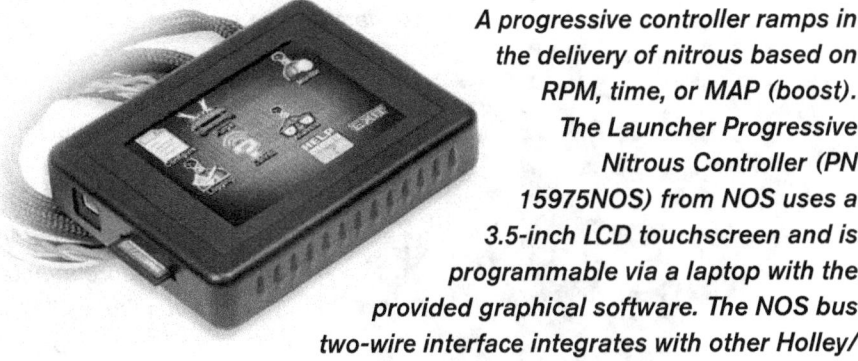

A progressive controller ramps in the delivery of nitrous based on RPM, time, or MAP (boost). The Launcher Progressive Nitrous Controller (PN 15975NOS) from NOS uses a 3.5-inch LCD touchscreen and is programmable via a laptop with the provided graphical software. The NOS bus two-wire interface integrates with other Holley/NOS products, such as Holley EFI, and it has its own SD card slot for data logging without a laptop and saving various configuration files that you can swap on the fly. (Photo Courtesy Nitrous Oxide Systems)

A window switch is another great investment, as it prevents the nitrous system from spraying in between shifts and helps dial in your launch. MSD's RPM Activated Window Switch (PN 8956) is basically the originator, which lets you set a single low- and high-RPM limit. MSD also offers a digital version (PN 8969) designed specifically for late-model engines. (Photo Courtesy MSD Performance)

effective and ensure proper distribution to each cylinder. These custom systems add quite a bit of cost to the equation given the increased amount of plumbing, solenoids, and nozzles. The intake manifold needs to be drilled for the nitrous nozzles and lines need to be fabricated, so this isn't for the novice builder. For the ZL1, Nitrous Outlet offers a system that places a plate in between the lid and supercharger. Although the system is costly, it is considerably easier to install.

Speaking of cost, another misconception with nitrous is that it is less expensive than other forms of forced induction. In reality that isn't the case. The initial buy-in is certainly cheaper, but with every bottle refill the difference between nitrous and boost is much smaller. And your basic $500 to $600 nitrous kit probably does not include everything you need. A wide-open throttle (WOT) switch is essential to arm the nitrous system with the Camaro's electronic throttle. A window switch also helps determine the RPM in which the nitrous activates and deactivates. This helps keep your engine safe and helps you optimize traction.

Progressive controllers take this one step further by actually limiting

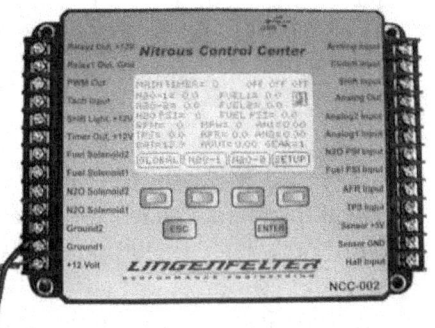

Although Lingenfelter's NCC-002 Nitrous Control Center (L460240000) does not have a touchscreen, it has just as many functions. In the right hands, this is a very capable piece of hardware. It features two independent progressive stages of nitrous and fuel control, independent control of nitrous and fuel duty cycle for each stage, a programmable voltage output for data acquisition, linking to the LNC-2000 timing retard, and much more. (Photo Courtesy Lingenfelter Performance Engineering)

Although a standard plate kit as you'd use on an SS model works on the ZL1, Nitrous Outlet offers this unique Supercharger Blower Plate System that flows up to 380 hp with jetting from 100 to 300 hp. The plate sits between the lid and the supercharger itself for optimum distribution, atomization, and flow. Although this example has the CTS-V–style lid, a different version is available for the ZL1 (PN 00-10174). (Photo Courtesy Nitrous Outlet)

Beyond plate kits, the next step is a direct-port system, which places nozzles next to each fuel injector in the intake manifold. This alleviates any concern for distribution and allows the maximum amount of flow. Although the plumbing is much more substantial, a Nitrous Outlet 8-Cylinder 4-Solenoid Direct Port System with Dual Injection Rails (PN 00-10474-L-R) flows up to 800 hp of nitrous, though it comes with 100- to 400-hp jetting. (Photo Courtesy Nitrous Outlet)

the flow of nitrous through the solenoid until full traction. The added complication adds cost, but they also take the place of window switches. NOS makes some of the best on the market, which also happen to be affordable.

Often used for class racing, direct-port kits are not allowed except in the upper echelons. In addition, they incur significant cost. A more traditional plate kit, as you'd use with a carburetor, is often used with classes such as Ultra Street or Real Street. The Nitrous Outlet Puck System is the first major innovation in years for this type of plate system. The 360-degree delivery from the center of the intake plenum gives it the best possible distribution. (Photo Courtesy Nitrous Outlet)

Bottle pressure is also essential to safety and proper operation, so having a liquid-filled gauge on the bottle itself is a great investment. Around 900 pounds is optimal, and in colder temperatures (below 80 degrees F) you need a bottle warmer to hit 900 pounds. Under no circumstances should you use a blowtorch to heat a bottle. In fact, you should replace bottles periodically to avoid a senseless tragedy. To prevent bottle explosions when the pressure is too high, you should also purchase a blow-down tube. The NHRA, as well as other sanctioning bodies, require it.

A purge kit helps clear air out of the line for a stronger initial hit, and to let everyone know you are packing nitrous. It's nice to have and looks cool, but it's not essential. The same goes for an auxiliary pressure gauge inside the cabin and remote bottle opener. A standalone fuel tank for the nitrous system can be another "nice to have" item with larger shots. It removes the strain on your in-tank fuel pump, so you can stick with a stock fuel pump yet spray 200 to 400 hp or more of nitrous. It is more reliable at maintaining pressure during activation when the pressure tends to drop at the fuel rail, which could lean out the air/fuel. It also allows you to use race gas as enrichment (without retuning) for added safety. Universal and application-specific kits are available.

Superchargers

Like nitrous, superchargers were invented for other purposes, but soon found their way onto internal combustion engines. Gottlieb Daimler received the German patent in 1885 for the Roots blower, and two supercharged Mercedes models were introduced in 1921. Meanwhile, Luis Renault patented the centrifugal supercharger in 1902, which found use in aircraft during World War II. Robert Paxton McCulloch and Paxton Superchargers were influential in bringing about automotive use for the centrifugal with the 1954–1955 Kaiser Manhattan, 1957 Studebaker Golden Hawk, Ford Thunderbird F-Type, Packard Clipper, and 1958 Packard Hawk.

The first screw-type compressor was patented in 1878, but many of the breakthroughs needed to make it practical came later, including the patents of Alf Lysholm starting in 1935.

Essentially, any supercharger is an air compressor that is directly or indirectly driven by the engine's crankshaft. The size of the pulleys (with a belt-driven blower), the blower's internal gear ratio, and the design of the compressor determine how many pounds of boost are generated per engine rotation. Atmospheric pressure at sea level is 14.7 psi, so every psi of boost adds to the absolute pressure. At elevation the atmospheric pressure decreases; however, boost is mostly fixed. So while the absolute pressure may decrease, boost remains the same. Temperature, on the other

POWER ADDERS

hand, can affect boost due to the difference in air density.

Roots Superchargers

Roots and hybrid Roots superchargers are known as positive displacements. This is an engineering term that is often used to describe pumps. A fixed amount of air is trapped in the cavity and then forced out via the rotors. Positive displacement pumps are considered constant-flow machines because they can theoretically produce the same flow at any RPM, though in practice that isn't the case. Nevertheless, they produce boost much sooner in the RPM band than other methods. The Roots and hybrid Roots superchargers use two intermeshing lobes inside the casing.

By the time the 2010 Camaro SS was released, the industry had come a long way from the ancient 4-71 and 6-71 blowers that General Motors

The Magnuson TVS2300 uses the Eaton four-lobe high-helix rotors with 160 degrees of twist inside its proprietary high-flow housing. The original Camaro design uses a jackshaft to propel the rear drive, along with an open plenum and a large liquid-to-air intercooler directly below the rotors. A straight airflow path is provided by the 180-degree rotation of the rotors and front entry. A front-mounted heat exchanger, intercooler reservoir, and pump are the few parts external to the blower, which helps make for an easier install. (Photo Courtesy Joseph Potak)

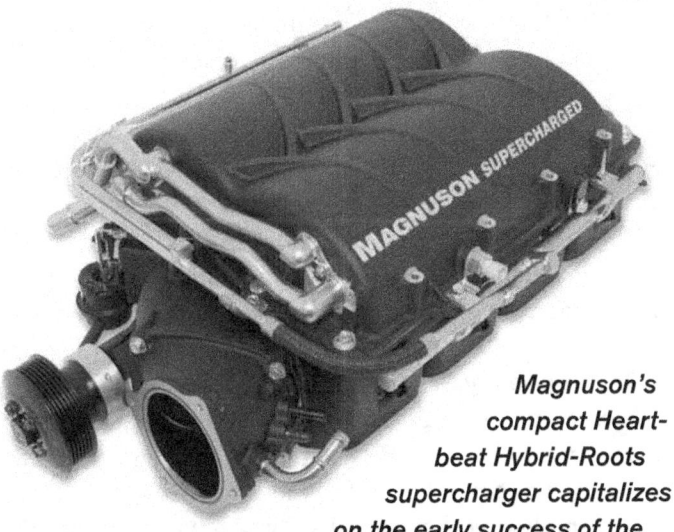

Magnuson's compact Heartbeat Hybrid-Roots supercharger capitalizes on the early success of the original blower by reversing the orientation, placing the rotors at the bottom and the intercoolers on top, as does the OEM Eaton. Instead of using a jackshaft with cog gears and a belt at the back, the pulley directly drives the rotors. Magnuson says the Heartbeat makes 25 hp more than the standard TVS2300 and 46 hp more than its competitors. (Photo Courtesy Magnuson)

SLP's TVS2300 (PN 92000A) uses a direct drive at the front of the supercharger to eliminate the jackshaft, extra bearings, pulleys, and rear belt. The rotors are still at the top of the housing with a port-matched intake manifold below and a large intercooler. This kit is 50-state legal and boosts power to 575 hp with the LS3, and 550 hp with the L99. (Photo Courtesy SLP Performance)

used on diesels. The Eaton Twin Vortices Series (TVS) supercharger uses two high-helix four-lobe rotors that are twisted 160 degrees. It was a huge leap forward in efficiency from previous designs, which made it the go-to for OEMs, and the aftermarket followed.

Edelbrock, Magnuson, and SLP all use the Eaton TVS rotor package inside their proprietary designs, as well as the ZL1's LSA. The inlet and outlet design of the supercharger housing has proven to drastically affect performance. There is some debate on how much impact the intake manifold has, as some blowers use an open design, flowing right out of the blower and into an open plenum to the cylinder heads. Others, such as the Edelbrock version, actually have tuned intake runner lengths.

Another notable difference is that some suck air in through the top and blow down through the intercooler and into the runners (like the ZL1), while others suck air in through the bottom and blow up through the intercoolers. Edelbrock was the first to use the latter design, but Magnuson has since followed with the HeartBeat. Thus far, testing has proven that the front-drive HeartBeat performs much better than Magnuson's previous rear-drive design.

Although nearly all aftermarket supercharger kits use the Eaton TVS2300 rotors (such as the 2009–2013 Corvette ZR1's LS9), the ZL1's factory LSA supercharger uses the smaller TVS1900 rotors. Just as with an engine, there is no replacement for displacement. The 1.9L blower can't compare to the potential of the 2.3L, which is exactly why Magnuson offers a HeartBeat TVS2300 conversion.

Lingenfelter went another route in developing a front cover that bolts to an LS9 supercharger while running the Camaro's accessory drive system. During testing, boost went from 8 to 12 psi (using the same pulleys), while boasting an improvement of 87 hp and 105 ft-lbs of torque with a modified engine. The beauty of this system is that it also allows you to easily retrofit the 638-hp LS9 crate engine into your Camaro.

Edelbrock introduced a new top and coil cover design in 2014. Functionally it is the same as this, with a pair of Eaton TVS rotors and 2.3L of displacement. The Edelbrock E-Force blower was designed to fit under the stock hood, and its compact design is similar to OEM blowers. It is reliable and has excellent belt wrap, so that you don't have to worry about belt slip. (Photo Courtesy Edelbrock)

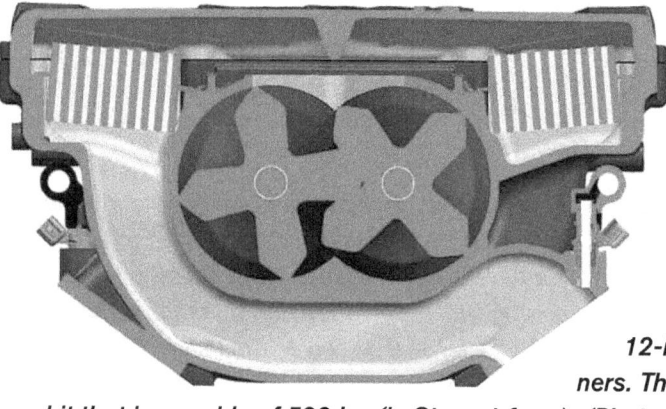

The front-entry Edelbrock blower places the rotors at the bottom, which blow air up through twin high-capacity bar and plate intercoolers and into 12-inch-long intake runners. This is a 50-state-legal kit that is capable of 599 hp (in Stage 1 form). (Photo Courtesy Edelbrock)

Screw-Type Superchargers

Screw-type superchargers can also be used as a bolt-on upgrade to the factory LSA supercharger or another means of adding boost to the SS. Like the Roots, the twin-screw design is a positive displacement type, but instead of paddling the air into the engine with two identical rotors it uses male and female screws. Whipple uses three lobes on the male rotor and five

POWER ADDERS

Alf Lysholm was the inventor of twin-screw supercharging. Although the concept is similar to the Roots-style Eaton supercharger, the difference is that screw-type blowers are compressors. In contrast to having rotors that paddle air in and build pressure as a function of resistance to flow, screw-type blowers compress the air trapped between two intermeshing screws. The Lysholm kit makes 580 hp on the LS3 and 550 hp on the L99 with 7 to 9 psi; however, it is capable of more than 700 hp with higher boost levels and other modifications. (Photo Courtesy Lysholm Technologies)

on the female. Kenne Bell uses four on the male and six on the female. Although there is radial symmetry that allows the two screws to mesh, they are laterally asymmetric, hence the different number of lobes.

The volume between the lobes actually compresses the air by moving from a larger volume to a smaller one before reaching the output. A Roots blower, by comparison, is just an air mover and uses the resistance to flow to create pressure. The precision required for machining the screws to fit so tightly together tends to make them more expensive. However, their inherent design is more efficient. It takes less power to turn the supercharger, also known as parasitic loss. Most proponents say there is no loss in bottom-end power with better performance on the top end and less heat.

In a Roots supercharger, the internal leakage between each rotor and the natural reversion from the manifold to the casing works against itself as it progresses through the RPM band, which accounts for the boost drop-off in the upper RPM and

Whipple is another huge player in the twin-screw business with more than 26 years of experience. It is the choice of Chevrolet Performance for the COPO program. The base 2.9L kit is 50-state legal, though there are plenty of upgrades available to increase the power, as well as tuner and hot rod kits. It uses a jackshaft (stainless steel or carbon fiber) with helical-cut gears instead of a belt for reliability. It fits under the factory hood with no modifications except with 2014–2015 models, which require modifying the OEM hood vent or the use of a Whipple vent. (Photo Courtesy Whipple Superchargers)

CHAPTER 6

Whipple prides itself on the size of its air-to-water intercooler, which uses a bar-and-plate design, and the air bypass (integrated into the plenum) that reduces burst knock. The 3 x 5 rotor combo, Whipple says, is superior to 4 x 6 designs used by other companies at airflow under the curve. By using a center-down discharge, you have less pressure loss, better distribution to all cylinders, and cooler operation. (Photo Courtesy Whipple Superchargers)

overall lack of adiabatic efficiency. Although the screw-type does not suffer this issue, its placement on top of the engine means that it is subject to the same heat-soak problems and the discharge temperature is not typically as cool as with a centrifugal, although you can get away with more compression than with a Roots-blown engine.

Three brands of twin-screw superchargers are available: Whipple, Kenne Bell, and Lysholm. Because of its initial invention, the technology went largely unused with both OEMs and aftermarket manufacturers until the late 1980s to early 1990s when Whipple and Kenne Bell stepped in. Lysholm Technologies was founded in 1995, but its roots go all the way back to Svenska Rotor Maskiner (SRM) and its chief engineer Alf Lysholm (hence the name).

SRM was one of the only manufacturers of screw compressors and an original supplier to companies such as Whipple. Since Lysholm was founded, it partnered with Eaton to develop the OEM supercharger for the Ford GT in 2004 and was later purchased by AirPower Group, which also owns Vortech Engineering and Paxton Automotive. Now Lysholm makes aftermarket systems to compete with the privately owned Whipple and Kenne Bell that made their bones boosting naturally aspirated engines and upgrading factory supercharged engines.

Lysholm's Camaro supercharger kit makes 580 hp with a stock LS3 and 550 hp with a stock L99 with a rear entry 2.3L design. Kenne Bell's offerings, however, are much more extensive, starting at 2.8L and also offering liquid-cooled 3.6L and 4.2L options for both the SS and ZL1. The larger units support more cubic inches and higher boost levels, as high as 30 psi. More than 1,000 hp has been made with a 3.6L blower set to 17 psi with pump gas. Of these three manufacturers, Whipple makes the only front-entry design, with just one size (2.9L) that supports more than 1,000 hp.

Chevrolet Performance also offers a rear-entry 4.0L Whipple developed for the COPO Camaro program. NCC Racing even makes a 4.5L kit for the truly insane. The NCC Racing version keeps all factory equipment in place, such as the windshield wipers, and is capable of 1,500 hp and more than 25 psi.

Centrifugal Superchargers

Because packaging isn't nearly as much of a concern as with positive displacement blowers, the potential of a centrifugal is nearly limitless. ProCharger's bad-boy F-3R-136, for example, is capable of 3,000 hp, 50 psi, and 4,000 cfm. You might have a difficult time fitting this in your street car, but it certainly illustrates the point.

Centrifugals are true compressors. An impeller compresses the air by adding velocity. Air is drawn into the snail-like compressor housing (volute) by the spinning impeller where the vanes of the impeller convert the low-pressure low-speed air into low-pressure high-speed air. A diffuser then converts that air into high-pressure low-speed, which is fed into the engine. Because a centrifugal spins at three to four times the speed of, say, a TVS2300, it needs its own transmission to apply a step-ratio (usually more than 3:1) capable of achieving that RPM from each engine revolution.

ProCharger offers self-contained lubrication for the gears and bearings exclusively; Vortech and Paxton have both self-contained models and those that require accessing engine oil. Self-contained oiling offers an easier installation, better reliability, and a more ideal choice of oil with less frictional loss and heat. It also does not transfer heat from the engine to the supercharger. The only drawback is (of course) having to change this oil every 6,000 miles. Much like the TVS series blower being much quieter than its predecessors, helical gear sets offer the same convenience with centrifugal blowers.

Centrifugal superchargers are by far the most efficient form of supercharging. Some experts say that a centrifugal takes around 30 percent less horsepower to drive than a Roots supercharger. And unlike a positive displacement blower, heat transfer is minimal from the engine to the supercharger.

Street-based centrifugal kits typically use an air-to-air intercooler, which is more effective than an air-to-water. Due to the design limits of positive displacement blowers, air-to-water (or more accurately air-to-water-to-air) intercoolers are the only option. So not only do

Vortech Superchargers offers several variations on this kit, including one that features the V-3 Si-Trim centrifugal supercharger. This gear-driven self-contained head unit can support up to 775 hp, but regularly boosts power to 581 hp on stock Camaros. The kit is upgradable to the V-7 YSI-trim blower with a cog drive, which is capable of 1,200 hp. The standard system uses a dedicated 10-rib supercharger drive with an automatic belt tensioner and SFI-approved balancer. (Photo Courtesy Vortech Superchargers)

If you think this kit looks similar to the Vortech kit, don't adjust your glasses. Paxton Superchargers is owned by the same parent company. The one major difference between the two kits is the head unit. Paxton employs the NOVI-1200SL, which is a self-lubricating supercharger capable of 775 hp and 1,150 cfm. Paxton says it adds 47 percent more horsepower at 6.5 to 7.5 psi, which equates to well over 500 rwhp. A 10-rib dedicated drive with an ATI Performance balancer allows for maximum belt traction and stability. (Photo Courtesy Paxton Superchargers)

ProCharger was early out of the gate with its intercooled P-1-SC-1 system that boasts a 50-percent horsepower gain thanks to 7 psi of boost through the three-core air-to-air intercooler. The supercharger and bracket come in satin, polished, and black. And a helical gear set is available for less supercharger whine and a more stealthy approach. The standard kit uses a 6-rib drive but can be upgraded to 8-rib or even 12-rib (or cog). (Photo Courtesy ATI ProCharger)

CHAPTER 6

they have lower discharge temperatures from the blower itself, but also even lower intake temperatures compared to positive displacement superchargers.

Critics of centrifugal superchargers say that the linear power delivery is too "peaky," and lacks low-end power. Although it will never compare to a positive displacement blower's off-idle grunt, a large portion of the boost lag can be offset by having properly matched parts. A stock or bolt-on Camaro SS, ZL1, or Z/28 is best matched to a ProCharger P-1SC or D-1SC supercharger. The Vortech V-3 SI, Paxton NOVI-1200, and Paxton NOVI-1500 are comparable units.

Although each of these companies offer kits that accommodate these blowers as well as some larger models, A&A Superchargers and East Coast Supercharging make their own to accommodate Paxton and Vortech head units. IPF Tuning even makes a kit for the V-6 using a Vortech V-3 SI.

With such a wide array of choices in supercharger kits, it is important to take into account several factors before purchasing. The size and placement of the intercooler, completeness of the kit, OEM parts removed or relocated, ability to upgrade, and the drive system vary greatly among them.

Some kits have a bad reputation over the years from throwing belts. This can be a concern with any supercharger; however, thankfully over the years the manufacturers have become much better at improving belt wrap. The better the belt wrap, the more traction it has. For higher boost levels and heavy-duty use, an upgrade from the factory 6-rib belt to an 8-, 10-, or even 12-rib is a welcome improvement.

ATI Performance, among others, manufactures balancer and pulley upgrades to fit most kits. The crank should be pinned with any supercharger to keep the balancer from spinning independent of the crank. A noisy cog drive is unnecessary except for dedicated race cars, though some still keep a 10-rib and have even logged 7-second quarter-mile times. A gear drive kit from ProCharger, Chris Alston Chassisworks, or The Supercharger Store eliminates any chance of belt slip; again, it is suitable for dedicated drag cars only.

Unlike nitrous or simply raising the compression, superchargers produce pressure through all four engine cycles. Thus supercharged engines ingest more air than a high-compression naturally aspirated combo by using the entire intake stroke, and unlike nitrous it aids in scavenging by blowing through the exhaust stroke. This key difference

ProCharger offers a kit for the Z/28, which starts with the Stage II P-1SC-1 set to 6.5 psi to add 120 hp. This is an eight-rib system built with road racing in mind and works with all the factory parts and pieces; no trimming or cutting. (Photo Courtesy ATI ProCharger)

ProCharger's revolutionary i-1 debuted on the fifth-gen and is perfectly suited to more stock-based Camaros that want up to 900 hp with the technology to create instant boost with a centrifugal supercharger. Instead of a set gear ratio (such as the 4.10 in the D-1SC), the i-1 uses a variable ratio, such as a CVT transmission, that optimizes on the fly for the desired performance. Using the included touchscreen, you can adjust the boost level and the way it ramps in for better acceleration, cruising, and safety when handing the keys to the valet. (Photo Courtesy ATI ProCharger)

drastically changes optimum camshaft and cylinder head specs, ignition, tuning, and many other areas. It is another example of how supercharging increases the volumetric efficiency of the engine, well beyond what is capable naturally aspirated.

Although some purists may prefer the "14.7 psi that God gave them," there's no way to make any engine (let alone an LS engine) big enough to surpass the performance of supercharging. Many are starting to believe the same about nitrous. In the LSX Challenge Series, for example, it has become evident that even the fastest nitrous cars can't compete with boost in the quarter- and perhaps even the eighth-mile with all else being equal.

Turbochargers

In appearance and operation, a turbocharger is much like a centrifugal supercharger. Of course, instead of being driven by the engine's crankshaft, a turbo is driven by a turbine placed into the flow of exhaust gas. As the turbine spins, so, too, does the shaft that connects it to the compressor. Unlike a centrifugal supercharger, there are no gears. The compressor spins at a 1:1 ratio to the turbine. Because it isn't driven by the crankshaft, there is no parasitic loss. However, being reliant on exhaust gas to produce boost is not without complication.

The turbo was invented as an alternative to supercharging and patented in 1905 by Alfred Büchi for use on diesel engines. It took 20 years to catch on in the aircraft industry, and even longer in the automotive industry. The high-temperature metals needed for a turbine proved to be a large obstacle. Many stigmas resulted from a lack of understanding and use.

For example, many consider heat to be a considerable issue with turbocharging, but it actually has a substantially better adiabatic efficiency than Roots superchargers. As the technology behind compressor design has improved, even less heat is transferred to the compressed air. With a quality intercooler, heat soak should be no more of an issue than with any form of boost.

Perhaps the biggest stigma about turbocharging is "turbo lag." And there is no doubt that this reputation was earned. Early turbos were crude by today's standards, particularly in the aftermarket. Unlike today, there was a lack of options initially, which forced users to adapt turbos intended for other purposes, rather than use a custom-designed setup.

The first passenger cars to be produced with a turbo were the 1962 Oldsmobile Jetfire Turbo and the Chevrolet Monza Spyder. A whopping 5 psi at just 2,200 rpm! Porsche and Saab followed suit in the 1970s before General Motors struck gold with the 1980s Buick Regal, T-type, and Grand National. These G-Bodies helped ignite the aftermarket turbo craze. As turbos became bigger and boost went higher, lag increased. Eventually manufacturers began offering more aspect ratios, more turbine and compressor combinations, more ball bearings to spin easier, and more efficient wheel designs. A modern turbo that is properly sized should not have excessive lag.

Of course, this is not an absolute statement. As the horsepower demands grow, twin-turbocharging becomes necessary to negate lag and eventually it becomes somewhat unavoidable. But, of course, those levels are reserved for full-on drag cars with high-stall converters, 2- and 3-speed transmissions, transbrakes, two-step rev limiters, and anti-lag. The diesel and import markets resort to compound boost to negate lag. A small turbo is run in-line with a larger turbo for top-end power. The compressor literally feeds the inducer of the larger turbo, and they even attach the turbine housings to decrease spool time. The boost multiplies instead of adding together, so 8 psi from one and 20 psi from another could be well over 30 psi total. Twin-scroll turbos can also help negate lag, although they are more prevalent in OEMs.

BMW has been a leader as of late, strategically pairing the exhaust from each cylinder to the two scrolls so that the exhaust pulses complement instead of interfere. BMW and Valeo (supplier of Audi) each have a stake in electric turbo technology that uses an electric motor to spin the compressor for instant spool-up, and could hit the market in late 2016.

The design of the turbo system as a whole can greatly affect performance and reliability. For example, if the hot-side piping is too large, it could make it difficult for the turbo to spool and reach the desired boost level (to say nothing of lag). Too small and it could cause excessive backpressure. Every turbo system must have an effective waste gate. Some are internal, common in OEM applications such as the Grand National, which means they are part of the turbocharger.

External waste gates are most common among custom systems and kits. A waste gate regulates the turbine, and the boost pressure in turn, by opening or closing its valve in the exhaust stream that feeds the

CHAPTER 6

Turbo manufacturer Turbonetics offers a CARB-legal single-turbo system for the 2010–2013 Camaro SS. Both full and tuner versions are available for the LS3 and L99, which are conservatively rated at 550 hp. Installation time is estimated at 12 to 15 hours and includes a Turbonetics T76 ceramic ball-bearing turbo, Spearco 26 x 11 x 4.5-inch air-to-air intercooler, two Turbonetics Evolution 35-mm waste gates, Turbosmart bypass valve, TIG-welded T304 stainless steel exhaust, aluminum charge pipes, 630-cc injectors, NGK TR6 plugs, and a DiabloSport programmer with a custom calibration for the CARB-legal version. (Photo Courtesy Turbonetics)

turbo. A spring determines the max boost pressure, which can be manipulated by a solenoid or carbon dioxide when using a boost controller.

The sound that turbos are perhaps most known for, the whoosh when you let off the gas, is from a blow-off valve (BOV). These are placed on the cold side and vent boost to the atmosphere (usually) when the throttle closes. A BOV prevents surging, where the boost goes back to the compressor and causes damage to the turbo.

Last, but not least, an intercooler is a necessary part of a turbo system unless you plan on running straight methanol. Otherwise it will be nearly impossible to use a respectable amount of boost without causing detonation. Just as with a supercharger, an air-to-air intercooler is preferable for street cars, autocross, road racing, drifting, etc. Air-to-water intercoolers are better suited to drag racing and the standing mile.

The largest manufacturers of turbochargers are Garrett (owned by Honeywell), BorgWarner, and Mitsubishi supplying, all of the OEMs and industrial applications. Garrett and BorgWarner are large players in the aftermarket as well, with plenty of sizes appropriate to the Camaro. Turbonetics and Precision Turbo also toe the line between the OEM and aftermarket sectors, though Precision is mainly geared toward the performance market.

Comp Turbo and Bullseye Power also serve different segments; Comp is more budget-oriented and Bullseye is more boutique and race-oriented. Each manufacturer offers unique compressor wheel designs, whether cast or billet aluminum, and bearing systems. Billet allows for an infinite possibility of wheel designs that can be exponentially more efficient than cast.

Turbine wheels live in harsh environments up to nearly 2,000 degrees, so special high-nickel alloys are used, such as Inconel. BorgWarner uses lightweight titanium aluminide on some of its turbos to reduce inertia and improve response.

The number of specs for each turbo is staggering (from the inducer diameter to the exducer, A/R, inlet type, outlet type, etc.) so selecting the correct turbo is best left up to a professional.

Most turbo manufacturers offer waste gates, blow-off valves, and even intercoolers. TiAL is by far the biggest name in waste gates and blow-off valves. The company even offers stainless steel turbine housings for a handful of Garrett turbos.

Turbosmart also offers an impressive lineup of waste gates and BOVs that are a great match to its manual

POWER ADDERS

and electronic boost controllers. Just as with turbos, sizing is crucial to proper waste gate operation (i.e., preventing boost creep). Boost creep is a common phenomenon with internal waste gates but could also occur with an undersized external. If you are commanding 12 psi, it is easy to understand how detrimental it can be for the engine to see 13 to 15 psi.

Spearco (Turbonetics) and Precision are perhaps the two biggest providers of aftermarket intercoolers. Precision and Chiseled Performance are the go-to sources for high-horsepower air-to-water units. For street applications, Garrett, Bell Intercoolers, Treadstone, and Vibrant Performance have various sizes and shapes to fit. Designs vary, but among the air-to-air intercoolers, bar and plate types are generally considered superior to the conventional tube and fin types. The area, as well as

Hellion Power Systems offers a turbo kit that, even in base form, supports more than 1,400 hp with its twin Precision 62-mm billet turbos. An upgrade to ball bearings for faster spool-up is available, along with larger 64- and 67-mm turbos. Perhaps its next greatest feature is in the location of turbos, which make them a highly visible part of the engine bay. To accomplish this, Hellion uses stainless steel 4-into-1 tubular headers. The downpipes connect to the factory cats and H-pipe. A larger, vertical, dual-inlet intercooler and twin Turbosmart VEE bypass valves handle the charged air. (Photo Courtesy Hellion Power Systems)

Unlike the Hellion kit, AGP mounts the turbos on the underside, as with many modern OEM systems. In fact, its emphasis is on OEM-like durability and reliability, which is why it uses the factory exhaust manifolds with cast-iron "turbo adaptors" (also available separately). Billet turbos are standard, though AGP offers many other options from Garrett, BorgWarner, and Precision, depending on power level and performance. The system is capable of 700 to 1,500 hp with other options, including four intercooler sizes. Stock engines can regularly make 700 to 800 hp according to AGP. (Photo Courtesy AGP Turbochargers)

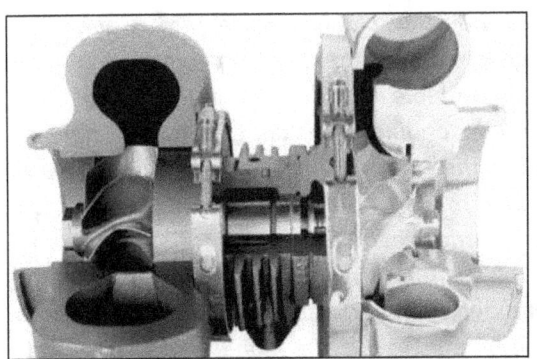

This cross-section of a Garrett turbo shows the basic components. The turbine (left) is the part that comes in contact with exhaust gas. The CHRA (center) houses the bearings that surround the turbine shaft and spin the compressor. Ball bearings help reduce friction for quicker spool-up. The compressor (right) is the shiny part, and the inducer diameter is the way most people refer to the size of a turbo. (Photo Courtesy Garrett by Honeywell)

If you are fabricating a custom single-turbo kit, the Precision Turbo PT7675 Competition Engineered Aerodynamics (CEA) is a great place to start. Rated at 1,200 hp, it features the CEA compressor wheel machined from 2618 aluminum with a 76-mm inducer. The higher efficiency and faster transient response allows for better top end and spool-up. (Photo Courtesy Precision Turbo)

For a twin-turbo system, Precision recommends the PT6266 as a starting point. With both CEA compressor and turbines, Precision says the 6266 offers 30 to 45 hp increases over similarly sized turbos. Like the 7675, the compressor is machined from a 2618 forging but has a smaller 62-mm inducer that is capable of 735 hp on its own (1,470 hp combined). (Photo Courtesy Precision Turbo)

A reliable waste gate is essential to proper boost control. In the old days, over-boosting, which could destroy your engine, was a serious concern. Thankfully companies such as Precision really have a handle on external waste gates, such as this PW46 (46 mm). The valve body is cast from high-grade 347 stainless steel, and the valve is made from nickel chromium alloy. The 17-7 precipitation hardened springs are used to adjust the boost level, which is capped by a satin anodized piece of 6061 billet aluminum. (Photo Courtesy Precision Turbo)

The blow-off valve, like the waste gate, is also a safety item. Except, instead of protecting the engine, it protects the turbo. When the throttle blade on the engine slams shut, boost that has built up in the charge tubing has nowhere to go but backward. This phenomenon is known as compressor surge, and it can damage the turbo. Precision's PB64 solves that by using a Kevlar-reinforced silicon diaphragm and hard-anodized valvestem to vent the boost into the atmosphere, giving off that trademark "whoosh" sound that makes turbos so cool. (Photo Courtesy Precision Turbo)

POWER ADDERS

Turbosmart makes quite a few turbo products; however, it is most known for the eBoost2. This compact electronic boost controller fits in any 60- or 66-mm gauge pod, and not only sets max boost, it limits boost by RPM, time, or gear. There is even an RPM compensation feature to prevent boost drop-off at high RPM and safety features to prevent waste-gate creep. (Photo Courtesy Turbosmart USA)

the thickness, dictates its efficiency and how much power it can accommodate. Intercoolers are available as cores only or as a universal fitment with end tanks and mounting tabs welded on.

Although most performance applications are lucky to have a single turbo kit on the market, there are quite a few for the fifth-gen Camaro. Turbonetics makes one of the only 50-state legal kits, which uses their T76 ceramic ball-bearing turbo, Evolution waste gates, and Duo 35 bypass valve. In order to obtain its CARB EO number, Turbonetics routed the post-cat exhaust back to the engine bay for the front-mounted T76 and Spearco air-to-air intercooler. The bolt-on kit for stock LS3s and L99s comes with injectors and tuning, good enough for 614 hp.

STS Turbo invented and patented remote-mounted turbo systems, placing the turbos downstream of the exhaust system (usually where the mufflers are located similar to the Camaro kit). The complete single turbo V-6 kit and twin-turbo SS kit also carry CARB EO numbers and retain all factory emissions equipment, such as the cats. The intercooled V-6 kit makes around 400 rwhp and the V-8 kit makes more than 530 rwhp with an otherwise stock engine.

Critics of the design say that the extra tubing increases turbo lag, which seems to be evident in the torque curve. For the average consumer, however, this is probably not an issue given the limits of traction and is on par with a centrifugal supercharger. STS Turbo went into bankruptcy in 2015. The founder, Rick Squires, who sold the business in 2012, has purchased the patents and inventory. The kits are offered through Squires Performance.

There are only a few players in the single turbo market, both of which use a similar design that are more economical than your typical kit. Fastlane and On 3 Performance retain the factory exhaust manifold on the passenger's side and fabricate a stainless steel turbo manifold on the driver's side and a 2.5-inch crossover pipe to merge into a turbo just behind the driver's headlight. Both kits use a front-mount air-to-air intercooler and high-quality V-band exhaust clamps that merge to the stock exhaust with a regular clamp, but that is where the similarities stop.

Fastlane's kit has a 3.5-inch downpipe, a flex pipe to keep the hot-side from cracking, BorgWarner 72-mm turbo, TiAL waste gate, and BOV. Just 7 psi is enough for 580 rwhp with a stock LS3 (530 hp with an L99). On 3 says its base kit is capable of 650 rwhp with a 3.0-inch downpipe and its own branded 70-mm turbo, 44-mm waste gate, and 50-mm BOV. A 76-mm turbo is optional, as well as a few A/R ratios.

The twin-turbo market is literally flooded, so I'll just do a brief review of the biggest players. Hellion is a major player in the Mustang market and brings the same thoughtful, high-end approach to the Camaro. Its design has some impressive headroom thanks to a pair of Precision billet 62-mm turbos (larger 64- and 67-mm turbos are also available). This system replaces the exhaust manifolds with 4-into-1 style tubular headers that place the turbos behind the headlights. Yet it still connects to the factory cats and exhaust. Hellion says the kit makes more than 600 hp with just 5 psi of boost but has the potential to make well over 1,000.

AGP and Fabberge are also newcomers to the General Motors world, offering twin-turbo systems as well. The AGP kit connects to the stock exhaust manifolds with its "turbo adapters," which can be purchased separately. A number of turbo options are available from 800 to 1,400-rwhp, along with fuel system upgrades and air-to-air intercoolers. The Fabberge kit uses the factory manifolds as well to place the turbos by the transmission, where the factory cats would normally reside. The entry-level kit offers Garrett turbos, TiAL waste gates, and BOV capable of 1,000 hp. Comp journal and ball-bearing turbos are also available, along with other upgrade options including ARH shorty headers. A Dominator version is available with 1,500-hp-capable Garrett 3582R compressors and TiAL SS 1.03 A/R housings, which was used on the former record-holding IPS Motorsports–built Camaro of Terri Mensing.

Despite the many choices of off-the-shelf kits, some still elect to build custom kits. For the extremely skilled DIY'er, it's the opportunity to do some fabrication work and get exactly what you want. Because the Camaro was not designed by General Motors with a turbo system, compromises are made with every kit. Whether it is a relocated washer tank or a restricted radiator that you take offense with, the custom kit makes the design choices yours. And for those with full-on race cars, a custom kit could be needed for class rules and optimum performance.

For example, Lingenfelter Performance Engineering went the custom route when building a Camaro for the NMCA's LSX Real Street class. A front-mounted 76-mm certainly isn't appropriate for a street car, but it kept the hot-side piping short and allowed the turbo to source cold, high-pressure air from the nose of the car. Although a pump gas street car might use a similarly sized turbo to make less than 700 hp, this race gas–gulping 358 cubic-inch flat-plane crank LSX makes more than 1,000 hp while screaming more than 8,500 rpm. The impeller speeds are quite a bit different as you can imagine, so care needs to be taken or the turbo can be over-spun and damaged. Because twin-turbo systems are not class legal, Lingenfelter built the engine combination right to the edge for the best performance possible.

Lingenfelter, Vengeance Racing, KraftWorks, Redline Motorsports, Speed Inc., IPS Motorsports, Late Model Racecraft, Nelson Racing Engines, and Shearer Fabrications are responsible for some of the finest turbo fabrication among late-model GMs.

Some builders resort to combining forced-induction methods to get the most out of a given setup. In a factory supercharged car such as the ZL1, a turbo could be used to exceed the capabilities of the OEM 1.9L blower. Nitrous is sometimes used to aid spool-up with a larger turbo. The first LSX to ever run 6s in the quarter-mile used nitrous to get the big 80-mm turbos spinning with the small 352-ci engine combination. Although this method has fallen out of favor because of the improvements in turbo technology, it has made a comeback with the standing-mile crowd. Nitrous has the added cooling benefit and is sometimes used to cool air-to-air intercoolers. When boost first started to catch on, nitrous was actually used in place of an intercooler. Thousands of blown head gaskets later, enthusiasts and builders have realized that adding cylinder pressure for the sake of cooling isn't necessarily a good idea.

ZL1 LS9 Supercharger Swap

Although you can make a considerable amount of power with the factory 1.9L supercharger, the ZL1's LSA is ultimately limited by the smaller housing and the heat that it generates. With the right upgrades, the LS9 has proven to be capable of 800- to 1,000-rwhp on boost alone, thanks to its 2.3L TVS supercharger. Unfortunately, dropping one of these blowers on an LSA is not a simple swap. To solve this, Lingenfelter Performance Engineering cast a high-flow snout that allows you to drop the larger blower onto the LSA crate engine, retaining the factory accessory drive system. At nearly $1,500 not including the supercharger, it is not exactly a budget upgrade. But it allows you to keep with factory parts for reliability. The other advantage of this kit is that it also allows you to drop an LS9 crate engine into your ZL1 by simply swapping out the snout, in which case, the price tag on the snout is a drop in the bucket. ∎

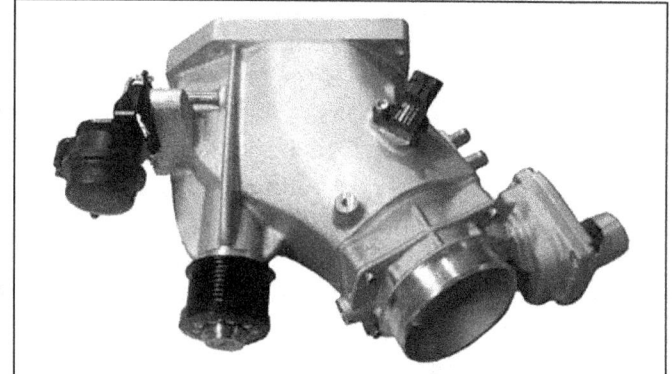

LPE's supercharger isolator coupling comes installed on the snout, but it does not include the 10-bolt supercharger pulley, which is available separately in 2.55- or 2.35-inch diameter. The EVAP purge solenoid is relocated for better internal airflow and cleaner appearance. Clearance is also provided for the LS9 intercooler lines.

POWER ADDERS

How-To Projects

Nitrous Install

All photos for this project are courtesy of Joseph Potak.

To some this may appear as an intimidating pile of parts, but to others this is exactly what the doctor ordered. Most nitrous kits are anything but application-specific. Nitrous Outlet offers a completely plug-and-play plate kit for the fifth-gen that eliminates the guesswork and fabrication. Every part you need is included in one easy-to-order kit, from wiring to hard lines, solenoid brackets, 10-pound bottle, and even a blow-down tube.

For this install, I use a remote bottle opener, NOS window switch, and Lingenfelter LNC-2000 to retard timing.

This is Nitrous Outlet's standard 10-pound bottle with high-flow valve. Believe it or not, the valve can be a real bottleneck (no pun intended) with budget systems. This 45-degree valve supports up to 800 hp of nitrous and has two 1/8 NPT ports for gauges and pressure assist systems, as well as a port for the blow-down tube. Each bottle is made from machined aluminum and powder-coated gloss black. It weighs 14.5 pounds empty, 24 pounds full.

This is a wet system, which means it has solenoids for fuel and nitrous that are contained on a bracket made specifically for the Camaro.

A billet aluminum plate with six specially designed discharge ports for nitrous and fuel allow for the best atomization and cylinder-to-cylinder distribution possible. With the right jetting, this kit supports 400 hp of nitrous.

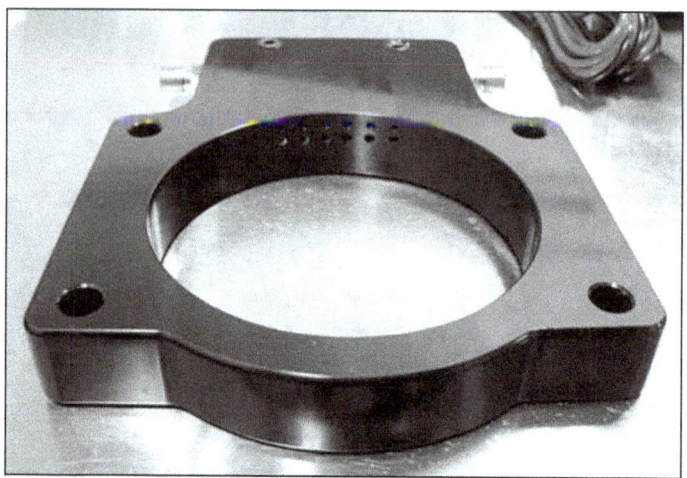

A single input on each side plugs into the nitrous and fuel solenoid. A dual-stage system is also available with two additional ports for timed delay of up to 400 hp.

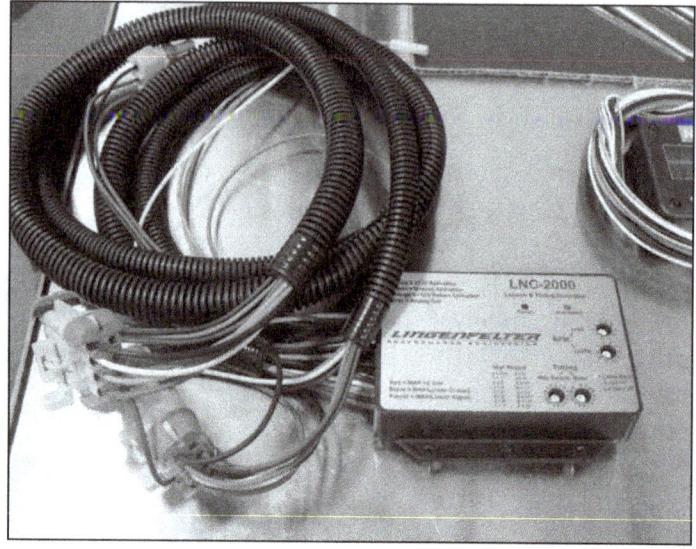

Nitrous Outlet sells the LNC-2000 Launch & Timing Controller, which functions as a two-step rev limiter and a timing retard. For consistent launching, a two-step certainly comes in handy. However, retarding the timing is crucial to spraying nitrous. This is one of the most common mistakes that owners make, which leads to engine carnage and the negative connotation to nitrous. The general rule is to retard timing by 2 degrees for every 50 hp of nitrous.

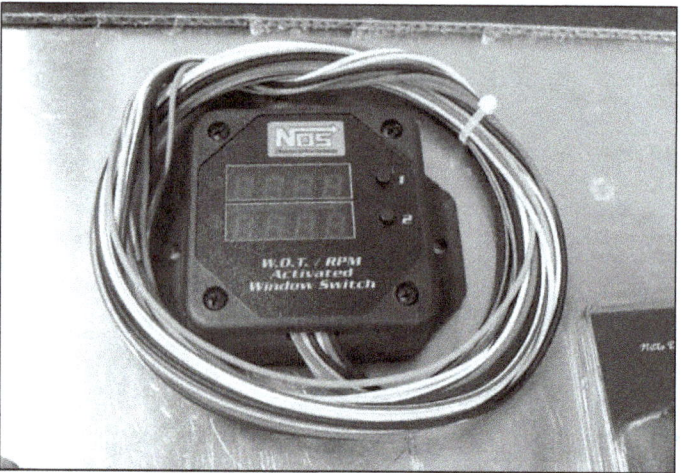

This two-stage window switch from NOS is also available through Nitrous Outlet and includes a TPS input for activation, so it also serves as the arming mechanism to put everything in one streamlined package. NOS actually includes this in some of its drive-by-wire kits.

A remote bottle opener is not essential but is certainly a nice convenience. With the flick of a switch you can open and close the nitrous bottle.

1 To get started, remove the air intake and unbolt the throttle body.

POWER ADDERS

3 The Nitrous Outlet plate simply bolts in between the throttle body and the intake manifold with the inlet ports on top.

2 The nitrous plate moves the throttle body forward by 3/4 inch, which can cause interference with the idler pulley (top left) and the actuator motor. The throttle body will be rotated 180 degrees upon reinstallation. In the meantime, you need to plug in the provided TPS wire extension harness.

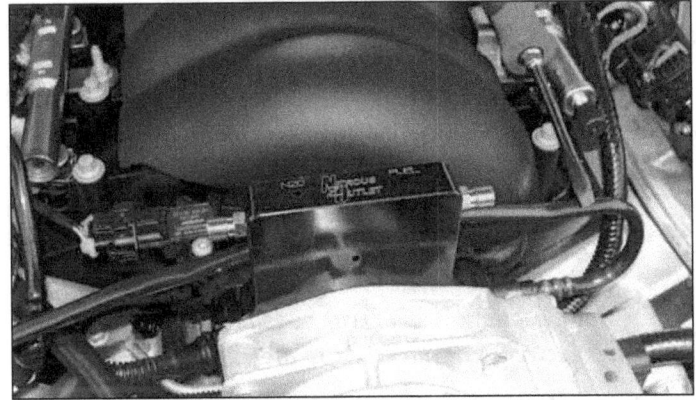

When you open the hood the nitrous system is fairly obvious. If that is a problem, Nitrous Outlet has quite a few custom (hidden) options.

4 The kit includes hard lines and solenoid brackets, which should be installed loosely at first before the final tighten. Again, since this kit is application-specific, it has the right fuel rail adapter to screw right into place and tap the fuel source at the Schrader valve. There is an optional fuel pressure safety switch to shut off the nitrous if there is insufficient pressure.

5 Tighten the solenoids to the brackets using these two Phillips-head screws. These solenoids have a bottom discharge (mounted on its side), which Nitrous Outlet says is more efficient than other designs.

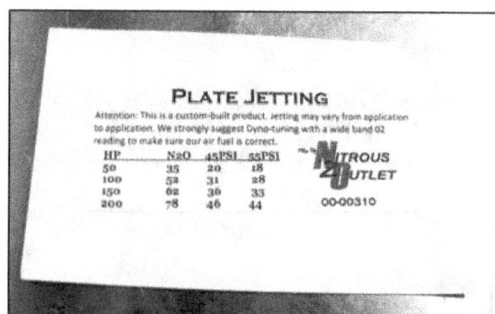 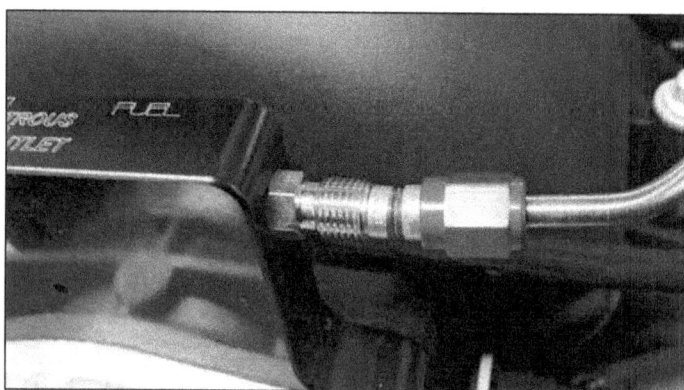

6 Nitrous Outlet provides this handy jet guide. In case you are wondering, you want to use the jets for 55 psi of fuel pressure unless you have a standalone nitrous fuel system. In my experience these jets are pretty close, but it is better to be safe than sorry. As it says on the card, you want to at least make a few pulls on the dyno with a wideband oxygen sensor to make sure.

7 The brass jets go right into the inputs to the plate where the hard lines screw in, so they are easy to access.

 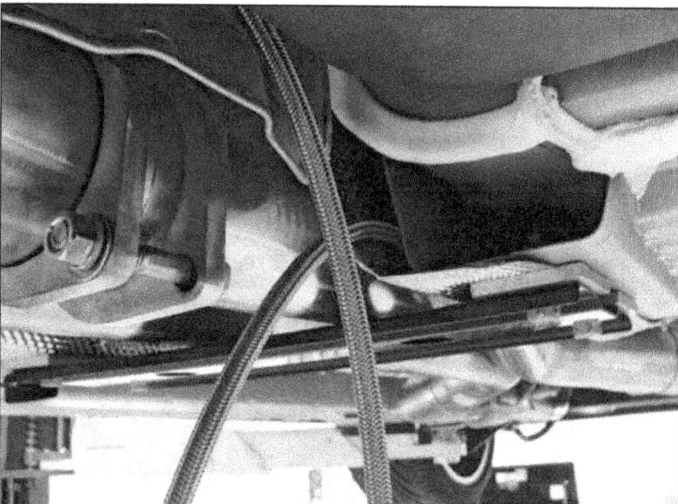

8 This nitrous purge kit uses a small solenoid that plugs into the side of the nitrous solenoid. You bend a hard line to exit the engine bay.

9 Run a braided stainless steel line the length of the floor, protected wherever possible. You don't want it to be easy to snag or run close to the exhaust.

 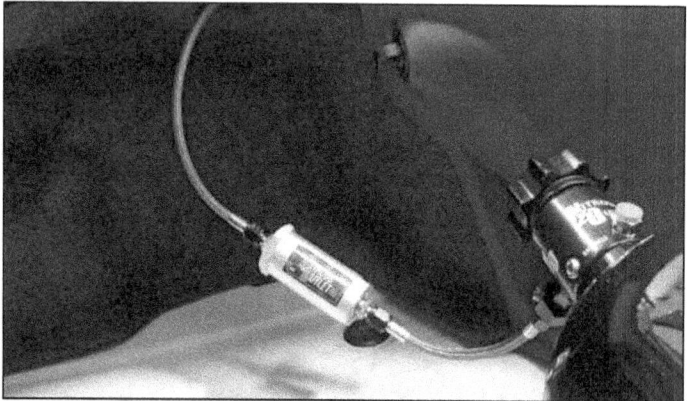

10 You then run the nitrous line to the solenoid along the firewall.

11 In the rear of the car, you run the line up and into the trunk with the bottle mocked up. It is important to always run a nitrous filter to protect the solenoid, just as with fuel.

POWER ADDERS

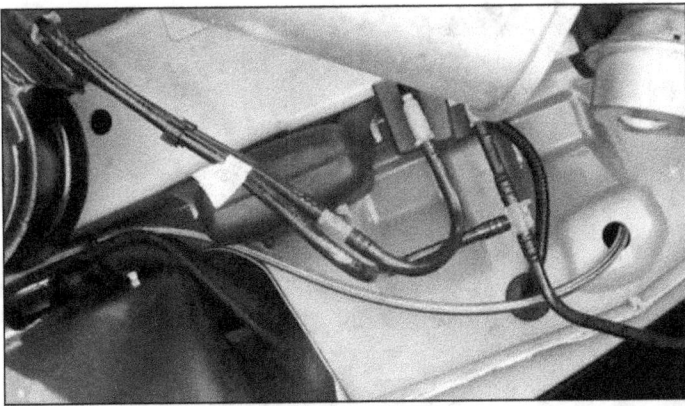

12 Here you can see the line through the floor. Although some choose to run nitrous line under the carpet in the interior, for safety sake it is better to run the line under the floorpan, using the factory heat shield whenever possible.

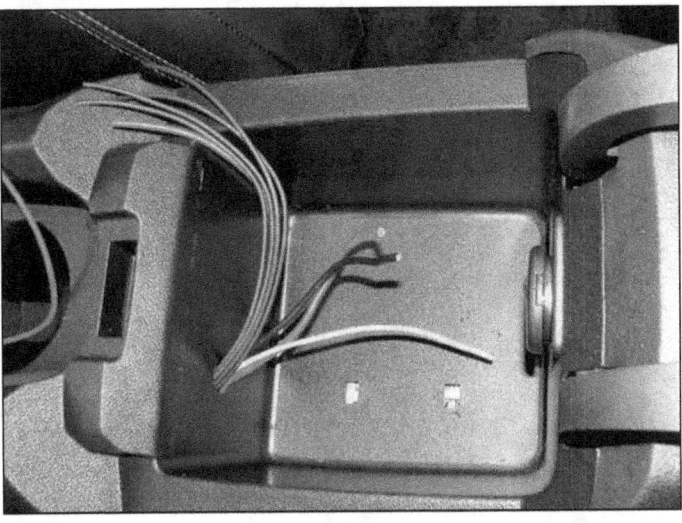

13 Nitrous Outlet has an application-specific switch plate with wiring that sits in the center console.

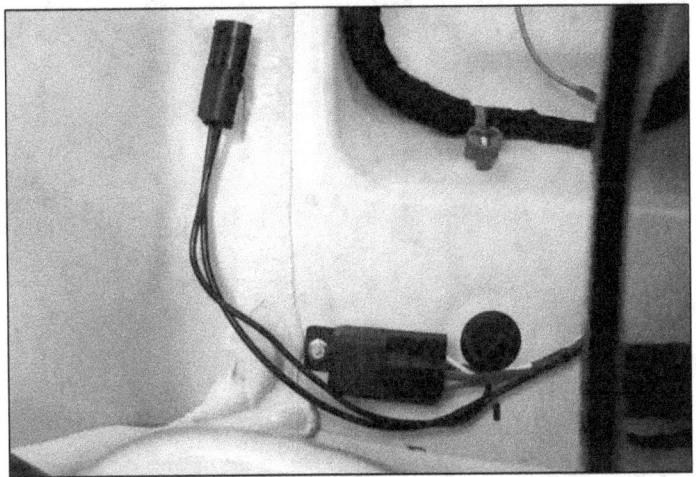

14 The Nitrous Outlet kit includes many heavy-duty relays, most of which you mount in the engine bay, except these for the remote bottle opener and heater.

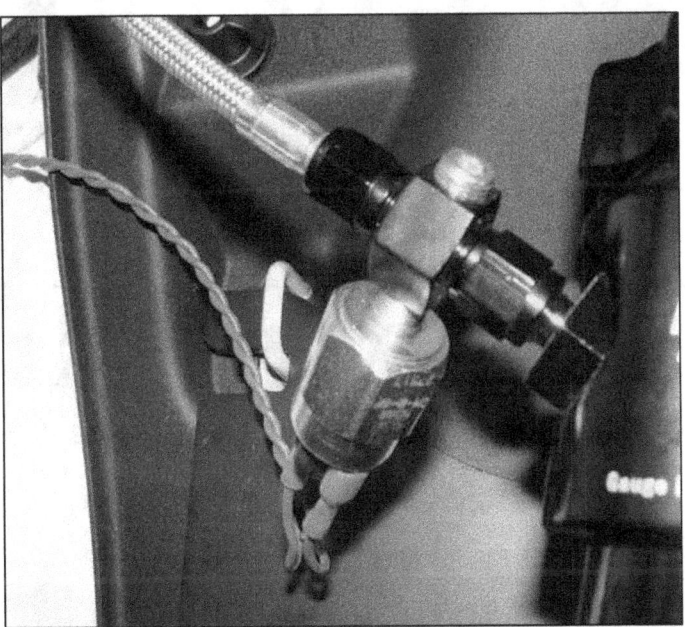

15 If you opt to use Nitrous Outlet's bottle heater, you need a nitrous pressure sensor to activate and deactivate the system.

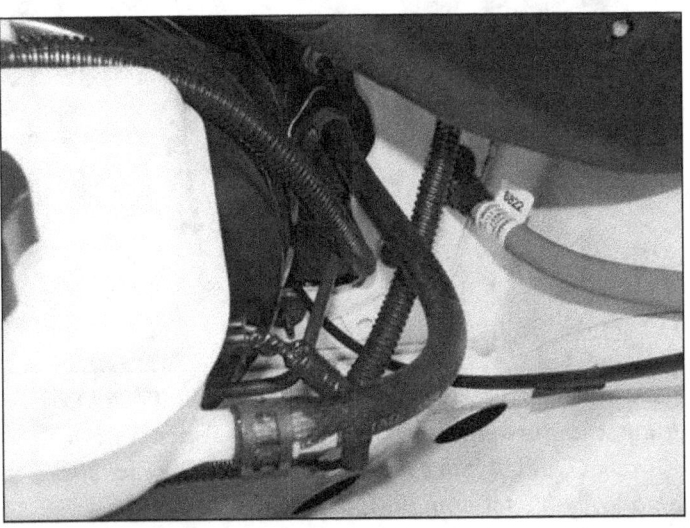

16 These wires must be run all the way up to the engine bay and covered in a wire loom for protection.

CAMARO 5TH GEN 2010-2015: HOW TO BUILD AND MODIFY

CHAPTER 6

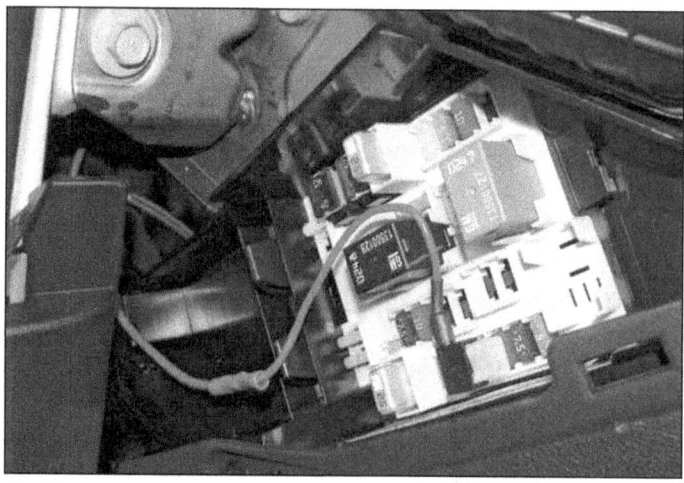

17 Use a fuse tap to grab a switched ignition source of power.

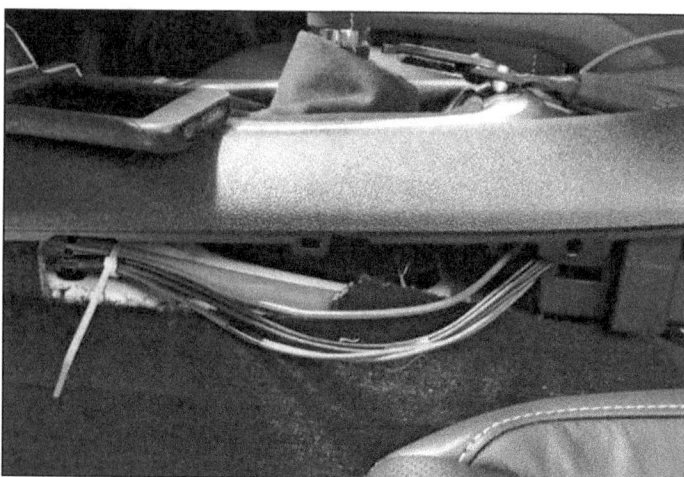

18 Run the wiring for the switch panel underneath the center console.

19 Here you can see how these heavy-duty wires tap into each switch of the panel.

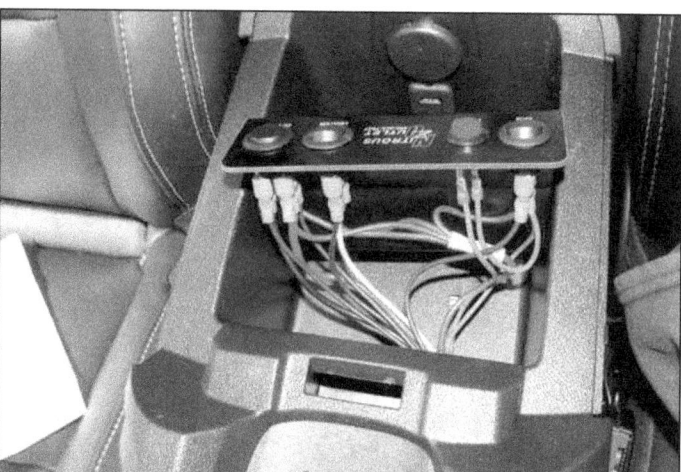

20 With the switch panel all wired up, it can go back into place for final installation.

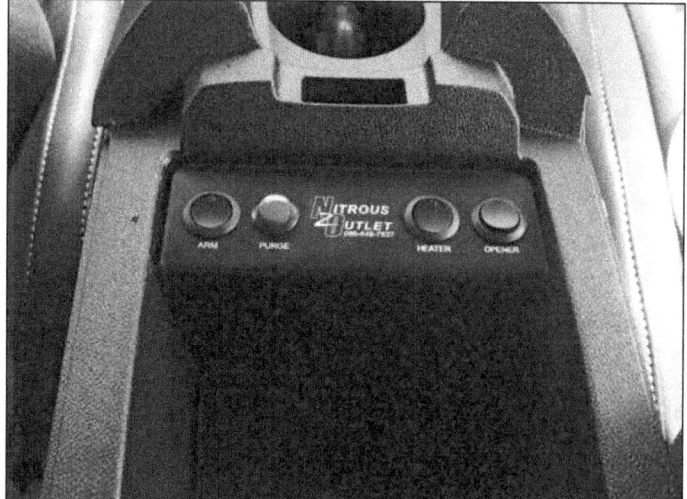

The switch panel still allows room for plenty of items in the center console and access to the power and USB inputs.

Fully installed, you can see the 10-pound bottle in the trunk with the heated bottle bracket and opener from Nitrous Outlet. A billet version of the heated bracket is also available for about twice the price.

POWER ADDERS

21 Run the flexible hard line for the purge solenoid through the cowl, after drilling a hole.

22 Black plastic helps to disguise the purge line while still keeping it fully functional on the cowl, spraying a plume of frosty nitrous up over the windshield.

TVS2300 Supercharger Install

All photos for this project are courtesy of Redline Motorsports.

Edelbrock redesigned the top and coil cover design on its popular E-Force supercharger for 2014, which was just in time for the introduction of the Z/28. At that time, Edelbrock did not have a Z/28 kit but Redline Motorsports was able to adapt the basic LS7 kit (PN 15490). In doing so, Redline was able to maintain the dry-sump oiling system and the litany of coolers that the Z/28 employs to go lap after lap on the road course without concern. Yet when Redline was done, the stock Z/28 went from 455-rwhp (stock) to 652 with additional help from a camshaft and long-tube headers.

Although this supercharger is capable of much more, the LS7's high-compression thin cylinders and fragile exhaust valves don't lend themselves to more than 4 to 5 psi.

Here is a better look at the OEM-quality bracket, fully installed. The Z/28's accessory drive system is the same as the 2006–2013 Corvette Z06.

1 Bolt this bracket to the water pump, which mounts a new tensioner for the supercharger belt. Edelbrock's proprietary valley cover with flush-mounted bolts allow the blower to sit lower and fit under stock hoods.

CAMARO 5TH GEN 2010–2015: HOW TO BUILD AND MODIFY

2 After plugging in the MAP sensor, which has a different connector than the factory version and requires a slight rewiring, lower the assembled blower. Cut O-ring grooves into the E-Force's intake flange to use the OEM individual gaskets rather than a traditional one-piece gasket. Here, Siemens 60 lbs/hr injectors were installed to match the blower's airflow.

3 The massive Z/28 radiator comes with a single fan on the front and many coolers. Mounting a heat exchanger on the front is significantly different than with the standard Camaro kit.

4 To mount the heat exchanger weld a bracket to it, which taps the radiator support. Space it out a bit instead of mounting it flush.

5 After dropping the radiator, fans, and coolers back into place, slide the heat exchanger behind the bumper support. This is a good look at the various brackets.

6 It is crucial that the heat exchanger does not affect the air dam and underbody aero.

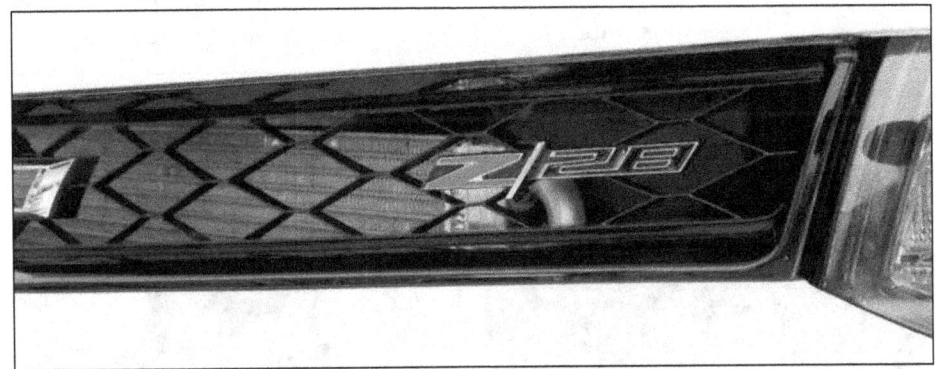

7 The heat exchanger now lurks behind the Z/28's thin upper grille and emblem, tipping off would-be challengers.

8 You need a custom intake of tube to join the MAF and factory cold-air kit to the throttle body. With the dry-sump oil tank and all items back in place, you get a sense of the finished product.

9 Remove the factory carbon heat extractor so you can close the hood. It takes some modification, but it can be reinstalled and still used.

10 Redline dialed in this 2015 Camaro Z/28's calibration on its in-house DYNOmite chassis dyno. Quality tuning and a conservative 4 to 5 psi are key to keeping the LS7 alive. By retarding the timing and adding some fuel, the blower and other mods helped this Z hit 652 hp on pump gas.

Custom 4.5L Whipple Supercharger Install

All photos for this project are courtesy of NCC Racing.

When it comes to power adders, size most certainly matters. That's exactly why NCC Racing is looking to offer the biggest positive displacement supercharger kit on the market for the fifth-gen Camaro. A 4.5L Whipple supercharger has proven to be capable of more than 1,400-rwhp and 25 psi on NCC's in-house prototype. Vinny Colella says his kit is similar to the 4.0L COPO, except that it keeps all factory options, such as the windshield wipers and accessories. This makes it appropriate for street cars as well as dedicated race cars.

NCC has a custom ATI Performance balancer and 12-rib belt drive setup to go along with the twin-throttle body rear blower inlet housing, heat exchanger, and coolant reservoir.

Whipple provides the 4.5L supercharger and intake manifold for the LS7 heads. This blower is typically used on the Ford GT kit with a different, lower snout and entry. Unlike the out-of-the-box Whipple kit for the Camaro, this is a rear-entry version. NCC Racing fabricates the twin throttle body inlet to support massive airflow.

POWER ADDERS

This is a look at the backside of the prototype rear blower inlet housing, which gives you an idea of what was required to make this work (lots of fabrication) and probably why there isn't anyone else making a comparable kit.

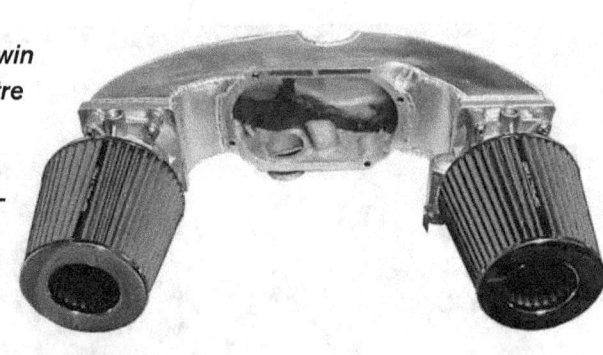

Here is a closer look at the twin throttle body inlet with Spectre high-flow air filters. The kit uses Corvette ZR1 (LS9) throttle bodies with a "piggy-back throttle body controller to operate the second throttle body as a mirror image of the main throttle body."

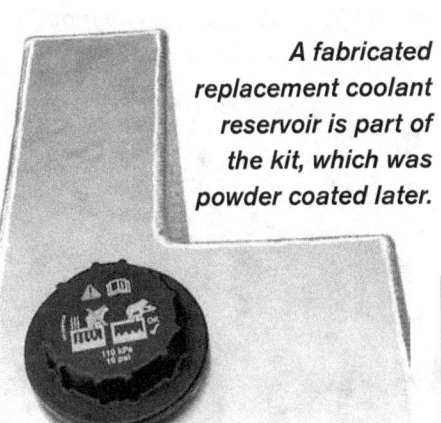

A fabricated replacement coolant reservoir is part of the kit, which was powder coated later.

From the rear you can see that the MAP sensor mounts in the back of the intake manifold. The bypass is at the back of the blower as well.

A massive Fluidyne heat exchanger is used, which requires some modification to the bumper support.

With the ZL1 bumper on, you can see that the exchanger tucks completely behind it without any issues.

CAMARO 5TH GEN 2010–2015: HOW TO BUILD AND MODIFY

Because the blower is so massive and it is a rear-entry component, some modification is required to the firewall.

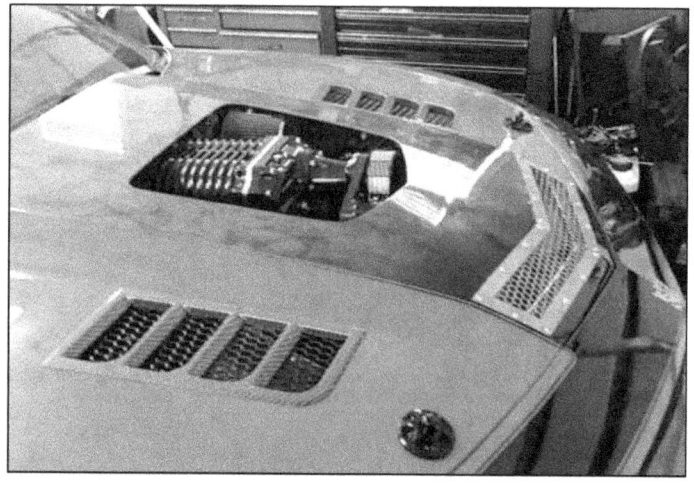

With a taller fiberglass hood, you can basically cut out a symmetrical window to clear the blower. Some sort of scoop or raised section can then be molded in.

The stock hood can also be modified to fit the NCC Racing 4.5L Whipple kit. Notice that massive Gates 12-rib belt. That's key to making more than 25 psi of boost.

Here is the fully installed system on the NCC Racing prototype with an LSX 454, dry-sump oiling and Mast Black Label LS7 heads. Custom tuning is required (with the factory ECM) to run in Speed Density because the MAF sensor has been deleted.

CHAPTER 7

FUEL SYSTEM, IGNITION AND TUNING

When it comes to fuel and ignition, there may be quite a bit going on that you are not used to with a traditional hot rod. LS engines operate at 4 bar of fuel pressure, that's a whopping 58 psi! Like most modern cars, the fuel system is return-less. These two factors greatly affect the injector flow rates and fuel system upgrades. On the ignition side, eight individual coils are mounted on the valvecovers for an extremely efficient ignition system. The factory coils and wires are high quality compared to yesteryear, when such upgrades were worth quite a few horsepower.

The biggest concern, though, is the spark plugs. Choosing the right plugs is essential to resisting detonation and its harmful effects. Unlike previous small-blocks, ignition timing is not controlled by the distributor (there is no distributor). That, along with fueling, is completely contained within the ECM's operating system. Thankfully a host of tuning options makes tuning the flash-based ECM much easier than in years past.

Engine Management System Tuning

As I mentioned in Chapter 4, the OEM flash-based computer (aka ECM, PCM, or ECU) can be recalibrated through the ALDL OBD-II port under the dash with tuning software. A cable plugs into the port, which then goes to either a handheld device or a proprietary conversion box that connects to a laptop. This was a huge step up from the old PROM-based computer on tuned port injection engines, which required much less precise methods, including chip burning. Even the OBD-I computers (Gen II LT1) didn't offer nearly the amount of control and speed, not to mention software options.

Moates.net even offers a Road-Runner emulator for the LS1 PCM that allows for real-time tuning. Instead of shutting off the engine, modifying the calibration on your laptop, and then waiting for it to upload to the computer, you can

Dyno tuning is a key component to any successful build. By using a load-bearing dyno you can best simulate road conditions while monitoring the health of the engine in a controlled environment and measuring any performance change.

CHAPTER 7

simply make changes on the fly. This makes for a much more efficient process of dyno tuning a new combination. Unfortunately RoadRunner is not available for fifth-gen ECMs, which are more complex computers and sometimes require a dealer to unlock. Some have deemed them less aftermarket-friendly as a result, but on the other hand, they are faster and have even better fueling control. The software is pre-engineered for larger injectors and more fuel.

Although tuning is essential with camshafts, engine swaps, and forced induction, plenty can be gained from EFI tuning less modified vehicles. HP Tuners, for example, allows you to eliminate GM's torque limiting functions, known as "torque management," in a number of areas. These functions were meant to preserve driveline components (such as those weak, stock SS axles) for warranty purposes by limiting the engine's torque; terrible for performance purposes. In addition, tables control the electronic throttle's response, at what coolant temperature the ECM starts retarding spark, and power enrichment (commanded air/fuel ratio) that can also improve the driving experience on even a stock Camaro.

With more modified vehicles MAF tuning becomes an essential part of the equation, which is needed to align your commanded air/fuel ratio with the actual air/fuel. Camshafts, ported heads, strokers, and forced induction require adjustments to the main spark and volumetric efficiency (VE) tables as well. RPM and airflow dictate the spark advance, while fueling (VE) is dictated by manifold pressure and RPM.

Of course, getting the fueling spot-on requires properly scaling the injectors. With stock injectors, General Motors has already done the work for you. When upgrading to higher-flowing injectors, though, these parameters need to be changed based on the flow data. The easy solution is to either use another OEM GM injector or an aftermarket high-impedance injector with flow data.

Because the factory LS3 and LS7 injectors are already 42 lbs/hr, the only OEM upgrade available is the LSA and LS9 59 lbs/hr injectors. Injector Dynamics, Deatschwerks, Fuel Injector Clinic, and Infinity all offer complete data sheets with their injectors to copy and paste into your tuning software.

For high RPM and lots of boost, an aftermarket engine management system is ideal. Although it may not contain all of the emissions and liability concern features of an OEM, the capabilities and added features are nearly endless. Many have internal memory, so that you don't need to be hooked up to a laptop for data logging. Boost, nitrous, and methanol control can be combined into one unit instead of separate ones. Wideband oxygen sensors allow instant fueling correction, even at WOT (when the factory ECM does not). Many have Flex Fuel capabilities and switchable maps, so that you can have preloaded tunes for various types of fuel or boost levels rather than having to carry a laptop with you to make changes. Most can run low-impedance injectors (essential for big-power combos), and there are typically no RPM limitations.

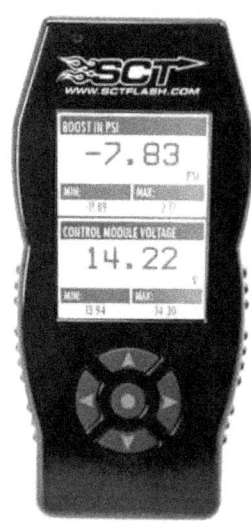

SCT's X4 is a premium handheld tuner that comes preloaded with tune files that have been developed during dyno testing to increase power. You can store up to 10 custom tune files from your local SCT dealer, so you can flip between pump and race gas, high/low boost, or various shots of nitrous. It has a full-color backlit display that helps make adjustments and also scan the ECM to provide real-time vehicle data and even log it. Exhaust gas temperature (EGT), air/fuel ratio, and any other 0–5 volt source can be monitored. It can also be used to read and clear diagnostic trouble codes. (Photo Courtesy SCT Flash)

Not happy with the throttle response of your Camaro? The JMS PedalMAX is another way to modify the ECM's commands without touching the programming, which would void the warranty. This digital microprocessor improves the throttle reaction, which can even be adjusted with the optional control knob. It uses a proprietary sealed enclosure with a plug-and-play wiring harness. (Photo Courtesy JMS Chip)

FUEL SYSTEM, IGNITION AND TUNING

SCT's Livewire TS Plus has a color 4-inch touchscreen that can be mounted on the windshield or dashboard to switch between tunes on the fly. It has many of the same features as the X4, such as data-logging, storage for up to 10 custom tunes, preloaded tunes, and the ability to adjust the tune. It also has a rearview camera input, performance calculator, adjustable warnings/alerts, and selectable graphics and gauge layouts to display high-speed engine monitoring. (Photo Courtesy SCT Flash)

The most popular systems include AEM Infinity, BigStuff3, FAST XFI, Haltech, Holley EFI, and Motec. Unfortunately not all of these systems are compatible with electronic throttle bodies and transmissions (such as the 6L80E, 4L60E, and 4L80E), which make those units more race-oriented. And only two or three can be integrated with the factory Body Control Module (BCM) for full operation of interior electronics, gauges, ABS, etc.

The Haltech Sport 2000 has become particularly attractive for

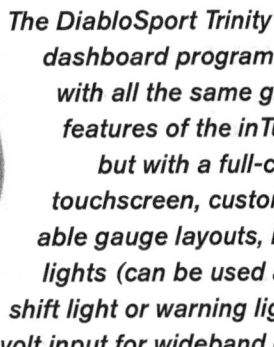

The DiabloSport Trinity is a dashboard programmer with all the same great features of the inTune, but with a full-color touchscreen, customizable gauge layouts, LED lights (can be used as a shift light or warning light), 5-volt input for wideband oxygen and other sensors, and it can hold up to five custom tunes in addition to the canned tunes. The Racing Mode is one of the coolest features, which turns the device into a piece of testing equipment to measure 0–60, 0–100, 1/8-, and 1/4-mile times. (Photo Courtesy DiabloSport)

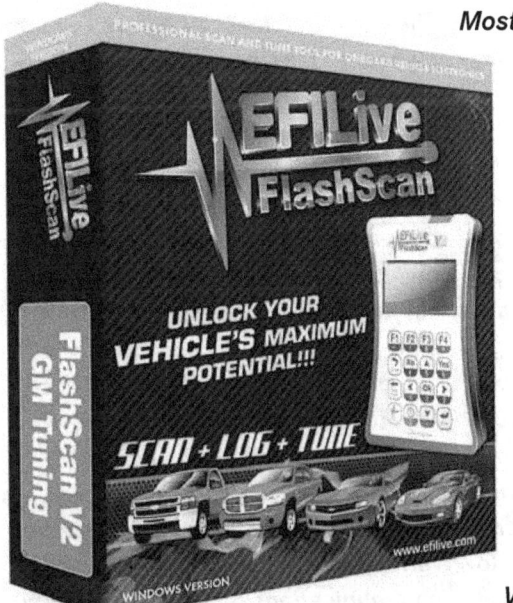

Most professional GM tuners use some sort of laptop-based software such as EFI Live to tune factory ECMs. The FlashScan V2 is the hardware needed to interface with a PC laptop. FlashScan can be used to pass through or on its own and is capable of logging up to 2,000 hours of data at full speed with a 2GB SD card. There are four 0–5-v analog inputs, two K-type thermocouple inputs, two 12-v digital inputs, and a serial input. The software can integrate wideband oxygen sensors and has a Virtual VE Table for the Camaro E38 and E67 operating systems. (Photo Courtesy EFI Live)

DiabloSport produced one of the first handheld tuners for GM applications, and its encore performance is the slender inTune. By being smaller than most smart phones, it is easy to stow when you are not using it, yet it has all the features you'd expect of a handheld, such as canned tunes for your application and the ability to make extensive adjustments. You can calibrate for larger injectors, disable AFM, and adjust cam timing, as well as the usual parameters such as ignition timing, shift points, speedometer calibration, throttle booster, speed limiter, and torque management. A DiabloSport dealer can also upload a custom tune. (Photo Courtesy DiabloSport)

CHAPTER 7

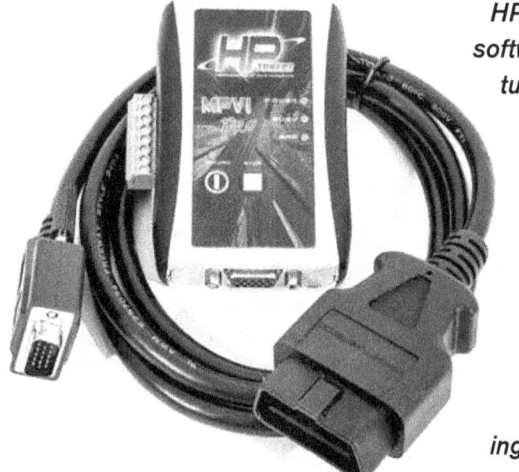

HP Tuners is perhaps the most popular software choice among professional GM tuners in the United States. It uses the VCM Scanner to transmit data from your OBD-II port to a laptop. Like EFI Live, HP Tuners' VCM Suite is free to download and works only with Windows software. However, you must purchase tuning credits as well as the VCM Scanner to actually tune your Camaro. The advantage of this laptop-based tuning software is that you can tune pretty much any engine parameter. (Photo Courtesy HP Tuners)

The AEM Infinity has also been used in a piggyback scenario but was originally designed to function on its own. It has the ability to interact with factory components such as DBW throttle bodies, VVT, traction control, and knock sensors. But it adds the ability to fire low-impedance injectors, read up to 17 voltage inputs and 6 temp inputs, adjust fueling with dual wideband oxygen sensors, and has several methods of engine protection. Boost control (by RPM, timing, gear, VSS, switch input, or Flex Fuel input), nitrous control (up to four stages), and launch control are added features you won't find in any factory ECM. (Photo Courtesy AEM)

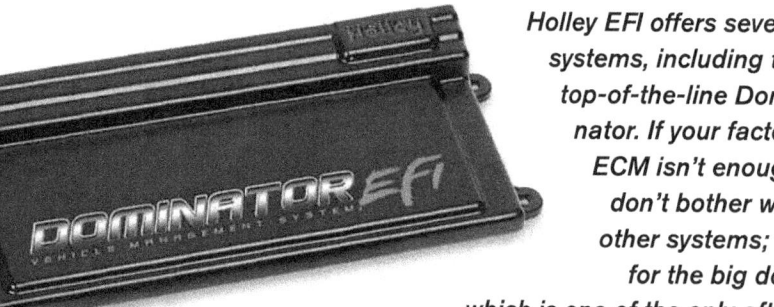

Holley EFI offers several systems, including the top-of-the-line Dominator. If your factory ECM isn't enough, don't bother with other systems; go for the big dog, which is one of the only aftermarket EFI systems that can control electronic GM transmissions such as the 4L80E and 4L60E. The Dominator is the ECU of choice for cars making well over 2,000 hp, so you know it can handle anything you can throw at it. It can control DBW throttle bodies (up to two) and integrates with OEM sensors and ignition coils as well as aftermarket versions. (Photo Courtesy Holley)

this reason, as it piggybacks with the factory ECM. It even has barometric and air temperature correction and safety features to protect the engine when a fuel pump fails, oil pressure drops, etc. The Haltech unit has all of the benefits of aftermarket engine management, with virtually none of the drawbacks.

Although the factory ECM may be void of race-friendly features such

The Haltech Elite ECU allows Camaro owners to take advantage of the features of a top-quality aftermarket EFI system without losing the functionality of factory equipment such as the ABS and gauge cluster. Although it can be run on its own, several late-model builders have been running this in conjunction with the factory ECM in high-powered street combinations. It has all the essentials you need to run in your Camaro such as drive-by-wire throttle control, eight ignition coil outputs, eight fuel injector outputs, six engine position inputs, knock control, variable cam control, dual CAN Bus communications, and OBD-II capability. (Photo Courtesy Haltech)

FUEL SYSTEM, IGNITION AND TUNING

as a two-step rev limiter, some electronics can augment its operation safely and easily without breaking the bank. MSD Ignition offers the LS 2-Step Launch Control (PN 8733) and Timing Twister (PN 86251). Both use simple rotary dials to adjust and plug into the factory wiring harness. The 2-Step makes launching a breeze by limiting the RPM to the set limit at the starting line, though it should be noted this is for a race application with no catalytic converters.

The Timing Twister has a number of uses, but most practically for timing retard with boost or nitrous. Your normal timing is locked into the ECM. However, when you arrive at the track and want to turn on the nitrous, increase boost, or add race fuel, you can advance or retard the timing as needed while leaving the idle and low-speed timing as-is.

Lingenfelter has a number of similar devices, from the RPM-003 window switch, to the adjustable launch controller. If you decide to convert the TR6060 to face-plated gears, for example, you want to select the Torque Cut Module that doubles as a two-step rev limiter and launch controller for consistent launches.

Ignition Systems

Although there is plenty of advertising to suggest otherwise, ignition upgrades aren't worth much horsepower. The factory LS3, LS7, and LSA coils are reliable and powerful enough for more than 1,000 hp. Both MSD and ACCEL sell coils that boast more energy, but it doesn't always show up on the dyno. This is not to say that these aren't great products, it's just that they seem to fix a problem that doesn't exist on mildly modified engines.

Plug wires aren't usually worth any horsepower either, and aftermarket wires can have issues with the immense electronic interference on your GPS- and satellite radio–equipped fifth-gen. As power output climbs toward 2,000 hp and factory electronics become less of an issue, this is a whole different matter.

Holley EFI and AEM high-output coils become necessary with high-powered and aftermarket EFI-equipped LS engines. Some have even resorted to a Jesel or MSD distributor conversion for better high-RPM stability. These setups have an external belt drive and single coil to fire the plugs, which is definitely not

Unlike previous generations, OEM ignition coils are pretty efficient and powerful, but that doesn't mean there isn't room for improvement. MSD says its patented winding design and materials help generate improved spark energy and voltage output. Multiple sparks at idle allow for quick starts, smoother idle, and a more efficient combustion process. (Photo Courtesy MSD Performance)

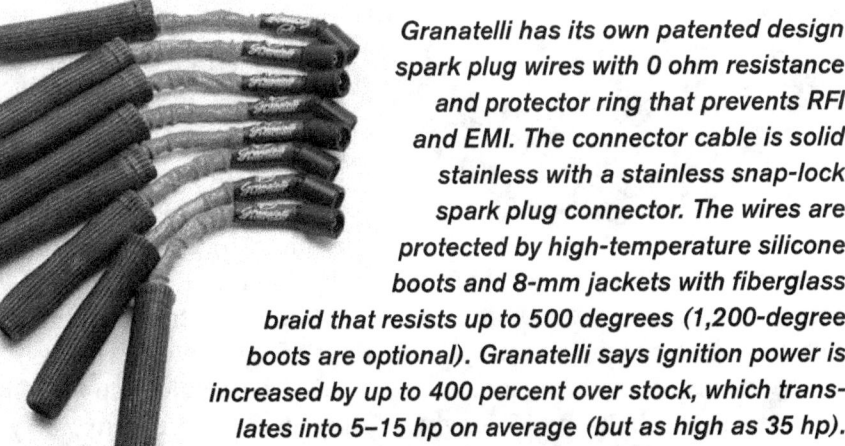

Granatelli Motor Sports created the Malevolent coils to increase spark energy on LS engines for better fuel economy, throttle response, and idle by way of increasing the efficiency of combustion. Two versions are available that are rated at 80,000 and 85,000 volts in blue and black. Average power gains are reported as 6 to 8 hp, though they are capable of up to 18 hp. (Photo Courtesy Granatelli Motor Sports)

Granatelli has its own patented design spark plug wires with 0 ohm resistance and protector ring that prevents RFI and EMI. The connector cable is solid stainless with a stainless snap-lock spark plug connector. The wires are protected by high-temperature silicone boots and 8-mm jackets with fiberglass braid that resists up to 500 degrees (1,200-degree boots are optional). Granatelli says ignition power is increased by up to 400 percent over stock, which translates into 5–15 hp on average (but as high as 35 hp). (Photo Courtesy Granatelli Motor Sports)

CHAPTER 7

The folks at FAST (Fuel Air Spark Technologies) had high-horsepower cars in mind when they designed the XR-1A High-Output Ignition Coil. High compression, naturally aspirated, and forced induction benefits greatly from the high spark energy, delivering up to 44,000 volts and 103 mJ of energy. FAST says these coils are comparable to CDI systems and support up to 19 amps of current and 17 volts.

The MSD LS 2-Step Launch Control (PN 8733) is your ticket to consistency at the dragstrip. This plug-and-play module allows you to set a specific launch rev limiter in 100- and 1,000-rpm increments via the rotary dials. Once engaged, you can leave it at any RPM you want by simply holding the gas pedal down. With a stick car, this is the only way to fly. Note: Two-step rev limiters are not recommended with catalytic converters. (Photo Courtesy MSD Performance)

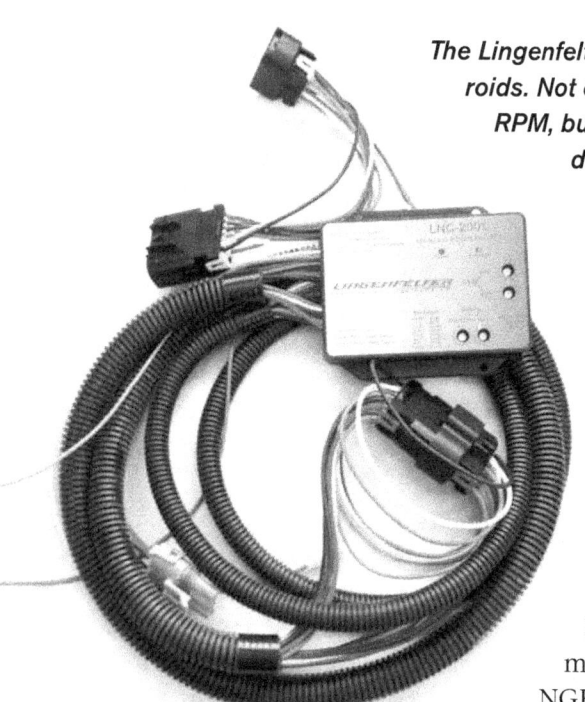

The Lingenfelter LNC-2001 is a two-step on steroids. Not only can you set and adjust launch RPM, but it also can retard timing up to 15 degrees. The retard function can be triggered with nitrous activation or inline with boost using a 3-bar MAP sensor input. Turbo cars can use the timing retard to help build boost at the line, too. (Photo Courtesy Lingenfelter Performance Engineering)

street-friendly. Intense heat from turbo systems may also require some heavy-duty spark plug wires.

Speaking of spark plugs, nearly any stock or bolt-on LS engine responds well to NGK TR5 spark plugs. With smaller combustion chambers and forced induction, you need a colder plug such as the NGK TR6. Higher boost levels and 200 or more of nitrous require at least an NGK BR7EF or B8EFS. With nitrous the rule is to go one step colder for every 100 hp.

Brisk is another quality manufacturer of spark plugs, which (like the NGKs) use a single strap with a nickel-alloy non-projected tip. Stay away from iridium and platinum plugs.

Fuel Systems

When it comes to the fuel system, the choices are many. As previously stated, the fuel system is return-less, which means that a pump control module is built into the pump assembly to regulate the pressure. The first option to upgrade the pump's capacity is to employ a voltage booster from MSD, Lingenfelter (Kenne Bell), or JMS.

JMS says it can increase output by up to 85 percent with its PowerMAX. Most tuners say a voltage booster is sufficient for smaller superchargers and turbos with mostly stock engines. The next step up for the SS is retrofitting the ZL1 fuel pump, which Chevrolet Performance has made extremely easy and affordable at around $420 (PN 19260557). This single 250-lph pump is pulse-width modulated, comes complete with everything you need to drop in, and supports up to 650 hp without a voltage booster.

FUEL SYSTEM, IGNITION AND TUNING

Lingenfelter offers a drop-in twin-pump setup with 190-lph pumps that support 850 to 1,000 hp with a voltage booster and 750 to 900 hp on its own. Switching to a return fuel system is a necessary task with high-powered applications and has the added advantage of boost referencing to provide more pressure when you need it most.

The Chevrolet Performance ZL1 fuel pump (PN 19258436) is easily the best upgrade option for any SS, boasting 250 lph at 65 psi. It is a direct, bolt-in swap that includes the module, sender, tank seal, and instruction sheet. By most accounts it easily supports 650 hp at the flywheel. The pump is pulse-width modulated, so you don't have to convert to a traditional fuel pressure regulator and return-style system. (Photo Courtesy Chevrolet Performance)

When the ZL1 pump won't cut it, Squash Performance offers a plug-and-play return-style setup using two Walbro 450-lph pumps that work with gas and E85. This system supports 1,100 rwhp on E85, and even more with gas. The hanger is made from CNC-machined 6061 aluminum, anodized for corrosion protection, sealed with a Viton O-ring, and fitted to a modified OEM bucket. Either -8 or -6 fittings are available, and it can even come pre-wired with a 15-foot pigtail and sealed connector to activate the second pump at 1 to 2 psi with a Hobbs pressure switch. (Photo Courtesy Squash Performance)

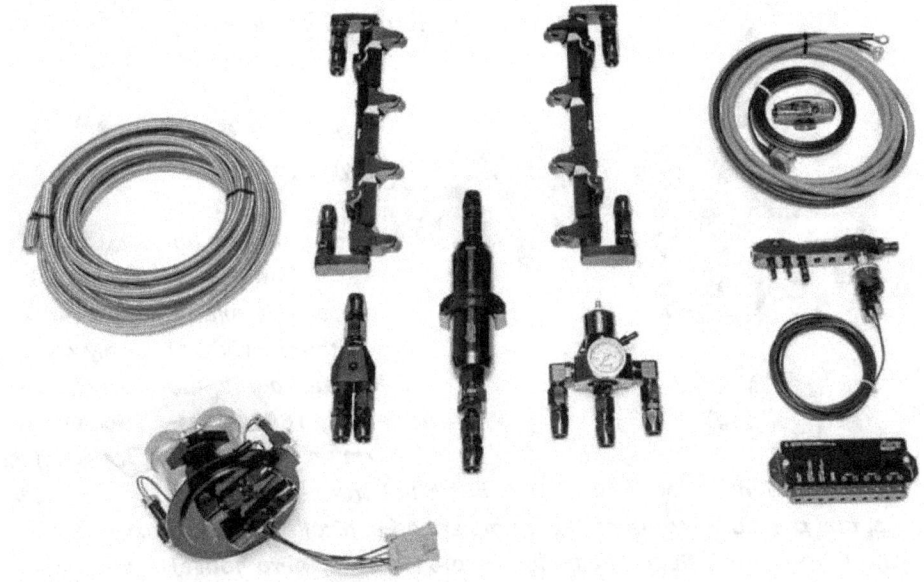

Fore Innovations offers double and triple fuel pump solutions for the fifth-gen Camaro using multiple types of pumps, wiring, fuel lines, filters, and other options. The top-of-the-line system supports more than 1,800 hp, as well as multiple fuel types, including E85. Fore offers an FC2 controller or FC3 Staged controller with add-ons for a pressure switch, Flex Fuel sensor, boost/vacuum manifold, etc. Some kits are designed to work with stock fuel rails; others have aftermarket rails routed in series or parallel. All, however, are return-style systems. (Photo Courtesy Fore Innovations)

CAMARO 5TH GEN 2010–2015: HOW TO BUILD AND MODIFY

CHAPTER 7

How to Pick a Good Tuner

Let's face it, you may be able to turn a wrench, but tuning an EFI engine can be a complicated endeavor. With the fifth-gen Camaro you not only have to worry about destroying a perfectly good (and rather expensive) engine, but it would be easy to create a runaway throttle and other issues that could prove to be dangerous to a driver on the road. Thankfully there are a growing number of resources out there, including tuning schools, that can help an aspiring calibrator learn the craft. EFI University is one of the oldest of its kind and offers beginning to advanced-level classes. These, along with Calibrated for Success, are theory-based classes. The Tuning School takes a much more hands-on approach with specific tuning software. Often a quality calibrator has a certificate from either of these schools, which makes the selection process easier. Here are a few more tips:

They say the proof of the pudding is in the taste, so why not take a look at some cars that they have calibrated? Are they fast? Do they idle properly? How about part-throttle? How similar are the combos to yours? You wouldn't buy a car without test-driving it first, so it makes sense that you should at least get a ride in a car that has been tuned by this person, and preferably one that is similar to yours.

Ask the potential candidates questions. What software do they use? What hardware do they use? Do they use a wideband oxygen sensor? Is the tuning done on the dyno, the street, or both? What type of dyno do they have? Ideally the majority of tuning should be done on a load-bearing dyno, which best imitates the friction of the road without the hazards and limitations. The tune should also be validated with a test drive and data logging on the street.

Find someone you trust and stick with them. At the end of the day, you want to be happy with the end result of your hard-earned money spent. You could hire the best tuner in the world, but if they throw their hands up in the air halfway through, say your car is a piece of junk, and kick you out, then this isn't going to be an enjoyable experience. Plus, in the event that something catastrophic does happen, even if it is not the tuner's fault, you want someone on your side that is going to be helpful.

Tuners don't have the best reputation. It can be a thankless job. If a car runs well, the engine builder seems to get all the credit. If it's fast at the dragstrip, the chassis guy gets the praise. At the same time, when the car isn't running right, it is the tuner's fault. The builder (or owner) doesn't take the blame for using a set of injectors they found on the shop floor. And the engine builder doesn't take the blame for choosing a cam suitable for Pro Stock. So definitely take caution in what blame is assigned to the tuner and involve them early in the build process. They can help steer you toward a combination that is going to meet your needs and avoid pitfalls. Remember their reputation is attributed to each car they tune, so they want your build to be a success as much as you do. ■

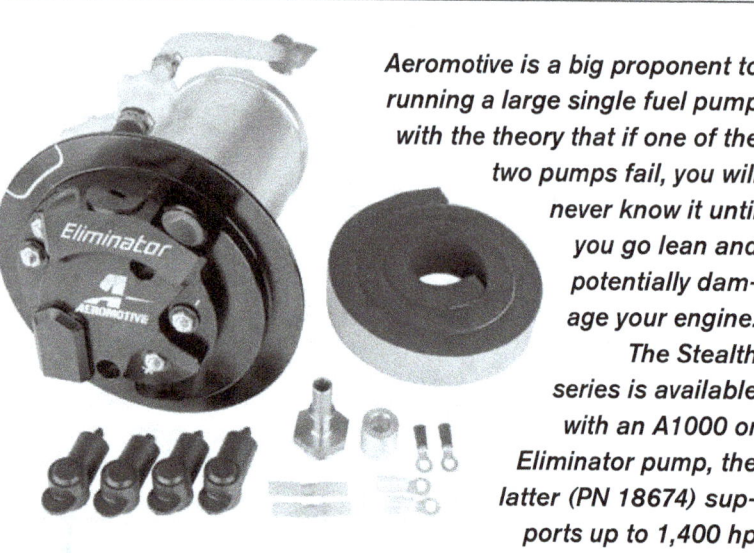

Aeromotive is a big proponent to running a large single fuel pump with the theory that if one of the two pumps fail, you will never know it until you go lean and potentially damage your engine. The Stealth series is available with an A1000 or Eliminator pump, the latter (PN 18674) supports up to 1,400 hp with forced induction. A billet fuel filter, billet bracket, billet fuel rails, fuel pressure regulator, fuel pump speed controller, Y-block, and fittings are included in the kit. (Photo Courtesy Aeromotive)

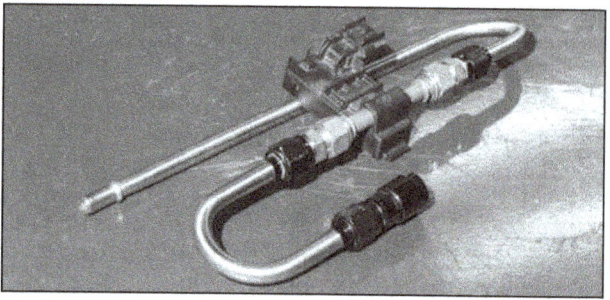

If you'd like to take advantage of the high-octane and cooling potential of E85, a Flex Fuel conversion is the only way to go. You can rotate between pump gasoline and E85 without having to switch the tune, and you don't even have to drain the tank. The ECM automatically adjusts the fueling and spark advance based on the ethanol content. This kit is from KraftWorks, which also offers tuning and fuel system upgrades to support the increased volume needed for ethanol.

FUEL SYSTEM, IGNITION AND TUNING

To get the most out of your stock or aftermarket fuel pump, you need a voltage controller. You have several options, but MSD's (PN 2351) was one of the first and is still a favorite. It was designed specifically to increase voltage in relation to boost pressure with an adjustable potentiometer range of 1.5 to 22 V and 5 to 30 psi. Software and a USB cable are included so that you can make adjustments on a laptop. (Photo Courtesy MSD Performance)

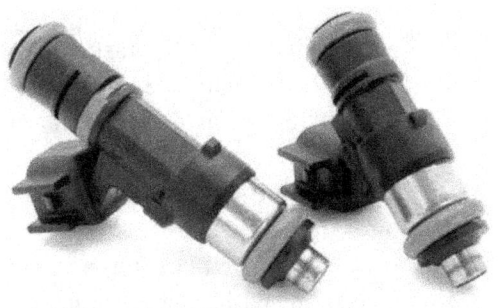

Fuel Air Spark Technology (aka FAST) has plug-and-play LS3/L99/LS7 injectors from 39 to 85 lbs/hr, which are rated at the appropriate 58 psi of fuel pressure. These high-impedance injectors have the correct EV6/USCAR connector, so you don't need adapters to plug into your wiring harness. A set of 50 (PN 30507-8) or 65 lbs/hr injectors (PN 30657-8) handles anything you can throw at it naturally aspirated. The 85 lbs/hr injectors (PN 3057-8) are ideal for boosted applications making more than 600 hp. (Photo Courtesy FAST)

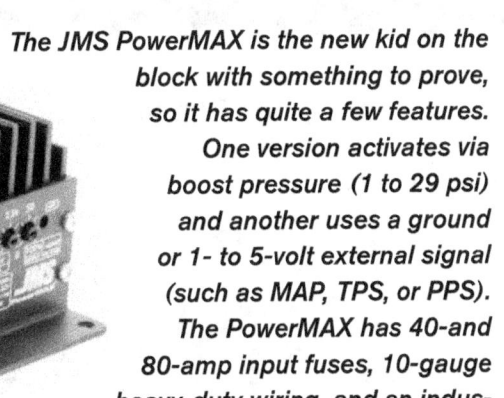

The JMS PowerMAX is the new kid on the block with something to prove, so it has quite a few features. One version activates via boost pressure (1 to 29 psi) and another uses a ground or 1- to 5-volt external signal (such as MAP, TPS, or PPS). The PowerMAX has 40-and 80-amp input fuses, 10-gauge heavy-duty wiring, and an industrial heat sink. (Photo Courtesy JMS Chip)

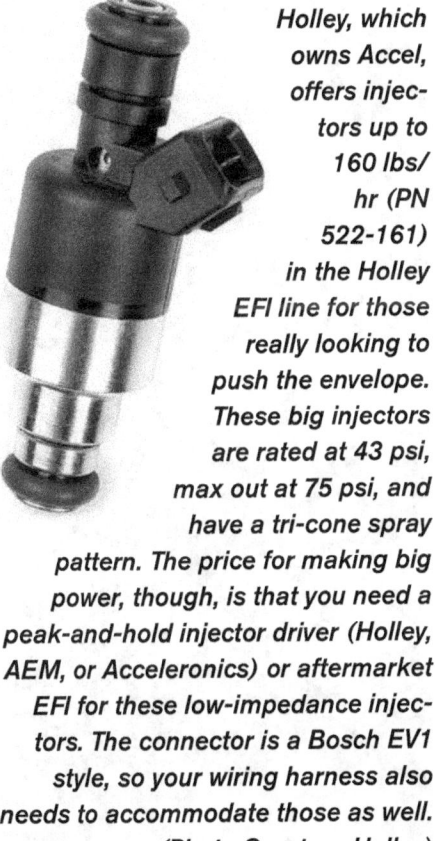

Accel offers 80 lbs/hr injectors (PN 151880), which are closer to 92 lbs/hr at 58 psi. Accel says its design does not lose metering control at higher fuel pressure, which is ideal for boost applications. These high-impedance injectors have a USCAR connection to plug into the Camaro's wiring harness, as well as an anti-plugging design to prevent carbon buildup. Some 55 lbs/hr (PN 151848) and 70 lbs/hr (PN 151861) injectors are also available. (Photo Courtesy Holley)

Holley, which owns Accel, offers injectors up to 160 lbs/hr (PN 522-161) in the Holley EFI line for those really looking to push the envelope. These big injectors are rated at 43 psi, max out at 75 psi, and have a tri-cone spray pattern. The price for making big power, though, is that you need a peak-and-hold injector driver (Holley, AEM, or Acceleronics) or aftermarket EFI for these low-impedance injectors. The connector is a Bosch EV1 style, so your wiring harness also needs to accommodate those as well. (Photo Courtesy Holley)

Aeromotive makes the task much simpler with its drop-in Stealth Fuel Pump Kit, which is available with an A1000 pump for up to 1,000 hp (with forced induction) or an Eliminator pump for max effort.

Squash Performance offers a dual-pump system with Walbro pumps that use the stock supply line with a -6 return (stock or aftermarket fuel rails) or -8 supply line for aftermarket rails. The Squash setup fits into a modified stock bucket and uses a Hobbs pressure switch to activate the second pump at 1 to 2 psi of boost.

Fore Innovations has one of the most expensive yet high-quality, complete, and customizable return system options.

Walbro, AEM, and TI Auto fuel pumps are available along with a controller, Teflon, or Startlite lines, pressure switch, and Flex Fuel sensor kit, to name a few.

The most basic dual-pump kit supports more than 800 rwhp, although triple-pump kits exceed 1,800 rwhp. Of course, if you switch to a fuel cell and external pump, the possibilities are endless.

Aeromotive's Atomic mechanical hex drive supports more than 5,000 hp with gasoline and 2,500 hp with methanol.

Magnafuel's Outlaw series is stated to support more than 3,000 hp.

How-To Projects

Fuel Pump Install

All photos for this project are courtesy of Joseph Potak.

If you have never replaced the fuel pump in a late-model GM vehicle, the process may be a bit intimidating. The fifth-gen Camaro has a plastic fuel tank that sits just in front of the differential and has two humps to allow clearance for the driveshaft in the middle. As such, there is a heat shield protecting the tank from the driveshaft and exhaust. The good news is that you don't have to remove the entire rear cradle or anything crazy to remove the tank. It is pretty much your standard fare: exhaust, driveshaft, filler neck, wiring, and tank straps.

FUEL SYSTEM, IGNITION AND TUNING

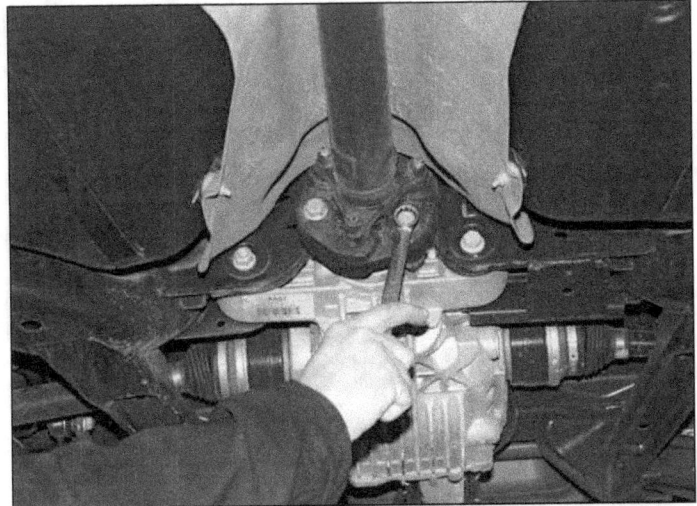

1 Step one is to remove the exhaust and driveshaft.

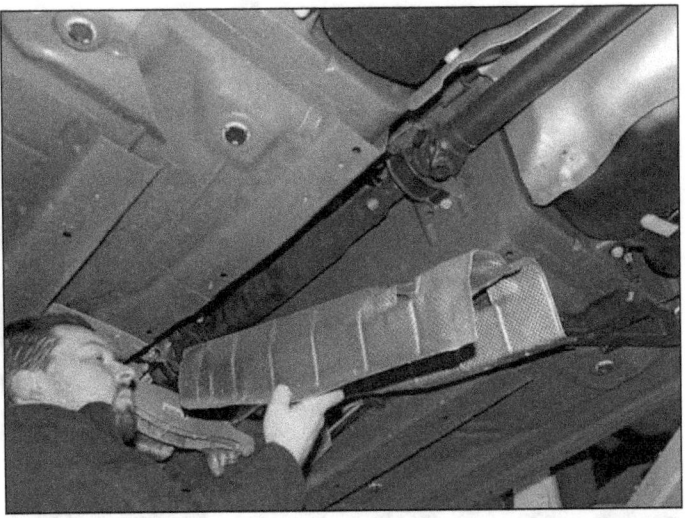

2 Because the Camaro has a two-piece driveshaft, this takes a few more steps than normal. After the flange has been unbolted from the diff, remove the front heat shield as well as the mounting bracket for the driveshaft coupler.

3 Finally unbolt the front coupler from the transmission.

4 Remove the heat shield that is covering the fuel tank.

5 Remove the front bolts that connect the rear subframe to the chassis to allow it to hang down and give ample clearance.

CHAPTER 7

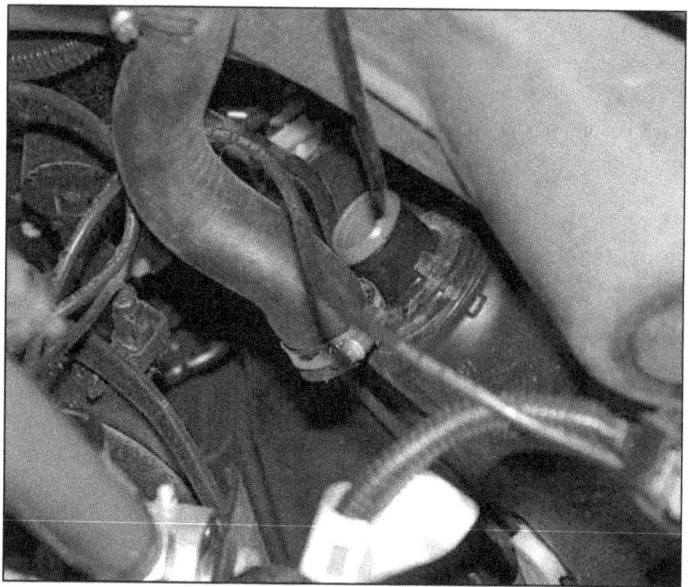

6 The filler neck can then be reached to loosen the clamp and pull off the hose.

7 Next you unhook the evaporative system.

8 Remove the electrical connections for the pump.

9 And finally, unbolt the straps so that the tank can drop. Notice that the diff is supported here.

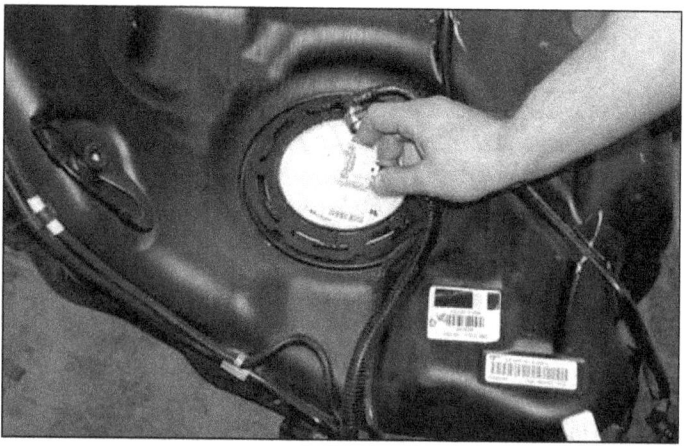

10 The fuel pump plug can be unhooked by hand.

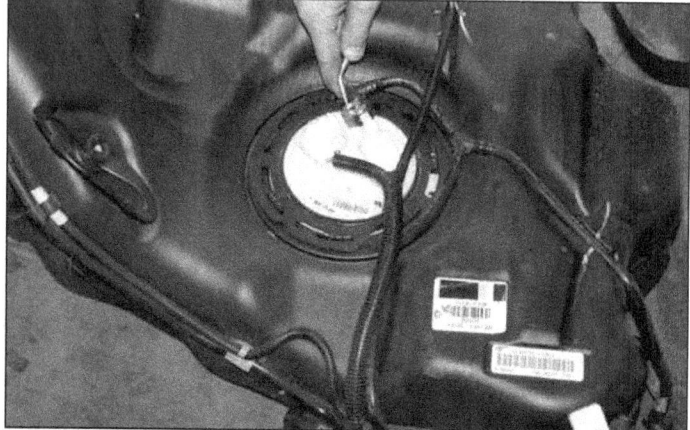

11 You want to use a two-pronged hose/line disconnect tool for the fuel line.

FUEL SYSTEM, IGNITION AND TUNING

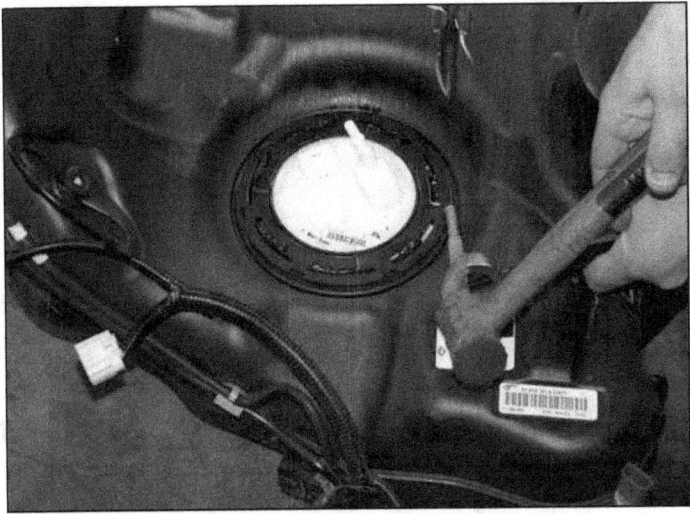

12 Use a brass chisel to spin the locking ring on the fuel pump.

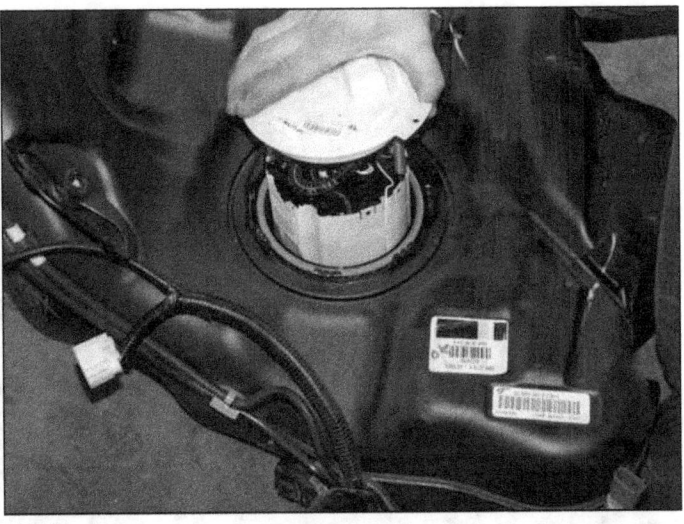

13 After removing the locking ring, lift the fuel pump straight up and out of the tank.

14 Before the pump can be completely liberated, it must be unhooked by hand at the bottom.

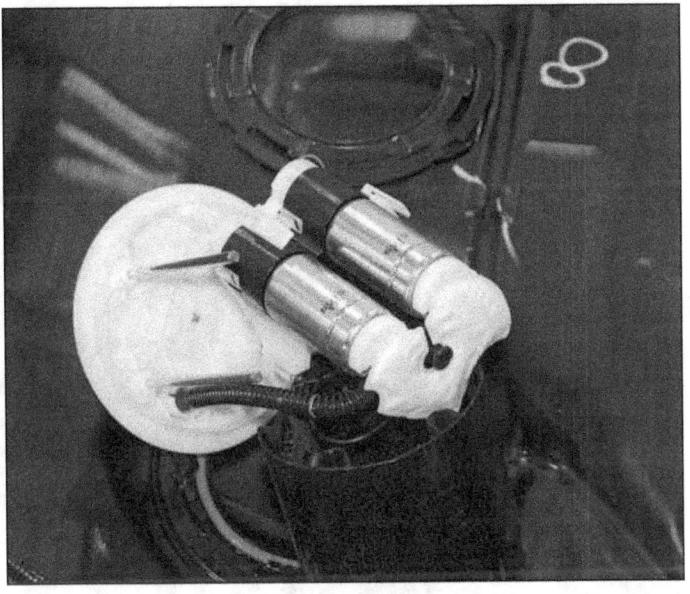

This is Lingenfelter's Camaro SS Twin Fuel Pump Module, which houses two 190-lph pumps in the primary module with a crossover fuel line, secondary module assembly, high-current capacity fuel pump control module, and all the required connectors. The electronically controlled version pumps out 270 lph a piece at 13.5 volts for 750 to 900 hp and 335 lph at 14.8 volts for 850 to 1,000 hp.

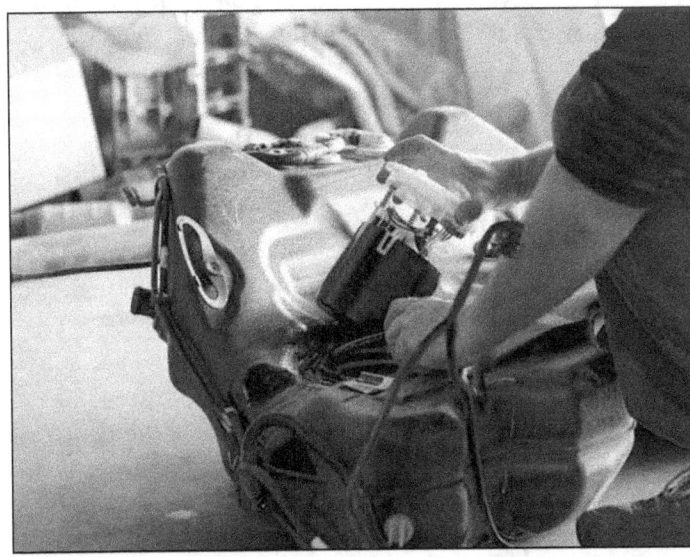

15 Just as with an OEM unit, the module slips down into the tank and everything is hooked back up.

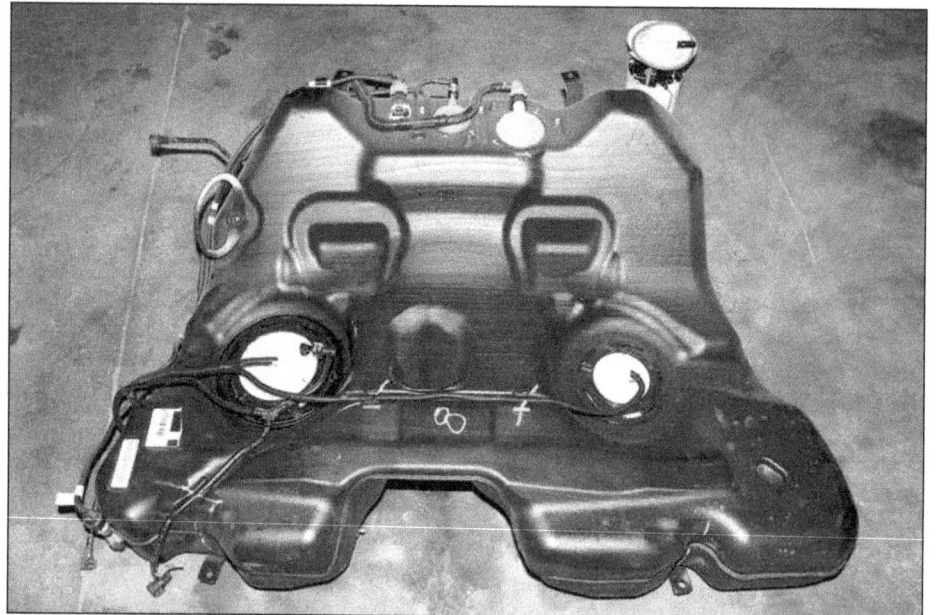

Because this is still a returnless-style fuel system with modified OEM pieces, you'd never know the difference. LPE reprograms the control module to work with the Camaro ECM, and pumps are specifically used to work with the pulse width modulated control system. Your traditional aftermarket pump does not, which is one reason that other aftermarket systems are return-style.

16 *Using a pole jack to support the tank, bolt it back up by the straps to begin reinstallation.*

Methanol Injection

Methanol injection is one subject not yet touched upon, which can certainly improve the performance of your Camaro. Snow Performance offers a water/methanol injection kit that is battle tested on the Camaro. Although applicable to any build, water/meth injection is best served on boosted applications, especially with positive displacement blowers.

The unfortunate side effect of bolting a supercharger directly to the top of your engine block is that it generates and absorbs quite a bit of heat, which makes it difficult for the intercooler to do its job. Between increasing intake air temperatures and raised cylinder pressure, the ignition timing must be backed off significantly. A water/meth kit helps absorb the heat in the intake charge and resist detonation so that you can add more ignition timing back into the engine and make more power. It can also be used as a measure of safety with varying quality of pump gas.

With your average TVS supercharged Camaro, the Snow Performance water/meth kit yields 25 to 30 hp with tuning. Although with higher boost some have seen well over a 40-hp increase.

FUEL SYSTEM, IGNITION AND TUNING

The basic Snow Performance Stage 1 kit starts out at around $360. It uses a basic, adjustable boost switch (from 1 to 15 psi) plus two nozzles, a 300-psi UHO pump, and everything in between, including tubing and wiring. For a couple of hundred more you get the Stage 2 with a progressive VC-20 controller. A built-in MAP sensor allows proportional injection of the water/meth mix, according to boost pressure. Stage 3 (shown) has four nozzles that inject using a 2D injection map based on boost and fuel injector pulse width. With each stage, Snow adds a greater level of precision to the injection. (Photo Courtesy Joseph Potak)

The Tuning School Method

If you are looking to get into EFI tuning but just don't know how, The Tuning School's GM Level 1 HP Tuners live seminar is an excellent introduction. The school also provides online learning options to further your education and to help those who cannot make it to the Odessa, Florida, headquarters or other available locations.

This two-day course is as hands-on as you can get. Instructors walk you through every step of the process, starting with engine theory basics and actually downloading and setting up the HP Tuners software on your laptop.

CHAPTER 7

It is important to have a thorough evaluation of the car via the owner's input and what you can visually inspect before you strap the car to the dyno. The Tuning School recommends using a load-bearing dyno for tuning, which best simulates road conditions and eliminates most on-road tuning. Assuming the car is in good working condition, you make a baseline pull using the HP Tuners' data-logging software.

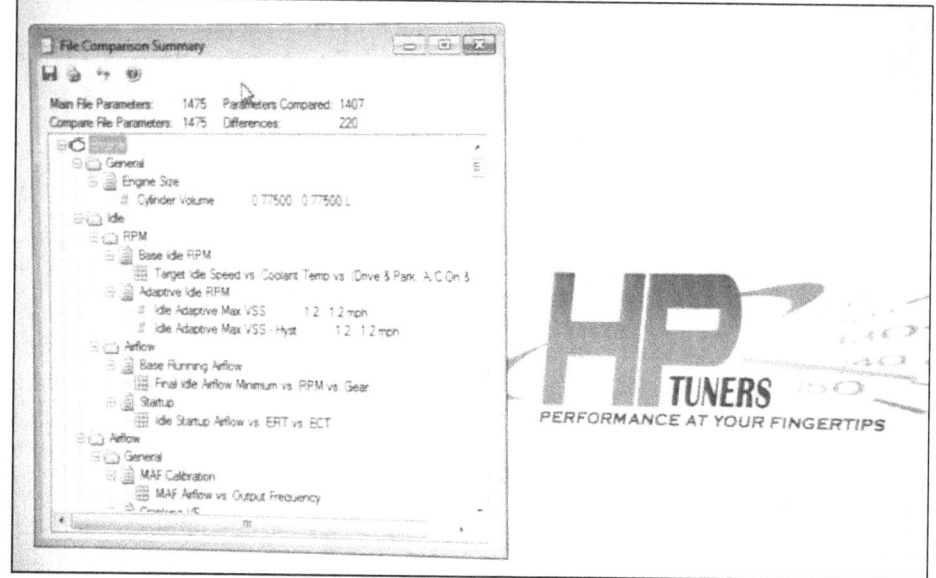

After scanning and downloading the vehicle's current tune, you want to compare it to the latest update of the OEM file. If it has already been modified, that may give you some clues about any modifications or issues that haven't been revealed.

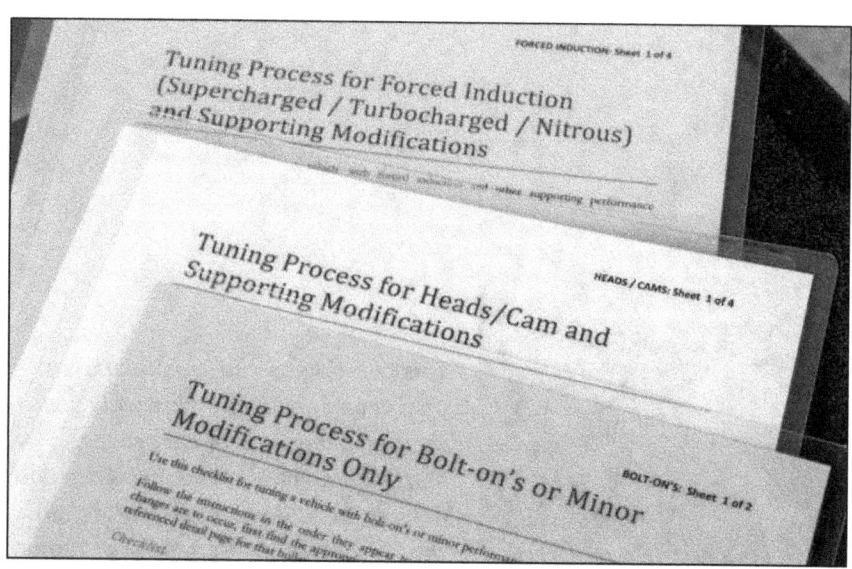

The Tuning School recommends starting with idle and part-throttle tuning. Heads/cam and forced induction usually requires more start-up and idle changes. The procedure varies, but generally speaking, it initially addresses performance changes, then WOT, and drivability last. Following the proper order of operations is crucial. For example, if you have not tuned the MAF first, it is difficult to implement the fueling changes you command later because that is the engine's first and most crucial input as to how much fuel to add.

FUEL SYSTEM, IGNITION AND TUNING

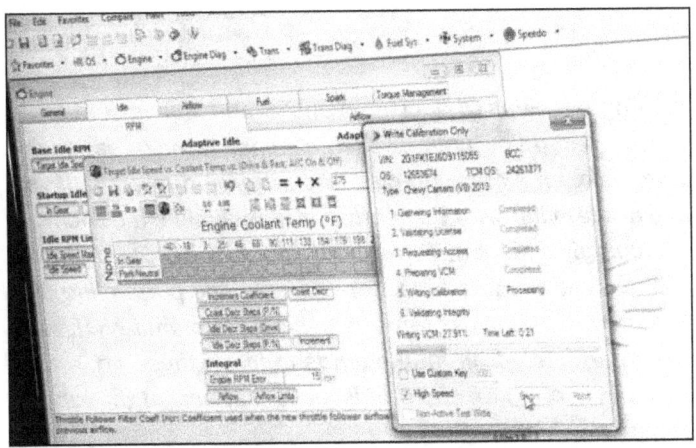

The 2013 Camaro SS on the dyno was equipped with a VVT camshaft, ported heads, headers, cold-air intake, and a torque converter. During my class the instructor went through the logic behind making some of the changes to the tune, and based on what I saw in the baseline testing, the class gave input as to what needed to be changed.

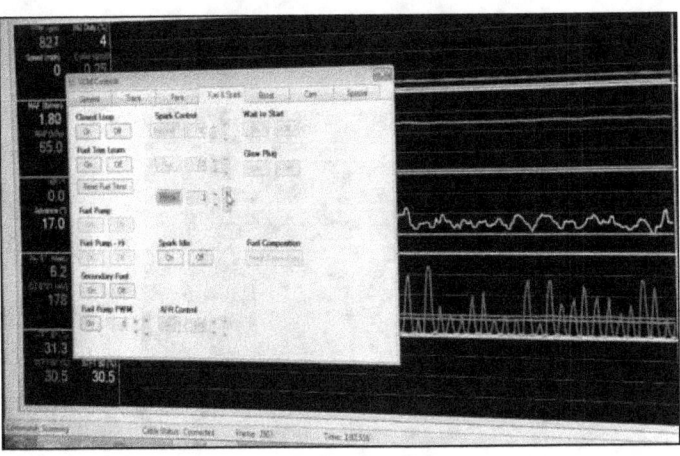

After uploading the first modified calibration, the VCM Control function was used for real-time tuning the idle to dial it in. The changes aren't permanent, but it is easy to go back and write these into the calibration then upload after the engine is turned off again. If you are not familiar with flash-based tuning, usually it can only be done with the power on and the engine off.

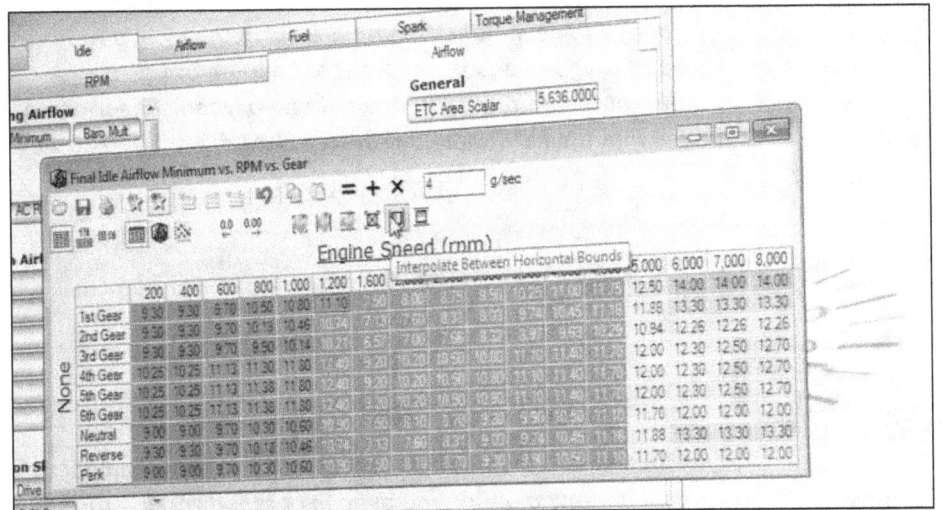

HP Tuners has many features built into the software to make your life easier, which the instructors love to point out. Among them is the interpolate function. This is a huge timesaver because you basically modify just a few points in whatever table you are working on and then use this function to fill in the rest of the values.

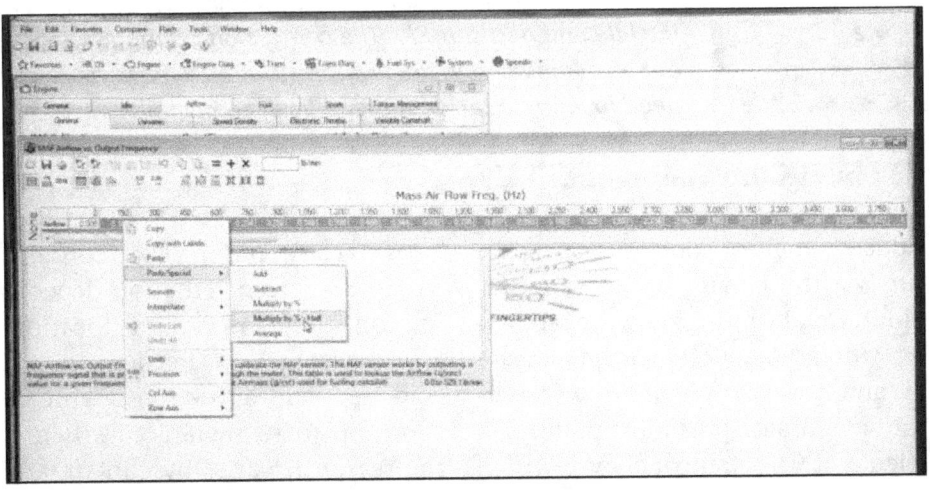

The histogram function is another nice feature, which the instructors demonstrated during MAF tuning. This allows you to take the data values from your logs and translate them directly into changes in the tune.

CHAPTER 7

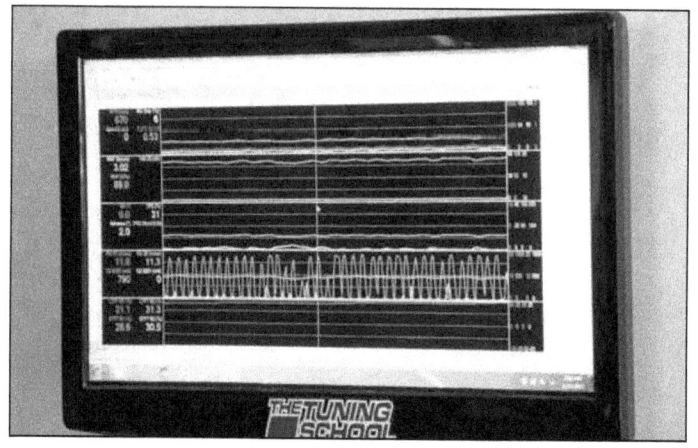

Making data-based decisions and changes is essential to this method of tuning, which eliminates the guesswork and makes it a more precise and efficient operation. If you are not familiar with this software, it looks like a bunch of squiggly lines, but The Tuning School teaches you how to interpret the data logs. For example, the purple line on the bottom is the fuel trims, which oscillate until WOT. An aftermarket cold-air intake tends to throw these off, and troubleshooting this kind of issue is just part of the job of tuning a vehicle.

When you are making WOT pulls, the configurable dashboard comes in handy. If you are using the dyno's wideband oxygen sensor, you want to keep an eye on knock (KR, at the bottom left). A wideband oxygen sensor can be fed into the HP Tuners' interface, logged, and read as well.

At the end of the session, you are able to see a measurable improvement on the dyno in horsepower and torque as well as both quantitative and qualitative assessment of the idle and part-throttle. The conclusion is empowering, but also humbling in the awareness of how much more you need to learn to tackle more difficult combinations.

Flex Fuel Conversion in EFI Live

Chances are even that your good old 93-octane pump gas has up to 10-percent ethanol. But unlike with E85, there are few to no benefits of adding corn liquor to the mixture. E85 is essentially cheap race gas you can buy at the pump that has the added benefit of cooling your intake air (via the latent heat of vaporization). Octane ratings vary, depending on whom you ask, what the mixture is, and how it is rated. But a conservative estimate puts most pump E85 blends at 95-octane or above.

Typically pump E85 contains 51- to 83-percent ethanol, depending on the season and location. More gasoline is needed to aid cold-start and allow the engine to come up to temperature, which is the reason it varies by climate and

FUEL SYSTEM, IGNITION AND TUNING

why they don't sell higher concentrations of ethanol at the pump. This cooling effect and the added octane allow you to run higher compression, more boost, and more timing, which can pay dividends on the dyno or track.

Recent dyno testing has revealed gains of more than 10 hp on bone-stock Camaros. The gains are even more impressive with boost, particularly combinations that easily become heat-soaked or exceed the capacity of the intercooler, such as a ZL1.

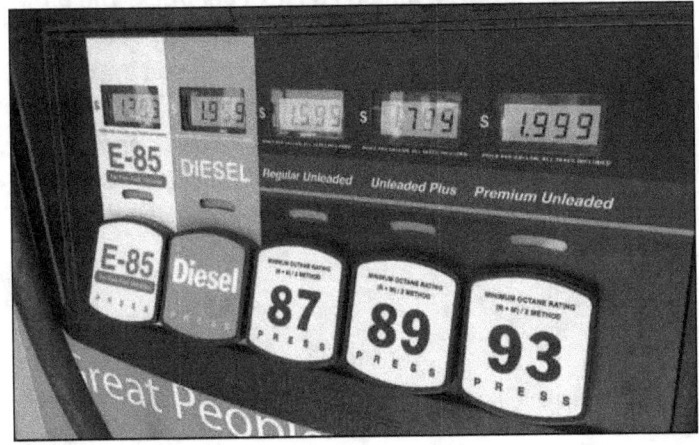

Because pump E85 varies so heavily in its concentration, a Flex Fuel conversion is the only way to reliably run it on a regular basis without having to manually retune the ECM for each mixture. Because General Motors offered Flex Fuel on other LS-based vehicles, it is just a matter of retrofitting the sensor, wiring into your factory ECM, and enabling the (previously dormant) features in your ECM's operating system. KraftWorks has become known for its Flex Fuel conversions on ZL1s and CTS-Vs, so tuner Jay Healy gave me a simplified walk-through of the process using EFI Live software.

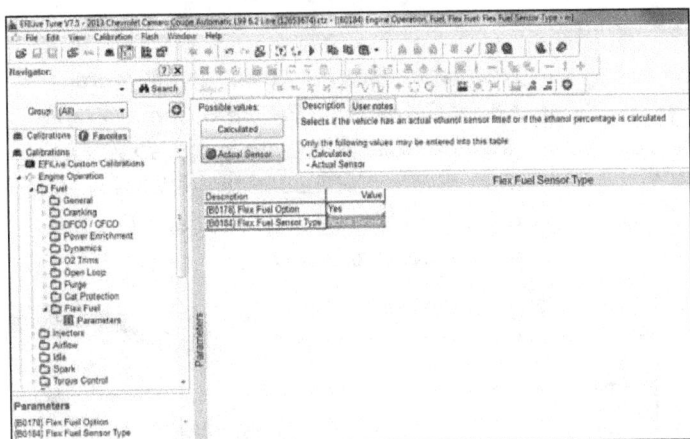

Once the sensor is installed and fully wired in, you need to enable the sensor. Under the navigator (on the left-hand side) you click Engine Operation/Fuel/Flex Fuel/Parameters to reach this screen. You click "Yes" to enable the Flex Fuel Option and then "Actual Sensor" under Flex Fuel Sensor Type to actually use its data.

Ethanol requires a different air/fuel ratio than gasoline due to its lower energy content. Thankfully the ECM already has this table built into its operating system, so that it can adjust the air/fuel by the percentage of ethanol. Once you've enabled the actual sensor, you just let the ECM do all the work in figuring out how much fuel to add.

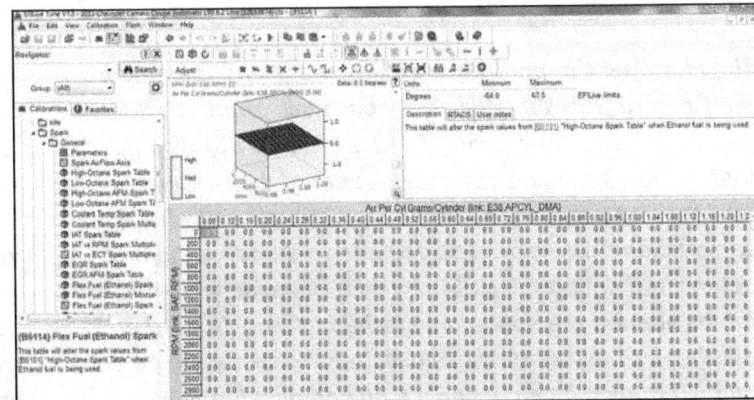

The spark table has three Flex Fuel tables under Engine/Spark/General, starting with Flex Fuel (Ethanol) Spark. This table is completely unpopulated, which alters the High Octane Spark Table with ethanol.

CHAPTER 7

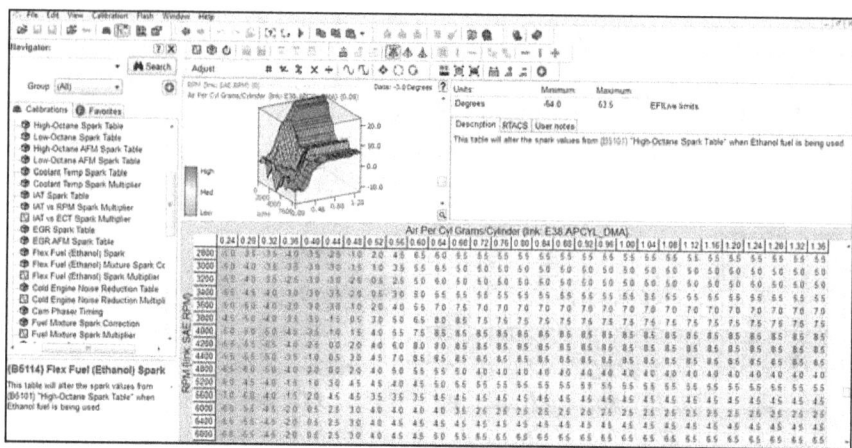

For comparison, here is the spark table from an OEM tune on a Flex Fuel truck. The difference in the 3D map is stark. In the upper portions of the table you can see that it is adding quite a bit of timing (in some cases 8.5 degrees). The 6.2L L94 truck engine can be a good starting point for populating this table, depending on the application.

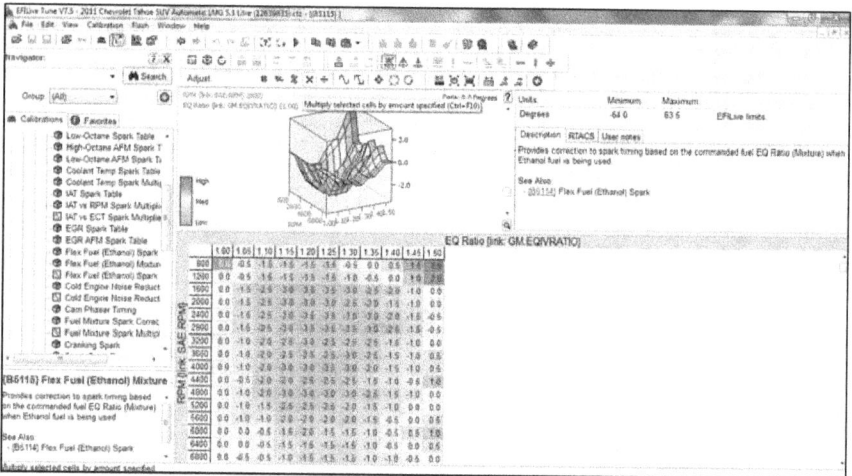

Next is the Flex Fuel (Ethanol) Mixture Spark Correction. The OEM Camaro table is going to be filled with zeros, so you need to populate it with something like this. This table corrects spark timing based on the commanded air/fuel ratio.

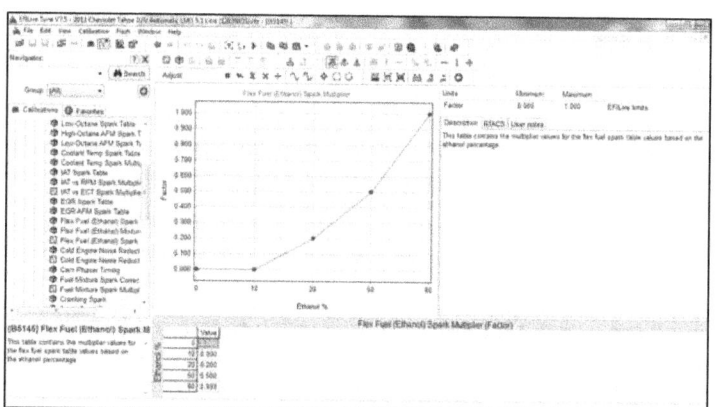

The Flex Fuel (Ethanol) Spark Multiplier is unpopulated in the Camaro. This table decides how much spark is added for the percentages of ethanol (0, 10, 20, 50, or 80). You notice that 0 and 10 percent both have a zero multiplier because ethanol-free premium and premium E10 generally have the same octane. The more E85 you add to the tank, the more octane and timing the ECM can add. Because you have two tables altering the spark timing when ethanol is used and another multiplying those values, depending on the percentage of ethanol, it can become a bit complicated.

The last step is activating the Engine Diagnostic/DTC for the P0178 and P0179 Fuel Composition Sensor, so that when you open the scan tool and fire up the engine you can read the ethanol percentage. This was a tank full of E10, hence its 9.8 ethanol percentage. From here you want to monitor the fuel trims and knock when testing to make corrections.

SOURCE GUIDE

aFe Power
232 Granite St.
Corona, CA 92879
888-901-7693
afepower.com

AEM Performance Electronics
2205 W. 126th St., Unit A
Hawthorne, CA 90250
310-484-2322
aemelectronics.com

Aeromotive
7805 Barton St.
Lenexa, KS 66214
913-647-7300
aeromotiveinc.com

AGP Turbochargers
1930 East 3rd St., #12
Tempe, AZ 85281
480-983-6083
agpturbo.com

AntiVenom Racing
1810 S. Parsons Ave., Ste. 108
Seffner, FL 33584
813-381-3995
antivenomefi.com

ATI ProCharger
14801 W. 114th Ter.
Lenexa, KS 66215
913-338-2886
procharger.com

BC Racing
321-206-6381
bcracing-na.com

BMR Suspension
928 Sligh Ave.
Seffner, FL 33584
813-986-9302
bmrsuspension.com

Century Transmissions
811 Plantation Dr.
Richmond, TX 77406
713-666-2616
centurytransmission.com

Chevrolet Performance
ChevroletPerformance.com

Circle D Specialties
14105 Packard St.
Houston, TX 77040
713-895-8834
circledspecialties.com

Competition Cams
3406 Democrat Rd.
Memphis, TN 38118
800-999-0853
compcams.com

Corsa Performance
140 Blaze Industrial Pkwy.
Berea, OH 44017
440-891-0999
corsaperformance.com

Dart Machinery
353 Oliver Dr.
Troy, MI 48084
248-362-1188
dartheads.com

DeatschWerks
1745 W. Sheridan Ave.
Oklahoma City, OK 73106
405-217-0701
deatschwerks.com

DiabloSport
1865 S.W. 4th Ave, Ste. D-2
Delray Beach, FL 33444
561-908-0041
diablosport.com

Edelbrock
2700 California St.
Torrance, CA 90503
310-781-2222
edelbrock.com

EFILive Limited
efilive.com

FAST
3400 Democrat Rd.
Memphis, TN 38118
877-334-8355
fuelairspark.com

Fore Innovations
12980 44th St. N.
Clearwater, FL 33762
727-258-4826
foreinnovations.com

Forgeline Motorsports
3522 S. Kettering Blvd., Ste. A
Dayton, OH 45439
800-886-0093
forgeline.com

GForce Engineering
519 N Hydraulic Ave.
Wichita, KS 67214
316-260-8433
shop.gforce1320.com

General Motors
gm.com

Goodyear Tire & Rubber
Company
200 Innovation Way
Akron, OH 44316
800/321-2136
goodyear.com

Granatelli Motor Sports
1000 Yarnell Pl.
Oxnard, CA 93033
805-486-6644
granatellimotorsports.com

Haltech USA
157 Venture Ct, Ste. 12
Lexington, KY 40511
760-598-1941
haltech.com

Hawk Performance
800-542-0972
hawkperformance.com

Hellion Power Systems
2735 Della Dr.
Albuquerque, NM 87105
505-873-4670
hellionpowersystems.com

Holley Performance Products
1801 Russellville Rd.
Bowling Green, KY 42102
270-782-2900
holley.com

Honeywell Turbo
Technologies
garrett.honeywell.com

Hotchkis Sport Suspension
8633 Sorensen Ave.
Santa Fe Springs, CA 90670
877-466-7655
hotchkis.net

HP Tuners
701 Dartmouth Ln.
Buffalo Grove, IL 60089
hptuners.com

JMS Chip & Performance
3247 Highway 63 S.
Lucendale, MS 39452
601-766-9424
jmschip.com

KraftWorks
1364 Gwenzell Ave.
Delray Beach, FL 33444
561-808-2399
kraftworks1.com

Lingenfelter Performance
Engineering
1557 Winchester Rd.
Decatur, IN 46733
260-724-2552
lingenfelter.com

SOURCE GUIDE

Lysholm Technologies
1650 Pacific Ave.
Oxnard, CA 93033
805-247-0226
lysholm.us

Magnuson Products
1990-A Knoll Dr.
Ventura, CA 93003
805-642-8833
magnusonproducts.com

Mast Motorsports
330 NW Stallings Dr.
Nacogdoches, TX 75964
936-560-2218
mastmotorsports.com

MGW LTD
4159 Mike Padgett Hwy.
Augusta, GA 30906
706-793-1770
mgwshifters.com

MSD Performance
888-258-3835
msdperformance.com

NCC Racing Products
Sherrills Ford, NC
508-922-9908
nccracing.com

Nitrous Express
5411 Seymour Hwy.
Wichita Falls, TX 76310
940-767-7694
nitrousexpress.com

Nitrous Outlet
305 S. 28th St.
Waco, TX 76710
866-648-7637
nitrousoutlet.com

Paxton Automotive
1650 Pacific Ave.
Oxnard, CA 93033
805-247-0669
paxtonauto.com

PCM of NC
618 Oak Ridge Farm Hwy.
Mooresville, NC 28115
704-307-4227
pcmofnc.com

Phastek Performance
6830 N. Eldridge Pkwy., #102
Houston, TX 77041
855-742-7835
phastekperformance.com

Precision Turbo
P.O. Box 425
Hebron, IN 46341
855-996-7832
precisionturbo.net

Quarter Master Industries
510 Telser Rd.
Lake Zurick, IL 60047
847-540-8999
quartermasterusa.com

Racing Head Service
3416 Democrat Rd.
Memphis, TN 38118
877-776-4323
racingheadservice.com

Ram Clutches
201 Business Park Blvd.
Columbia, SC 29203
803-788-6034
ramclutches.com

Redline Motorsports
1931 N.W. 40th Ct.
Pompano Beach, FL 33064
954-703-5560
redline-motorsports.net

Rockland Standard Gear
150 Rte. 17
Sloatsburg, NY 10974
877-774-4327
rsgear.com

RPM Transmissions
1426 W. 53rd St.
Anderson, IN 46013
765-640-5411
rpmtransmissions.com

SCT
4150 Church St., Ste. 1024
Sanford, FL 32771
407-774-2447
sctflash.com

SLP Performance
39555 Schoolcraft Rd.
Plymouth Township, MI 48170
855-757-7373
slponline.com

Snow Performance
1017 Hwy. 24 E., Unit A
Woodland Park, CO 80863
719-633-3811
snowperformance.net

Squash Performance
262-724-8035
squashperformance.com

STILLEN
3176 Airway Ave.
Costa Mesa, CA 92626
866-250-5542
stillen.com

Strange Engineering
8300 N. Austin Ave.
Morton Grove, IL 60053
847-663-1701
strangeengineering.com

TCI Automotive
151 Industrial Dr.
Ashland, MS 38603
888-776-9824
tciauto.com

Texas Speed & Performance
1621 Aviation Dr., Suite 105
Georgetown, TX 78628
512-863-0900
texas-speed.com

The Driveshaft Shop
4530 Southmark Dr.
Salisbury, NC 28147
800-564-2244
driveshaftshop.com

The Tuning School
2328 Destiny Way
Odessa, FL 33556
727-264-8875
thetuningschool.com

Toyo Tire & Rubber Company
toyotires.com

Turbonetics Inc.
14399 Princeton Ave.
Moorpark, CA 93021
805-581-0333
turboneticsinc.com

Turbosmart USA
8580 Milliken Ave.
Rancho Cucamonga, CA 91730
909-476-2570
turbosmartusa.com

Vortech Engineering
1650 Pacific Ave.
Oxnard, CA 93033
805-247-0226
vortechsuperchargers.com

Weapon X Motorsports
2105 Schapelle Ln.
Cincinnati, OH 45240
614-489-8360
weaponxmotorsports.com

Weld Racing
6600 Stadium Dr.
Kansas City, MO 64129
800-788-9353
weldwheels.com

Whipple Superchargers
3292 N. Weber
Fresno, CA 93722
559-442-1261
whipplesuperchargers.com

Wilwood Engineering
4700 Calle Bolero
Camarillo, CA 93012
805-388-1188
wilwood.com

Xtreme Innovations & Fabrication
250 N. Sugarbush Rd.
Luxemburg, WI 54217
920-845-5525
exremeinnovationsandfabrication.com

ZEX
3418 Democrat Rd.
Memphis, TN 38118
888-817-1008
zex.com

www.ingramcontent.com/pod-product-compliance
Lightning Source LLC
Chambersburg PA
CBHW081444070526
44586CB00019B/2227